DATE DUE			
MAR 2 0 1969			
FEB 9 1970			
DEC 2 1 1971			
APR			
APR 1 8 1972			
APR 9 1973			
MAY 0 3 2016			

20828

THE DAYS WE CELEBRATE

*Celebrations for Christmas
and Other High Days*

OUR AMERICAN HOLIDAYS

Edited by

ROBERT HAVEN SCHAUFFLER
AND OTHERS

A SERIES of anthologies for the use of students and teachers in schools and colleges; consisting of the best verse, plays, stories, addresses, special articles, orations, etc. Applicable to the holidays listed as follows:

CHRISTMAS	*December 25th*
DEMOCRACY DAYS	
EASTER	*March or April*
GOOD WILL DAYS	
HALLOWE'EN	*October 31st*
INDEPENDENCE DAY	*July 4th*
LINCOLN'S BIRTHDAY	*February 12th*
THE MAGIC OF BOOKS	*Book Week*
THE MAGIC OF MUSIC	*Music Week*
MEMORIAL DAY	*May 30th*
MOTHER'S DAY	*Second Sunday in May*
PAN-AMERICAN DAY	*April 14th*
PEACE DAYS	
ROOSEVELT DAY	*October 27th*
THANKSGIVING	*Last Thursday in November*
WASHINGTON'S BIRTHDAY	*February 22nd*

THE DAYS
WE CELEBRATE

☆

CELEBRATIONS FOR CHRISTMAS
and Other High Days

CHRISTMAS - ST. VALENTINE'S DAY
ST. PATRICK'S DAY - EASTER

Compiled and Edited by

ROBERT HAVEN SCHAUFFLER

EDITOR OF
OUR AMERICAN HOLIDAYS

DODD, MEAD & COMPANY
NEW YORK

ACKNOWLEDGMENTS

For their kind help in providing facilities and material for this compilation, special thanks are due to these New York librarians: Miss Thelma Edic, Librarian of the Magazine Reserve; Mr. Franklin F. Hopper, Chief of Circulation; Miss C. H. Meade, Librarian St. Agnes Branch, and her obliging and efficient staff; Miss Amelia Munson, Librarian Teachers' Reference Room, 58th Street Branch; and to the many other branches that kindly loaned books and magazines. Also to Miss Helen Mildred Owen, editor of *The Instructor* for her generosity in allowing so many extracts from a magazine pre-eminent for the quality of its holiday literature; and to these members of the Dodd, Mead staff: Miss Ruby N. Carr, Miss Madeline C. Duffy, and especially Miss Mary A. Brennan, for their invaluable co-operation in the business end of this undertaking.

For permission to use copyrighted material acknowledgment is made to:

The American Home Magazine and the Author: "I Wish You All a Merry Christmas," by Jean Austin.

Edith Mason Armstrong: "Christmas Adventure."

Mrs. George S. Burgess, literary executor of Katharine Lee Bates: "The Blind Boy of Bethlehem," by Katharine Lee Bates.

The Catholic World: "Lighting the Yule Log," and "The Swordless Christ," by John Moreland.

The Christian Century: "At Christmas," by Edith Lovejoy Pierce.

The Churchman: "In the Manger," by Una A. Harsen.

Estate of Joseph I. C. Clarke: "The Fighting Race," by Joseph I. C. Clarke.

Dodd, Mead and Company: "A Christmas Carol," by G. K. Chesterton (2 poems); "Christmas," "The Sending of the Magi," "The Wise Men from the East," "Easter Eve," and "Spring Song," by Bliss Carman; "The Trapper's Christmas Eve," by Robert Service; "A Little Christmas Basket," by Paul Laurence Dunbar; "The Joys of the Springtime," by Sarojini Naidu.

Katherine Edelman: "Christmas Candle," "Great-Grandmother's

Valentine," "A Day of Memories," "On St. Patrick's Day," "The Lane to Ballybree," and "Irish Mother."

Mildred Focht: "Aged Four," from "Four Trees and Other Poems."

Follett Publishing Company, Chicago: "Meeting the Easter Bunny," from "Around a Toadstool Table," by Rowena Bastin Bennett.

The Forum: "Joseph to Mary," by Sara Henderson Hay.

Wilfred Funk: "Christmas Packages."

Funk and Wagnalls Company: "Christmas," "Spring Thoughts," and "April," from "Broad-Cast," by Ernest Crosby.

Good Housekeeping and the Author: "The Three Kings' Road," by Anna Blake Mezquida.

"Spring in the City," by Eleanor Graham.

Mrs. J. H. Gower: "Parable in a Park," by Jean Milne Gower.

Julia Boynton Green: "Harrowing Reflections," "The Aftermath —December Twenty-Sixth," and "March Seventeenth."

Leigh Hanes: "Santa Claus," from "Green Girdle." (Lyric Press, Roanoke, Va.)

Mary Lindsay Hoffman: "The Day Before."

Henry Holt and Company: "Before Dawn," by Walter De la Mare, from "Poems," and "April, What Wonder-Working," by Lew Sarett, from "Wings Against the Moon."

Bruce Humphries, Inc.: "Babushka," from "Children of Christmas," by Edith M. Thomas. Copyright, 1907, by Edith M. Thomas.

The Irish Messenger of the Sacred Heart (Dublin): "The Breastplate of St. Patrick," and "The Irish Te Deum."

Reginald Wright Kauffman: "Resurrexit!"

Harry Kemp: "The Voice of Christmas."

Emilie E. King: "The Boy in Nazareth."

Alfred A. Knopf, Inc.: "Southern Cross," from "Slow Wall," and "March . . . April . . . ," from "Naked Heel," by Leonora Speyer. Reprinted by special arrangement with the authorized publishers, Alfred A. Knopf, Inc.

Mary Sinton Leitch: "The Thorn," from "The Unrisen Morrow."

Little, Brown and Company: "A Valentine," from "Tirra Lirra," by Laura E. Richards.

Dr. Francis Litz: "Evolution," by John B. Tabb.

Longmans, Green and Company: "Valentine in Form of Ballade," by Andrew Lang, from "Waifs and Strays."

Elbridge S. Lyon: "Only a Valentine," "The Dummy," and "Caramine, an Easter Pageant."

Mrs. Denis A. McCarthy: "The Green O' the Spring," by Denis Aloysius McCarthy.

The Macmillan Company: "The Palace and the Stable," from

"The Story of Mankind," by Hendrik Willem Van Loon, and "The Man Who Would Woo a Fair Maid," by W. S. Gilbert, from "The Bab Ballads."

Mary Frances Martin: "The Rann of the Christmas Tree."

Hazel Carter Maxon: "A St. Patrick Circus Party," "A Green Hat Party," and "A Happily-Ever-After Party."

Virginia Scott Miner: "Christmas Conservative."

Mabel M. Moran: "St. Valentine's Day Out."

John Richard Moreland: "Easter," from "Red Poppies in the Wheat," "O Who Would Think of Sorrow," and "Easter," (two poems), from "The Sea and April," "The Swordless Christ," from "The Catholic World," and "If a Man Die Shall He Live Again?," from "Newry."

Helene Mullins: "Christmas Carol."

The New York Times and the Author: "By Quill Pen or Wire, It's Still a Valentine," by Frederick Gruin, and "The Triumph of Life."

Moira O'Neill: "Corrymeela," from "Songs of the Glens of Antrim." (Wm. Blackwood, London).

The F. A. Owen Company, publishers of The Instructor: For "O Holy Night," by C. O. Richardson; "A Christmas-Card Pageant," by Elsie M. Hubachek; "The Doll's Christmas Tree," by Rebecca Deming Moore; "Primary Stories for Christmas Time," by Juanita Cunningham; "A Gift for Santa Claus," by Theda Pearson Hedden; "Christmas Games" and "Christmas Party Games," by Alice Crowell Hoffman; "A Christmas Toyshop," by Alice M. Corson; "Getting Ready for Easter," by Gardie Kirkman; "Easter Favors," by S. E. Evalyn Hammond; "Seasonal Games for December," by Harvey Haeberle; "Gifts Children Can Make," by Erma M. Stockwell; "A Novel Unit of Work," by Jack Hoskins; "Practical Handwork for Christmas," by Dorothy B. Hansen; "Christmas-Candle Candy," by Frances L. Sharpe; "Making Christmas Gifts," by Louise Broadbent; "Christmas Roll Call," by Juanita Cunningham; "Christmas Symbols," by Alberta Johnson; "An Arithmetic Christmas Tree," by Marian Elder Jones; "A Christmas Sand Table," by Florence L. Williamson; "Holiday Candlesticks," by Kathryn Mihm; "An Original Christmas Scene," by Kathleen Carmichael Dietz; "A Living Christmas Tree," by Louise Boelte; "Christmas Tree Ornaments," by Alice Crowell Hoffman; "A Valentine Party," by Theda Pearson Hedden; "Valentine Games," by Alice Hoffman; "Homemade Valentines," by Clifford Cook; "Using Old Valentines," by Frances Schuetze; "A Valentine Box," by Corinne Kidd; "St. Patrick's Day Games," by Berenice Mueller Ball; "Easter Parade," by Alma May Rodgers; "An Easter Booklet," by Inez Sundberg; and "Easter Greetings," by Marie Marsh.

Parents' Magazine and the Authors: "Christmas," by Dorothy Canfield; "Share Your Christmas," by Mrs. Thomas A. Edison; "The Heart of Christmas," by Henry C. Link; and "Keeping Christmas," by Willard L. Sperry.

Olive Price: "Footprints of Angels."

Ethel Robb: "Christmas 'Good Night.' "

Delle Oglesbee Ross: "The Goblin at the Grocer's," "Dawn in an Upper Room," and "Cupid Takes a Vacation."

Grace L. Schauffler: "Of Christmas," and "A Bit of Green."

Charles Scribner's Sons: "The Foolish Fir-Tree," by Henry Van Dyke.

Mary Stewart Sheldon: "What the Camels Brought to Miser Claus," and "The Power That Was Patrick."

Odell Shepard: "The Gifts."

Ruth Reno Smith: "In Behalf of St. Valentine."

Frederick A. Stokes Company: "Now Every Child," and "Six Green Singers," from "Come Christmas," by Eleanor Farjeon. Copyright, 1927, by Frederick A. Stokes Company. "I'm Wishing the Whole World Christmas," from "All Through the Year," by Annette Wynne. Copyright, 1932, by Annette Wynne.

Mirjane Strong: "Mr. Grasshopper's Easter Clothes."

Velma West Sykes and The Kansas City Star: "Nothing Ever Happens."

Dorothy Brown Thompson: "Upper Room," and "To Experience Easter."

Grace Torrey: "The Spirit of the Day."

Charles Hanson Towne: "An Easter Canticle."

Nancy Byrd Turner: "Childhood Christmas," "The Christmas Star," "They Sealed the Stone, They Set the Watch," "Spring's in My Garden," and "Easter Joy."

Lettie C. VanDerveer: "The On and Off of a Christmas Gift."

May Williams Ward: "The Miracle Again."

Irene Wilde: "Christmas Trees."

Woman's Home Companion and the Author: "Signs, Symbols and Psychology," by Anne Bryan McCall, and "The Spirit of Giving," by Anne Bryan McCall.

The Woman's Press and the Author: "The News That Came to Nazareth," by Ivy Bolton.

INTRODUCTION

Realizing that some readers consider any introduction an impertinent superfluity, I will try to be telegraphically brief.

The present series has been planned to complete and bring down to date the twenty-one volumes of OUR AMERICAN HOLIDAYS, and PLAYS FOR OUR AMERICAN HOLIDAYS. Except for occasions not covered by the first series, most of the plays, poems, stories, essays, articles, games, projects, exercises, activities, etc., which are provided here for each celebration, are of more recent date than the corresponding volume of the standard set. In THE DAYS WE CELEBRATE will be found some of the best work of such authors as Eleanor Farjeon, Rose Fyleman, A. E. Housman, Vachel Lindsay, Alfred Noyes, Walter De la Mare, John Masefield, Leonora Speyer, and Sara Teasdale—all written too recently for inclusion in the parent series.

There is a large proportion of easily staged-and-acted plays, pageants, masques, dances, and tableaux. These have nearly all been planned with an eye to economical production. Most of them have been written specially for these volumes. Much material has been provided for the use of teachers, and of children of all ages.

Together with its two parent series, I trust that THE DAYS WE CELEBRATE will provide a practical and down-to-the-minute library of holiday literature for everybody.

R. H. S.

CONTENTS

CELEBRATIONS FOR CHRISTMAS
PLAYS AND PAGEANTS

CONTENTS

PAGE

STORIES

GAMES AND OTHER ACTIVITIES

CELEBRATIONS FOR ST. VALENTINE'S DAY

PLAYS

POEMS

A VALENTINE STORY

ESSAYS

PARTIES, GAMES, AND OTHER ACTIVITIES

CELEBRATIONS FOR ST. PATRICK'S DAY

PLAYS

POEMS

ESSAYS

PARTIES AND GAMES

CELEBRATIONS FOR EASTER

PLAYS AND A PAGEANT

CONTENTS

POEMS

ESSAYS

ACTIVITIES

ACTIVITIES

Celebrations for Christmas

THE GOBLIN AT THE GROCER'S *

A Play

Adapted from the story by Hans Christian Andersen

BY DELLE OGLESBEE ROSS

PERSONS IN THE PLAY

THE GOBLIN
THE GROCER
THE GROCER'S WIFE
THE SERVANT MAID
THE STUDENT

VOICES OF—
- THE CASK
- THE COFFEE MILL
- THE WATER PAIL
- THE CUPBOARD
- THE WATCHMAN

TIME: *A hundred years—or more—ago.*

PLACE: *A town in Denmark.*

SCENE: *A Grocer's shop.*

NOTES: *The* GOBLIN *wears a tight gray suit, long pointed shoes, a tall pointed red cap with a big tassel. The* GROCER *and his* WIFE *wear the costumes of prosperous Danish peasants. The* SERVANT MAID *is also dressed in peasant costume, though in a*

---

* This play may be produced without royalty where no admission is charged. Otherwise a fee of three dollars must be paid to the author, 317 North Marion St., Oak Park, Ill.

3

poorer fashion. The STUDENT *wears a long smock, down-at-the-heel bedroom slippers, large spectacles, kerchief around his neck. His hair is long and tousled. The tongue may be made of some bright red material, long and shaped like a tongue. The poem read by the* STUDENT *is "The Noble Nature" by Ben Jonson.*

The shop, which is also the kitchen-living room in the GRO-CER'S *house, is warm and bright on Christmas Eve. At right a door opens into the* STUDENT'S *room, another door at right back opens to the street. Over this door is a little bell which tinkles when the door is opened. At center back is a window, well-curtained, with a wide sill. At right of the window is a low bench upon which is a cask, or tub. At left of window a shelf or table holds a water pail and coffee mill. A cupboard stands against the wall, left. At left, front, a door leads to the room of the* GROCER *and his* WIFE. *Across the center front of the room is a wide counter upon which are candles, a long loaf of bread, sausages and cheese. In the right corner of the room is a small table, covered with a gay cloth and set for two, with two chairs drawn up to it. There are lighted candles on table and counter.*

As the curtain rises the GOBLIN *is sitting cross-legged on the counter. He holds a bowl on his lap and is eating from it, busily, with much smacking of lips.*

GOBLIN. Um! Um! The Grocer's Wife makes good things to eat. (*He eats greedily, again smacking his lips.*) And she's thoughtful, too, for every Christmas she leaves a good big bowl of porridge with jam and butter for me. (*He rolls his eyes, takes off his cap, and loudly eats the porridge.*) Of course she couldn't if the Grocer did not allow it. He must be a generous fellow! (*The* GROCER *is heard talking to his* WIFE. *The* GOBLIN *puts on his cap, turns his bowl upside down on the counter, and leaps to his feet.*) They mustn't see me! Hundreds and hundreds and hundreds of years and no human has seen me! But they know when I am around—and whether I am displeased or not! Ha! Ha! Ha!

(*He leaps nimbly from the counter, then to the window sill and hides behind the curtains. The* GROCER *enters, left, followed by his* WIFE *who patters in fluttering her hands and talking breathlessly every chance she gets.*)

GROCER. I tell you times are too hard to feed a Goblin—

WIFE. But we must feed him, Husband, we must feed him, we'll have bad luck else—

GROCER. Well—perhaps at Christmas—

WIFE. Every holy day he should be fed—

GROCER. But—

WIFE. (*Talking fast.*) Every holy day, Husband. Else will the milk sour, the butter not come—and the mice eat the cheese—

(*The* GOBLIN *peeps out from the curtain and grimaces at them.*)

GROCER. Piff! Nonsense!

WIFE. (*Following him around as he takes food from the cupboard and puts it on the table.*) 'Tis never nonsense! My grandmother told me—and her mother told her—and her mother told her—and her mother told her—and—and—everyone *knows* if you'll feed the Goblin you'll have good luck!

GROCER. Nonsense—nonsense—say I!

WIFE. Oh, Husband—

GROCER. Where's that lazy servant lass?

WIFE. She went out to buy—

GROCER. She's never at hand when wanted—what is she going to buy?

WIFE. A mantilla—

GROCER. A mantilla! However does she have money enough for that?

WIFE. (*Pattering after him as he goes to the* CASK *and takes out some papers which he places on the counter.*) But, Husband, she has been saving for a long, long, long time—to buy a mantilla. Of course I will not say I have not helped out with a skilling now and again—a girl must have something new once in a while—

GROCER. Peace, Wife, your tongue goes like a mill clapper—

WIFE. And do you criticize my tongue, Herr Grocer? Many's the sharp bargain it drives for you—many's the time—

GROCER. Well, 'tis like to go at both ends—and if the Goblin should take it the house would be quiet—

(*The* WIFE *claps her hand over her mouth, the* GOBLIN *peeps out again. The* SERVANT MAID *comes in, right back, wearing her new red mantilla.*)

SERVANT. I am sorry to be late, Master, but I went to many shops before I found my red mantilla.

GROCER. Humph!

WIFE. (*Turning round and round the* SERVANT, *peering at her from all sides, and rubbing bits of the material between her fingers.*) 'Tis a gay one—that. I do not know if 'tis seemly for a servant maid—

SERVANT. Oh, Mistress!

WIFE. But then—even servant maids like pretty things— I say—

GROCER. Quiet now! You, my lass, go put your fine gauds away, then serve my supper.

(*The* SERVANT MAID *goes out, left, the* GOBLIN *starts out, then darts back as the bell tinkles again, and the* STUDENT *enters the door, right back.*)

GROCER. Good evening, Herr Scholar.

STUDENT. Good evening to you, Herr Grocer, and you, Mistress.

WIFE. 'Tis fine Christmas weather we are having—though 'tis not like summer—but then—what will you— I always say a little snow, now, on Christmas—

STUDENT. Yes, yes—

GROCER. What can I give you tonight?

STUDENT. Candles I must have. Bread and cheese, perhaps a link of your good sausage.

(*The* GROCER *gives him the candles, wraps the bread and cheese and sausage in one of the papers he has taken from the* CASK. *He hands the parcel to the* STUDENT, *who bows to them and starts off. He notices the paper and turns it in his hands.*)

STUDENT. Why—what have we here?

GROCER. 'Tis but a page torn from an old book—

STUDENT. Ah, but 'tis a rare old book. This is poetry.

WIFE. Poetry?

STUDENT. These lines breathe the divine fire. They were written hundreds of years ago—

WIFE. But then it is only old poetry—

STUDENT. Ah, madam, this will still be living when we are dead and gone—

GROCER. Yonder lies more of the same sort.

WIFE. I will get it—yes, wait—but one moment— (*She goes to the* CASK.)

GROCER. I gave an old woman a few coffee berries for it.

STUDENT. Coffee berries.

GROCER. You may have it all for eight skillings.

STUDENT. Thank you. Let me have it instead of the cheese and sausage.

WIFE. Then here it is, Herr Student. But won't you be hungry? (*She hands him a large tattered book.*)

STUDENT. I can very well sup on bread and butter. It would be a sin and a shame for such a book as this to be torn into scraps.

GROCER. (*Laughing.*) It makes good wrapping, Herr Student—

STUDENT. You are an excellent man—a practical man—but

as for poetry—you have no more taste for it than that tub!

(*He makes a low bow and goes into his room. The* Goblin *peeps out, shakes his fist at the* Student, *angry that his*
Grocer *should be talked to like that. But the* Grocer *stands
with his hands on his hips, laughing, for he knows a joke
when he hears one. The* Wife *stands nibbling at the cheese
and sausage on the counter. The* Goblin *hides again.*)

Grocer. Come, Wife, we'll go to rest for the night—and save
our appetites for breakfast.

Wife. Are you not hungry, Husband?

Grocer. Not now. 'Tis late, and that lazy wench is still
prinking in her new mantilla, I'll swear.

Wife. Well, I've heard an empty stomach is best to sleep
upon—but for my part—I do not know—

(*They go out left, the* Wife *still talking. The* Goblin
*leaps from the window sill, dances around the room on his
toes, peeps into the* Cupboard—*the* Cask—*the* Water Pail
—*gives the handle of the* Coffee Mill *a turn—dances to the
counter and peers into his empty porridge bowl. He dances
again, then stands with his finger aside his nose.*)

Goblin. The good Grocer! He really is generous. I shall
always stay with him. (*He cracks his heels as he leaps into the
air.*) Always! He gives me good porridge at Christmas—with
jam and a great piece of butter. (*He dances over to the door
left, and peeps through the keyhole.*) There—they are sound
asleep! I'll go in and take the Goodwife's tongue. She won't
need it now, and it is too quiet in here by far— (*He slips
through the door, returning at once with the* Wife's *long red
tongue. He runs over and puts the tongue on the* Cask.) Is it
really true that you do not know what poetry is?

Cask. Don't I know! It is something that is put into newspapers to fill them up.

Goblin. Indeed!

Cask. I should think I have more of it in me than the Student has—though I am only a tub at the Grocer's!

(*The* GOBLIN *puts the tongue on the* COFFEE MILL, *which whirrs and clatters.*)

GOBLIN. Do you know what poetry is?

COFFEE MILL. Of course I do—of course I do—of course I do—

GOBLIN. Stop it! Stop it! Who can listen to such a clatter! (*He takes the tongue from the* COFFEE MILL *and puts it on the* WATER PAIL.) Do you know what poetry is?

WATER PAIL. Gurgle—gurgle—gurgle—well I know! 'Tis the gliding brook—the rippling of waters over silver pebbles—the roar of the waterfall—

GOBLIN. Yes—yes—

WATER PAIL. The placid lake—the break of the waves on the shore—all poetry—gurgle—gurgle—

GOBLIN. What does the Cupboard say? (*He puts the tongue on the* CUPBOARD.) Do you know what poetry is?

CUPBOARD. Everything is poetry—if you can see it—

GOBLIN. Everything?

CUPBOARD. Everything, of course—

GOBLIN. (*Taking the tongue from the* CUPBOARD.) You all seem agreed. The opinion of the multitude must be respected. (*He stands solemnly for an instant, then runs to the door, left, slips in, returns without the tongue.*) Poor thing—supposing I had worn out her tongue on the Cask and the other furniture. But now for the Student! (*He hops and skips to the door, right, and peeps into the keyhole.*) Ah—he is reading the old poetry book. Now I shall know what it is all about—

(*He opens the door a wide crack. From the room glow changing colored lights. The* STUDENT *is heard reading.*)

STUDENT. "It is not growing like a tree
      In bulk, doth make Man better be;
      Or standing long an oak, three hundred year,
      To fall a log at last, dry, bald, and sere."

GOBLIN. It is like a mighty broad-stemmed tree—that Light —spreading its branches over the Student—

STUDENT. "A lily of a day
Is fairer far in May,
Although it fall and die that night—
It was the plant and flower of Light."

GOBLIN. Every leaf of the tree is fresh and green, and every flower like a graceful girlish head—

STUDENT. "In small proportions we just beauties see;
And in short measures Life may perfect be."

GOBLIN. The eyes of some are dark, thrilling—others are blue—serene and gentle— (*Music floats from the room.*) The fruit is like glittering stars! And the music—the music! (*The music is louder and more glorious.*) No—such beauty and glory as this I have never imagined! I believe I will stay with the Student from this time on— (*He starts to go through the door, then stops.*) But the Student has no porridge with jam and butter for me— (*He slowly closes the door. The light and music vanish.*) I must stay with the Grocer!

(*There is a loud clatter and commotion outside. A* WATCH-MAN *sounds his rattle.*)

WATCHMAN. Robbers! Robbers! Come, gentles, save thy goods. Robbers have descended on the town!

(*The* GOBLIN *runs to the window. The* GROCER *and his* WIFE *rush into the room, left. Their clothes are disarranged as though put on hastily, the* GROCER *wears a tasseled night cap, the* WIFE *one with frills.*)

GROCER. Is it our house that is being robbed?

WIFE. (*Running in circles.*) Where—where—where are the thieves?

GROCER. I must save my money— (*He rummages in the* CUPBOARD *and takes out a heavy box.*)

WIFE. I must save something—save something—save something—

(*She takes off her ear rings and puts them in her pocket. The* SERVANT MAID *runs in, dragging her mantilla after her. She has on a plain night cap, and a large apron over her night gown.*)

SERVANT. Oh—we are robbed—we are robbed!

WIFE. (*Running around, taking up things and putting them down again.*) Robbed! Robbed! Everything stolen! Oh—my poor husband who has worked so hard—

GROCER. This is a great thing to happen on Christmas Eve! I thought to feed the Goblin would keep off ill luck!

WIFE. Oh—the Goblin! The beautiful big bowl of porridge and jam and butter for Christmas—and then robbers on Christmas Eve. That isn't the way to celebrate Christmas!

GROCER. Perhaps we should have fed him oftener—

SERVANT. People say the more you feed him—

WIFE. The better luck—

GROCER. Well—we will not forget holy days this year—

(*The* GOBLIN *dances behind the curtains making them wave back and forth. Outside voices cry* "Thieves—thieves—catch the thieves." *The* SERVANT MAID *holds her mantilla closely to her.*)

SERVANT. We must hide— Oh—my beautiful mantilla! My beautiful mantilla! So gay—so red! They will steal it—

WIFE. We must save what we can—

(*She picks up the dishes from the table and throws them out of the window. There is a loud crash. The* GOBLIN *remains unseen, but it is a narrow escape. The* WIFE *folds up the table cloth and tucks it under her arm.*)

GROCER. Come—come—we must go! We must help catch the robbers!

SERVANT. Oh—no—Master—we must hide—they will rob us if we run to the street—

WIFE. Yes—yes—we must hide. Let the town guards catch them—they'll steal our money—our clothes—everything—

GROCER. I'll not desert my neighbors! They may be murderers as well as thieves!

WIFE. (*Running around.*) Oh—oh—we'll be murdered too—we'll be murdered too—

(*The clamor outside increases.*)

SERVANT. (*Clasping her hands.*) Oh, please, dear Master, let us hide—

GROCER. Where—? Nay—now—

WIFE. Where will we hide—where will we hide—we'll be murdered—robbed— Oh— Oh—

GROCER. Peace! Stop your clatter!

SERVANT. We'll hide in my clothes press. Robbers would never think to look in the servant's clothes press—

GROCER. Well—w-e-l-l—

WATCHMAN. (*Outside.*) Call the guard! Call the guard! Robbers are in the town—they have come from the hills—a band of robbers from the hills! Call the guard! Call the guard!

GROCER. (*Staring.*) Robbers from the hills!

OTHER VOICES OUTSIDE. Ho! The guards!

GROCER. (*Making up his mind.*) Come then—we will hide in the Servant Maid's clothes press.

(*He grabs his* WIFE *and starts out the door, left. The* SERVANT *grabs her mistress's skirts and out the door they go. The* GOBLIN *leaps to the floor.*)

WIFE. We'll all go together—we'll all go together—

GOBLIN. But I must save the most precious of all—the wonderful book! The poetry book! (*He flings the door, right, wide open.*) There he stands, calm as a June day, watching the crowds. But I shall save the book! (*The* GOBLIN *darts into the* STUDENT'S *room and back again with the book, which he carefully places in his cap.*) If the Student, who is *really* my Master, can watch the robbers so calmly, then so can I— (*He leaps to the window sill.*) I shall sit on the chimney top and protect the book. Our house may be the next one—one never

knows— (*He stands on the sill ready to jump.*) I will bring
the book back to my Master, the Student, but I shall stay with
my Master, the Grocer—for he has the jam and the porridge!
(*He peers out, looking up and down the street.*) But where is
this bold robber band? I see no one. The noise has ceased—the
Christmas chimes are beginning to ring. And the guard is chasing the robbers back to the hills— (*He leaps back into the
room, dances over to the* STUDENT'S *door.*) I must return the
wonderful book to my Master, the Student— (*He pops into
the room, leaves the book, and pops back. He capers around
the room.*) He is writing—more poetry, no doubt—and my
Master, the Grocer, is safe, for he is hiding in the Servant's
clothes press—and the robbers are gone—nothing is stolen—
(*He begins to dance. On the last figure of the dance he hesitates—continues—hesitates—then stops, places his finger beside his nose.*) I know what to do! 'Tis all decided! My Master,
the Student, will stay with my Master, the Grocer,—where
could he find better lodgings? So here will I stay also! And be
fed every holy day— (*He leaps in the air.*) So then will I have
two Masters—*and* the poetry—*and* the jam—*and* the porridge
—and so to all—a Merry Christmas! (*He starts to dance again
as the curtain falls.*)

THE ON AND OFF OF A CHRISTMAS GIFT *

By Lettie C. VanDerveer

CHARACTERS

Nicholas Peretto
Salvation Army Lassie (*heard but not seen*)

* For permission to produce, apply to the author, 11 South Illinois Ave.,
Atlantic City, N.J.

BOB HALE
LYALL HALE, his sister
MADGE LESTER, Lyall's friend
AN OLD LADY

SCENE: *A city side-walk stand on which are displayed a variety of Christmas tree trimmings, such as colored balls, silver moss, glass icicles, golden floss, etc., holly wreaths and red paper wreaths. A dark-eyed, black-haired young fellow is standing beside it, dividing his time between watching for possible buyers and rearranging his wares hopefully. He doesn't look very warmly clad, and has his coat collar turned up around his neck, and the coat buttoned tight about him. He has no overcoat nor gloves. He looks cold as he does a sort of jig-step from one foot to the other, sometimes whistling cheerily, sometimes calling out:* "This way for your Christmas tree trimmings. Anything you want." *From left of him comes the sound of a bell of the Salvation-Army-Christmas-Dinner kind accompanied by the intermittent call of a feminine voice, touched with Irish brogue, calling,* "Keep the pot a-boiling! Keep the pot a-boiling!"

NICHOLAS. (*Speaking to left.*) Business not so brisk this morning, Lassie. No coins jingling into that pot so far, eh what?

S. A. LASSIE'S VOICE. Never a one, boy. The colder the day the fewer the coins. (*In comradely raillery.*) But I've not noticed yourself runnin' down to the bank to make deposits very frequent.

NICK. (*Retorts in same spirit.*) Aw—that's because you can't see around the edge of that poke bonnet you're wearing. I'm th' : busy it keeps me hoppin'.

S. A. LASSIE. So I've noticed. Indeed'nd I'd hop meself if 't wasn't for the looks of it. This cold gets into the marrow of a body's bones. And never the price of so much as a drum-stick —let alone a Christmas dinner—has jingled into the pot this mornin'.

NICK. Begorra—you should add. Why don't ye spake the brogue, Lassie? Don't tell me you're ashamed of the Auld Countrie, bedad.

S. A. LASSIE. Ashamed of the Old Country? Indeed'nd I'm not. The nerve of ye! But how did ye ever guess I was born in the Old Country?

NICK. (*Impudently.*) Oh, ye've the map of the Imerald Isle on yer face, Lassie.

S. A. LASSIE. The impidence of the likes o' you tellin' me that. And here I've said not a word of you bein' Eyetalian from the black eyes and hair of ye to the Mussoleeny set of yer jaw. Old country yerself! (*She jingles the bell fiercely.*) Ye'd be wearin' sky-blue-pink clothes on ye if ye'd the nerve,—and rowin' yerself along in a gondoola.

NICK. (*Throws his head back and laughs heartily.*) Lassie, I'd geeva tha "eye" out of Eye*a*lian if I hada tha price of a beega woola sky-blue-pinka sweater theesa minuta.

BOB HALE. (*Appears at right, clearly of the well-to-do, comfortably clad class.*) Hello, Nick! I'll say you need a beega sky-blue-pink sweater this day. Whew! Doesn't the wind cut? How's business?

NICK. Well, if you're looking for a job I don't need help just this minute. (*With a grin and nod to left.*) Go jingle the bell for the Lassie yonder and maybe she'll put you on the Christmas dinner list.

BOB. (*Looks left, also grinning in friendly fashion, and lifting his hat.*) I guess the shoppers are few and far between this morning, Miss. Let's hope there'll be better days or Christmas dinners for the poor will be slim. (*As he speaks he takes some coins from his pocket.*) I want to pick out some holly wreaths on my way back, Nick. S'long! (*As he goes left the sound of his coins jingling into the pot is heard.*)

NICK. (*Calls after him.*) None better, so don't give the Lassie all your money. (*He draws his coat closer about his throat, shivering against his will.*)

BOB. (*His voice coming back.*) You'd better go get your overcoat, Nick. It's like the North Pole around this corner. . . . Say, want me to tend store while you go for it?

NICK. (*Blithely.*) Run along, pampered son of luxury,— this is nothing but a summer breeze. But thanks. (*He turns his shiver into a whistle, then says, with a shake of his head and whimsical nod in the direction* BOB *has gone.*) There's a guy who thinks overcoats grow on fire-hydrants.

S. A. LASSIE. Ain't it the truth! A warm heart and a ready hand with a dime in it, but never a bit of understanding in his good-lookin' head.

NICK. (*Finishes comically.*) "Begorry." says she. . . . Great chap, though Bob Hale is. He's a classmate of mine in High School. (*Suddenly he looks right, doffing his cap quickly.*) Hello, Madge! Hello, Lyall! (*Two pretty, well-dressed girls, arms full of parcels, stop at his stand.*) It takes more than a cold morning to keep you away from the bargain counters I see. I'd try to sell you some wreaths, Lyall, but honesty keeps me from it. Bob said he'd stop back for some. But there's nothing to stop you from investing, Madge. Best in the city. (*Holding a wreath up temptingly.*)

MADGE LESTER. (*Snuggling into her furs.*) Nothing but freezing my hands carrying them home this zero weather. But I'll pick out two or three. My word! (*Looking him over.*) Are you warm enough?

(LYALL, *too, looks at his outfit askance.*)

NICK. (*Turning a shiver into a shrug.*) Well, nobody's hollering for electric fans exactly today if you ask me. (*Waving a hand to right.*) Hold on, Jiggs, I'll give you a lift. (*To girls.*) Wait, I'll only be a minute. Jiggs Rudd is trying to unload those Christmas trees, and he's got a bad back from a fall—yesterday. (*He goes right quickly.*)

LYALL. (*Looking after him.*) Goodness! He does look cold,

Madge. You don't suppose . . . ?

MADGE. (*Her eyes also following* NICK, *the same thought in mind.*) Oh, he must have warmer clothes than that, Lyall. He always looks well enough dressed in school.

LYALL. (*Slowly, trying to reassure herself.*) Yes, he must have. (BOB *reappears, at her side.*) Oh, hello, Bob. Say, Bob, you ought to tell Nick Peretto to wear warmer clothes weather like this if he hasn't enough sense to know it himself.

BOB. Hi, Madge! Hi, Sis!

MADGE. You don't really suppose he hasn't them, do you?

BOB. (*Cheerfully.*) Oh gee, yes. He must have. (*But as* NICK *reappears he looks at him intently.*) Hey! You've got customers, Nicholas.

NICK. (*Shivering in spite of himself.*) Gee! I believe some of that snow clinging to those spruces got down my neck. Want your wreaths now, Bob?

BOB. (*Abstractedly.*) Wreaths? Oh yeah. . . . I tell you what, Sis, you pick out what we need and I'll be back for them.

LYALL. I've only got a minute, Bob. Besides I'm freezing to death. So don't be fussy about what I select.

BOB. (*Going.*) I won't. Nick'll help you. He's an honest guy even if he don't look it.

NICK. So's your old man.

(MADGE *has selected and piled up three wreaths.*)

MADGE. Lay these aside for me, please, Nick. I'll send Jeff for them. (*She pays him.*)

NICK. Thanks a lot, Madge. You're my first customer to-day.

LYALL. (*With chattering teeth.*) My stars! Your first? You pick ours out, will you, Nick? Four, I guess. I'm simply congealing. Come on, Madge, before you have to get an ice-pick to pry me loose. (*They hurry away with gay good-byes.*)

S. A. LASSIE. Beautiful—but dumb, ain't they? (*Jingling her bell.*) Keep the pot a-boiling! Keep the pot a-boiling!

NICK. Not so dumb. They're swell girls, those two.

S. A. LASSIE. (*Scornfully.*) All wrapped in furs and too cold to pick out their Christmas trimmings. Sst! Here they come back.

MADGE'S VOICE. We almost forgot about the Christmas dinner, Lassie. (*Their coins jingle into the pot.*)

LASSIE. Thank you very kindly, Miss—and you too, Miss.

LYALL'S VOICE. You're very welcome. And best of luck to you.

S. A. LASSIE. Now that's what I get for me mean words. Coals of fire—no less. The both of them fishin' out some money and their poor little slim coddled fingers tinglin' with cold the while.

NICK. Well hang on to the "coals of fire" . . . Hello! You're back soon, Bob. (*As BOB reappears.*) Goin' places? You look as if you've got your extra clothes in that bundle.

BOB. (*Pausing by the stand, an awkwardly wrapped bundle in his hands.*) Well—er—not exactly. (*He clears his throat, embarrassed, then plunges ahead.*) I say, Nick, would—would you—er—wear this sweater? You look so blame cold you've got me worried,—and—er—I was afraid you wouldn't take time to go home and get your own,—and it's awful weather for pneumonia. (*He keeps his eyes on the business of unwrapping the sweater.*)

NICK. (*Putting a hand on BOB's arm, shaking him a little.*) Bob Hale—what a two-faced rascal you've turned out to be. You're trying to give me a sweater without my knowing it,— ain't you now?

BOB. (*With a sheepish grin, hauling out a very heavy, very colorful sweater from its wrappings.*) Honest, Nick, you'd do me a favor to take it. You can chuck it any time you want to. I hate the thing. An old aunt of Mother's gave it to me last

Christmas, and every time I put it on I feel like part of the zoo.

NICK. (*Laughing heartily.*) And what'll that make me? The zebra or the giraffe?

BOB. (*Joining in the laugh.*) Oh gee. I didn't mean it that way,—insulting your taste,—believe me I didn't.

NICK. (*Proceeding to draw the sweater over his head.*) Boy, I'll wear your insult with joy. M-m! Does *it* stand between me and the cold, cold world! (*Calls left.*) Lassie, put the brakes on that bell and gaze on me—the sky-blue-pink sweater fer-ninst my Mussolini chin.

S. A. LASSIE. Indeed'nd it brings the smile on me map of Ireland to gaze on ye. Ye're the spittin' image of a circus parade I once seen. (*Jingle-jingle.*) Keep the pot a-boiling! Keep the pot a-boiling!

NICK. Listen to that now! The two of you ruin the joy bub-blin' up in my sunny Italian heart with your speeches. . . . Where are you off to, Bob, in such a hurry? I want to thank you properly.

BOB. (*As he hurries embarrassedly away.*) Aw, forget it! Honest, if you only knew how much I'd rather look at that sweater on you than on a hook in my wardrobe . . . ! S'long! (*Goes.*)

NICK. (*When* BOB *is out of hearing.*) What'd I tell you, Lassie? He's the best guy ever—Bob Hale is.

S. A. LASSIE. Faith and I'll take your word for it now. Seein's believin'! (*Ting-a-ling!*) Keep the pot a-boiling! . . . And it's lucky for you to be inside that rainbow this cold minute too.

NICK. Say, Lassie, you go inside that grocery store and get warm. I'll watch the pot. You look frozen.

S. A. LASSIE. Well—I will for a minute. Frambes'll be here any time now to take his turn, but I'm that cold my teeth are chatterin'. I'll be back as soon as I thaw out.

NICK. Don't hurry, now. (*He whistles cheerily as he beats his hands across his chest, looking down admiringly at his new possession the while. Presently he looks sharply to right.*) What now?

BOB. (*Rushing up breathlessly.*) Say, Nick,—gimme back that sweater quick, will you? (NICK *stares.*) I just met Lyall and she says she's sure she saw Aunt Cordelia getting off a trolley down town,—the old lady I told you gave it to me last year. Lyall's sure she's on her way to our house for Christmas. I'll take it home and wear it—sometimes—while she's around— and then I'll bring it back to you—see?

NICK. (*In smothered tones as he pulls the sweater up over his head.*) Gee! Sure. You don't want to get yourself in Dutch with Auntie,—giving away her Christmas present.

BOB. (*While he helps* NICK *out of it.*) I feel mean as the worst kind of Indian giver. You must think I'm nuts. . . . Say, you put on this coat of mine,—you'll miss the extra warmth of that sweater.

NICK. (*Waving him away.*) Nothin' doin'. I'm warm as toast now and when the Lassie comes out of that store I'll get her to mind my stand while I go toast my toes.

BOB. Well—just as you say. But I sure am sorry. S'long! (*He hurries away.*)

(NICK *again turns up his collar and hops from one foot to the other, beating his hands together for warmth. Presently the* LASSIE'S *voice is heard again.*)

S. A. LASSIE. Here I am again—and thanks to ye. Why— where's your sweater? Don't tell me they mistook ye for a tiger and skinned ye for the fur. . . . What's gone with it?

NICK. Can it,—somebody's coming. I'll tell you later. (*The* LASSIE *rings her bell again.*)

(*A voice speaks at left, a rather sharp, shaky, old-sounding voice, that of the* OLD LADY.)

OLD LADY. My girl, if you'd stop the din of that bell for a

minute maybe I could hear myself count out something to put in the pot.

S. A. LASSIE. Oh—I'm sorry, Ma'am. (*Jingle of coins.*) Thank you ever so much.

OLD LADY. Now for goodness' sakes tell whoever picks out the turkeys or chickens for your baskets to look at them good, and not get any of those bruised scrawny-looking ones. They're likely to stick 'em off on you if you don't watch out. And don't forget to put some candy in for the children. (*Another jingle of coins.*)

S. A. LASSIE. Indeed'nd I'll not. There'll likely be pie too if there's a few more passers-by like you. (*The* OLD LADY *comes into view, an odd-looking, old-fashioned figure in bonnet and shawl. She approaches* NICK'S *stand.*)

OLD LADY. (*Calling back to* LASSIE.) Oh, go 'long with your blarney now. Who knows but what I'll be stoppin' in some day askin' you for a cold bite? (*To* NICK.) Well, young fellow, what and all have you got here? . . . How any mortal being would buy such stuff as this (*Touching a box of tinsel.*) is more than I can understand. Howbeit it takes all kinds to make a world, as the old woman said when she kissed the cow. (*Shaking her head in annoyance.*) No, that ain't what she said at all. My goodness. I'm getting so forgetful. What did she say anyhow,—do you recollect?

NICK. She said "Everybody to his taste," didn't she?

OLD LADY. (*Regarding him keenly over her spectacles.*) Yes, that was it. But how in the world did you get onto such an old-time American saying as that? You're a foreigner, aren't you,—by the looks of you? Now don't think I'm insulting,— I've always thought dark slim foreigners a sight handsomer than our pudgy American men. (*Behind her hand.*) But don't spread it.

NICK. (*With a friendly amused grin.*) I won't. But you see I'm American—if I don't look it. Born here. I guess you expected me to say, "Me nota know what tha olda ladyee she say when she keesa tha cow—or tha cow she say when she keesa tha olda ladyee, yes."

OLD LADY. (*Laughing heartily and giving him a jovial push.*) Go long with you and get desa olda lady three or four wreaths, —and not these terrible red paper ones either. I'm on my way to my niece's to spend Christmas and I'm going to see to it that I don't have to look at any heathenish red paper wreaths in their windows while I'm there. Holly ones—with plenty of berries too, now mind you. (*As* NICK *picks them out carefully.*) My stars! Boy. Are you warm enough in just those thin clothes? You ought to bundle up more, weather like this.

NICK. Oh, I'm all right. You get used to cold weather after you've had it a few days.

OLD LADY. (*Skeptically.*) Um. Maybe. Well, of course it's none of my business—but if you'll take an old woman's advice you'll put on more clothes the first chance you get. (*She pays him for the wreaths out of a big worn purse.*) These are nice ones, same on both sides too. Well, good-by, boy.

NICK. Good-by, and thank you, and Merry Christmas! (*He watches as she goes and says to* S. A. LASSIE.) Odd as she is kindhearted. Look at that. She's waving the wreaths trying to get the eye of that taxi-driver. (*Starting right.*) Wonder if he sees her. . . . Yeah, he's stopping. (*Comes back to stand. For a while there is only the sound of the bell ringing, and the* LASSIE'S *call.*)

S. A. LASSIE. (*Presently.*) Well, you look froze without that sweater. Whatever in the world happened to it?

NICK. Had to lend it back to the guy again. The aunt that gave it to him last Christmas is on her way there for this Christmas. I'm due to get it again.

S. A. LASSIE. Mm, after you're froze. Them people never know their own minds.

NICK. Uh-uh, Lassie. Mind your tongue, or the gobbleuns'll

git you if you don't watch out. (*Calls to some passer-by.*) Hi, there, young fellow. Want some nice Christmas trimmings? Best in the city. . . . No—he doesn't. Next year I'm going to have a hot soup stand.

S. A. LASSIE. (*Jingling her bell.*) Keep the pot a-boiling! Keep the pot a-boiling!

NICK. That's the stuff. Your yodel will give them the idea, and naturally they'll turn toward my pot of soup. Fine!

S. A. LASSIE. (*Laughing.*) Whatever are you talking about any way? I can't tell whether it's me bell I hear jinglin' or your brains.

NICK. (*Adds.*) "Begorra!" Eh what? Well—look yonder! It's my old lady scrambling out of that taxi again. . . . She's coming this way too.

OLD LADY. (*Approaches, somewhat out of breath, carrying a hastily wrapped bundle. She starts talking as soon as she comes in sight.*) Young man—now I don't want you to think I'm taking liberties—and I *won't* take "no." I'm old enough to be your grandmother—and have to be humored in my whims or I might get a spell of some kind—at my age. (*Chuckling.*) I've brought you a Christmas present, and not a word back do I want out of you. (*All the while she has been unwrapping her bundle while* NICK's *fascinated gaze follows her fingers.*) You young folks don't know when you are inviting pneumonia— and somebody's got to take care of you—under Providence. (*Out comes a heavy colorful sweater.*)

NICK. Honest, I—I don't know what to say. I—I—

OLD LADY. Well—don't say anything. Just put it on. (*Behind her hand with a look right and left.*) I stole it.

NICK. (*Aghast.*) Stole it?

OLD LADY. Now don't start lookin' around for the police. Put it on. Put it on. (NICK *does so automatically.*) I tell you how it is. I came here from Philadelphia to spend Christmas with my niece and her family, to surprise 'em, and when I got to the house there wasn't a soul home but the maid, and as I went in the living room there was this sweater lying on a chair. Bob's—Emma's boy's, I suppose.

NICK. (*Under his breath.*) Bob?

OLD LADY. How in the world he ever came to choose a sweater like this with his complexion is more than I can imagine. Seems to me any way I gave him a nice sweater last Christmas—but this can't be it. Anyway, if it is he won't miss it for I've brought him another this time. I couldn't think of anything else except a necktie—or socks. . . . My! You look handsome in it. But now don't get vain at my saying so. It's your dark skin with those colors. (*Chuckling.*) But who'd ever have thought an old woman who'd lived a respectable law-abiding life as long as I have would sneak out of that house with a sweater the way I just did? Lucky this wrapping paper was lying nearby or I might have got caught hunting some.

NICK. But you got back so quick . . .

OLD LADY. Mm. Didn't I though? Regular gangster speed. You see my taxi man was tinkering with something wrong with his engine—a "knock" I believe he said. But you'd think the speed they go a knock or so wouldn't mean a thing to them. But anyway, as I come out the door here he was just about to pull away, so in I gets again,—and here I am.

NICK. Gee! I don't know what to say.

OLD LADY. (*Patting his shoulder with one hand and beckoning with the other.*) Well, don't say a word except "Merry Christmas!" And the same to you, child. Hi there. Taxi man, I'm ready.

THE END

THE SPIRIT OF THE DAY

A Play

By Grace Torrey

PERSONS IN THE PLAY

Plum Pudding
Indigestion
A French Doll
A Buster Brown Doll
The Present That Nobody Ever Wanted
A Child
A Tired Woman

Scene: *A shadowy room, littered with tissue paper, ribbons, packages, et cetera; in the lamplight a woman sews frantically, putting the last stitches into the costume of a French doll. As the clock strikes twelve, she puts the doll down, with a long, weary yawn.*

The Woman. That's done at last! (*She gets up, stretching.*) Oh! Oh! Oh! How tired I am! Eighty-one presents! It's enough to kill me. I believe next Christmas I'll go away. (*She moves about wearily, as if looking for something.*) Where in the world did I put that list? It would be too awful to have left out someone. (*She shuffles about the heaped-up articles on the table— tissue paper, thread, scraps of cloth, et cetera.*) It isn't as if anybody wanted a present. But it's the spirit— Oh, here it is. (*Reads from the list, making occasional comments.*) Tom—two dollars and fifty cents; that's really too little to spend on Tom. Grace Breckenridge, slippers. I had the yarn. Amy, ninety-eight cents; Bess, handkerchief; Roger, tie, one dollar and twenty-five cents; Maud—she always gives me something nice, so I simply had to come to the scratch this year. The Briggs children. Wretched little monsters! They have so much now, they don't know which way to turn. They'll never look at the things I'm sending. But I simply had to. The Briggses always remember Baby. I wonder if Baby really doesn't know I have that Buster Brown doll for her. Children are so sophisticated, nowadays. You can hardly surprise them any more. I doubt if Baby really believes in Santa Claus, any more than I do. But we have to keep it up, just to counteract the dreadful materialism of this age. After all, the spirit is the important— (*Goes on checking off. Stares suddenly, aghast, and holds her pencil poised.*) Aunt Lizzie! Aunt Lizzie! Of all people! I— have—no, I can't have—yes, I have! (*Puts both hands to her head, and says, half crying.*) Oh, I am so tired! Why must I always think of everything and everybody? No one else in this house will remember her; but if I don't, the family will never forgive it. Oh, dear! It's so late, now. I can't make anything. I've got to give her something in the house. And she knows everything I have. Oh, dear! (*Stands working her hands, and looking pitifully around, as if to find a Christmas present materializing in the air.*) I might— Oh! I know the very thing. That bag that Esther sent me last year. She never sees Aunt Lizzie. And I've never shown it to a soul. (*Goes to a heaped-up basket in the corner.*) It's very ugly: a bright red, green, and yellow chintz, with wide yellow ties. (*Draws out bag and looks at it. Shakes her head.*) I had forgotten it was so dreadful! Well— (*Begins to roll it up in tissue paper. Ties careful bow, and writes card, reading as she writes.*) "To dearest Aunt Lizzie. With oceans of love, and warmest Christmas Greetings from her devoted niece, Carrie." There! That ought to make anything welcome. And really, it isn't the gift that counts. It's the spirit. (*Puts the card under the ribbon and takes the package and the doll over to the back of the stage. Gathers up the mess on her table. Pushes the table back to the wall. Looks around, yawning and moaning.*) Well, I must go and get a little sleep. I can make things look better in the morning. Later in the morning, I mean. (*Very dolefully.*) It's Merry Christmas already—and Baby will be up at six, getting excited, and catching cold. And eating too much! I wish the plum pudding didn't always give her such dreadful indigestion. But it always has, and I suppose it will always have to. I wouldn't think of having it, if it weren't for the spirit. (*Yawns.*) Oh, I am—so—tired! (*Goes out yawning, and finishing diminuendo.*) The spirit—of—the—day—ha—hum!

(*As she disappears, enter, ponderously, from the side, PLUM PUDDING. He is round, pigeon-toed, pompous, with a fat voice. He stands facing the audience, but looking apprehensively out of the corners of his eyes toward the entrance by which he has come on. There rewards his gaze the thin, bent form of* INDIGESTION *in stringy clothes, her head tied up in a large cloth, her hands clasped over her stomach. She is pale and wears a woebegone expression. She, too, stands facing the audience with a sidelong eye for* PLUM PUDDING, *who speaks.*)

PLUM PUDDING. So there yer comes *hagain!*

INDIGESTION. (*Afraid, yet acid.*) Well, you heard what she said. I always have come after you. I suppose I'll always have to.

PLUM PUDDING. (*With slow backward gesture of the head toward woman's exit.*) 'Oo said? 'Er? (*With meaning eye for* INDIGESTION.) Womanfolk is all fools.

INDIGESTION. (*Infinitely satiric.*) I may look like a fool. But do you flatter yourself that I follow you around because I want to?

PLUM PUDDING. (*Fatly violent.*) W'at do Hi care w'y yer follers me haround? Yer follers me, doesn't yer? 'Oo cares w'ether yer wants ter, or doesn't want ter, hif honly yer goes hon follerin'? (*Mimicking* INDIGESTION, *but not being able, for physical reasons, to bend over.*) Do Hi flatter myself that she wants ter foller haround hafter me? No, hand don't flatter yerself has Hi wants yer, neither. Me, a respectable British gent, halways hand forever 'ounded by a female of no charm, no happearance. W'erever Hi ham, hit's halways the sime. Christmas day, heverybody smilin' hand pleasant. Hi comes hin hall decyryted with 'olly, hand burnin' bloo blazes. Heverybody claps 'is 'ands hand sez: " 'Urray for the plum puddin'!" Hi halways makes han hagreeable first himpression. Then wot 'appens? Within a hour, before folks 'as time ter go 'ome hand 'ave their troubles comfortable like, 'ere you comes hin, hand the sime hold song begins. Them as 'ave het the most hopens hup reg'lar: "That miserable plum puddin' his givin' me the hindigestion hagain. Hi houghtn't never ter 'ave nothink ter do with 'im. Hi never would, neither, honly ter be hin the Christmas spirit." Does hanybody think Hi likes hit—halways givin' my friends the stummick hache? (PLUM PUDDING, *much affected, would wipe his eyes, were he not so fat.*)

INDIGESTION. (*Weeping.*) Oh, I wish you wouldn't be so hard on me! I never wanted you to give me to anybody.

(*Voice from behind makes them both start and turn, to see a long figure, in rustling white, a red ribbon about his waist, a placard sticking cornerwise through the ribbon, on which it is possible to read the words of the* WOMAN'S *message to* AUNT LIZZIE. *The figure rustles up, saying.*)

UNKNOWN. Hold on there, hold on there! I must be in this!

PLUM PUDDING. (*Heavily.*) Hand 'oo, may Hi hask, hare yer?

UNKNOWN. Who am I? Who are you, you middle-class British institution? Who are you, to ask who I am? (*With scorn to* INDIGESTION.) Cry baby! What have you to wail about? (*Walks nervously around, ejaculating.*) Idiots! Nuisances! With warmest love! Stuff! With warmest maledictions! (*Turns upon* INDIGESTION.) You've nothing to cry about, I say. Nothing. I'm not even sorry for you. You come in the natural order of things. Plum Pudding—Indigestion—it's a cosmic process. It's cause and effect. You are, because you are predetermined to be. You must be. But I! I never even needed to exist! Once, oh, happy, happy once, I was not! (*He lifts his face, to address the heavens.*) Once there was no unhappy I. Once I *was not.* And now I have to be *am.* And unthinking conventions—pure, mechanical, instinctive, unreasoning habits—like you (*Stares at* PLUM PUDDING, *who is much outraged.*) are forever asking, 'Oo am I!

(*A giggle is heard from the corner, and a* VOICE *speaks.*)

VOICE. Silly, disagreeable old thing! Who do you suppose he is?

ANOTHER VOICE. I don't care. Kiss me again!

(*There is a loud sound of smacking, causing the group to turn, discovering the newly finished* DOLL *in the embrace of a* BUSTER BROWN. *They have entered, on tiptoe, hand in hand, at back of stage, during* UNKNOWN's *last speech.*)

PLUM PUDDING. (*Darkly.*) Hit's that misbehavin' French Doll hand that himmature piece of dry goods she's soft hon. For that matter, hall the girls hare fond of me—hat first.

INDIGESTION. (*Sourly.*) Sickening little sentimentalists!

UNKNOWN. How can you kiss each other that way? Don't you know how dangerous it is to kiss? How germicidal? How medieval? How commonplace? Don't you know that everybody kisses—the sick, the fat, the homely, the thin, the—

(*The* DOLLS *do not look at him, but rapturously at each other.*)

B. B. DOLL. But this is an especial kiss.

FRENCH DOLL. Yes. It expresses the spirit of the day!

(PLUM PUDDING *groans.* INDIGESTION *moans. The* UNKNOWN *strides toward them.*)

UNKNOWN. The spirit of the day, indeed! I'll spirit you! Come here. (*They come, terrified, to the front of the stage.*) Listen! You dare to love each other?

THE DOLLS. (*Trembling, but brave.*) We do!

UNKNOWN. Fools!

PLUM PUDDING. Come, come! Hit's happropriate to their youth hand propinquity. The young halways loves somebody. They loves me—hat first. (*Looks savagely at* INDIGESTION.)

INDIGESTION. (*Pettishly.*) I wish he wouldn't make these vulgar allusions to me.

UNKNOWN. Propinquity? Youth? Doll's face! (*To the* BUSTER BROWN DOLL.) You think she's pretty, do you?

B. B. DOLL. I *know* it, sir.

UNKNOWN. (*To* FRENCH DOLL.) You love him, do you?

FRENCH DOLL. (*Nodding.*) Oh, yes, dreadfully!

UNKNOWN. (*Tossing his head.*) Well, here's what your spirit of the time does for you. You (*Looking at* BUSTER BROWN DOLL.) are to stay here. You (*Looking at* FRENCH DOLL.) are to be given to the youngest and meanest Briggs.

(DOLLS *shriek and fall into each other's arms.*)

PLUM PUDDING. Well, my raisins! Hit hain't right. Poor young lovyers!

INDIGESTION. (*Sniffing.*) Oh, well, they'd probably quarrel in no time.

PLUM PUDDING. (*Furiously.*) Hi tells yer, they *wouldn't* probably. Halways cuttin' hin with yer would probablys! (*To* UNKNOWN.) And you, wild, rampagin' hupstart individial, 'oo hare yer, ter know so much, hanyways?

BOTH DOLLS. Yes, yes, you cruel man, who are you?

UNKNOWN. (*Desperately.*) Come here! (*All crowd about.*) I'll tell you who I am. I am the Present Nobody Ever Wanted!

PLUM PUDDING. (*Glaring at* INDIGESTION.) My word for hit, young feller, yer not the fust.

INDIGESTION. (*Clasping her stomach.*) Oh, how I ache for you!

B. B. DOLL. (*Embracing* FRENCH DOLL.) Brute! It serves him right.

FRENCH DOLL. (*Wiping her eyes, and shaking her head.*) I

don't believe him. Nobody ever didn't want a present.

UNKNOWN. Little ninny! Listen! Sixteen years ago this night—at this very hour—I was finished by Aunt Lizzie, sitting over there in that very chair.

FRENCH DOLL. What! Not that chair! Why, that's the chair I was finished in, too! (*To* BUSTER BROWN DOLL.) You see, dear, I've had the best of advantages. I was finished in one of the oldest and most established finishing places!

UNKNOWN. (*Glaring.*) If you will kindly let me finish! As I was saying, she didn't want to make me, but she had to do something for Cousin Jane. When I was finished, she said, "Thank Heaven!" and sent me off. I went, ignorant creature that I was, happy in the thought that I would be loved. But was I? I tell you, no! Cousin Jane put me away in a drawer for two years. She wrote Aunt Lizzie that I was lovely. She told me I was a perfect fright. At the end of two years she sent me to Cousin Sarah Alice, in Canada, because she was too far away for Aunt Lizzie to find out. Cousin Sarah Alice said, My word, I would stop a clock! and put me away for four years, when she sent me to Cousin Esther, in Iowa. Cousin Esther looked at me once, and said: H'm! The relations thought they could send her anything, just because she lived in Ioway. Then I was laid away again, this time for nine years.

FRENCH DOLL. Nine years! My! Isn't he old?

B. B. DOLL. Yes. Be patient with him, dearest. Only think, the poor creature is in his nonage. We must be very respectful and kind to him. The sight of youth, and life, and loveliness in such as you and I is among the very few pleasures left to the old and unlovely, such as he.

FRENCH DOLL. Stupid of him to be shut up for nine whole years. If anyone treated me that way, I should put an end to it in three minutes!

UNKNOWN. (*Desperately.*) End to it! End to it! Oh, you poor little inexperienced new-born thing! Did I not long to end it? Did I not *pray* for the end? But I was so horrible that the moths would not eat me. Then, last Christmas, Cousin Esther took me out of moth balls, aired me, and sent me here—to get even, she said. And *now*, I am done up to go back to Aunt Lizzie. There's your spirit of the time. I tell you— (*He tears off his wrappings, and comes out a very homely, limp bag, scarlet and green, with large yellow flowers.*) I tell you, I revolt! I will not be given away! I will not even lend myself to the machinations of the spirit of the time any longer. Nobody wants to give me nor get me. And I won't be given, nor gotten, any more. I hereby revolt!

(*Sensation in the group.*)

INDIGESTION. (*Hysterically.*) I won't neither, oh, I won't neither, I won't neither! I revolt!

PLUM PUDDING. (*Savagely to* INDIGESTION.) Be quiet. 'Oo hare yer, any'ow? Yer honly a consequence of me. Nothink but han heffect. Hand hif Hi decides ter be the cause, yer can't 'elp yerself.

INDIGESTION. (*To* PLUM PUDDING, *on her knees.*) Oh, please don't go on causing me. I don't want to be given to anybody. (*Clasping her stomach.*) It hurts so to be forever unwelcome. Please join me and this revolting gentleman.

B. B. DOLL. Come on, mister. I'm in for it, too. You see, the youngest Briggs has a horrible reputation for mutilating. It fairly makes one's sawdust burn to think of it. And—and I do love her. (*Embraces* FRENCH DOLL. *Very manly, but on the edge of tears.*)

FRENCH DOLL. Oh, Plum Pudding, dear, good Plum Pudding! Please join the revolution. I'm so young; so beautiful; so eager for life and love; so formed for a kindlier fate!

PLUM PUDDING. (*Sentimentally.*) I knows 'ow yer feels. Hi'm a kindly creeter, myself, naterally. (*Looks malevolently at* INDIGESTION *on her knees.*) Get up, there. Did Hi say for yer ter kneel down?

(Dolls *help* Indigestion *up. All form a supplicating group about* Plum Pudding.)

All. Oh, join with us, join with us!

Plum Pudding. Hit goes 'ard. Hi've kind of got the 'ang of comin' hin hon a platter, blazin' bloo hand bright. Hand hit's hagreeable ter 'ear them say has 'ow my blazin' represents the spirit of the time. Hand hall the laughin'— (*Shakes his head.*)

Unknown. Think how they turn on you later.

Plum Pudding. Ho, yes! Hi feels hit. Hif they didn't hall turn hon me, later! My 'olly! Hit's a shime to turn on a kindly creeter, like me! Blime, Hi'll join yer. 'Ere's my 'and hon hit!

(*While he has been talking, the* Child *has put her head in at the curtain at the rear of the stage, and looks on, smiling. When* Plum Pudding *extends his hand,* Child *speaks.*)

Child. What an interesting dream I am having!

Unknown. (*Takes* Plum Pudding's *hand, crying.*) Yours for the revolution! Down with the spirit of the time!

The Dolls. (*Embracing and dancing round and round.*) Yes, yes! Yours for the revolution!

Indigestion. Down with everybody's spirits! Down with all kinds of spirits!

Child. (*Coming in a little way, timid, but smiling.*) Merry Christmas, everybody!

(*Grand consternation.* Unknown *gets into the back of the group. The* Dolls *stiffen.* Indigestion *slinks to the side of* Plum Pudding, *who alone remains bland.*)

Plum Pudding. Merry Christmas yerself, Child, hif Hi may mike so free.

Child. (*Advancing.*) Are you Plum Pudding? (*Looking up at him and smiling.*) Mm! But you look good! I love you. (Plum Pudding *ecstatic.* Child *sees* Indigestion.) Oh! I know you! (*Mimics her characteristic posture.*) You're what he (*Points to* Plum Pudding.) gives me every year. But I don't mind. Lots of things give one Indigestion, all the time, that aren't half so jolly as Plum Pudding. Besides, I'd rather have Indigestion any day, than castor oil.

INDIGESTION. (*Quite beside herself with mingled indignation and pleasure.*) Castor oil! I should hope so. Slimy reptile! I can't bear to be mentioned in the same day with him. But you're a dear child! It has been so long since anyone appreciated my peculiar nature. Just for that, I promise not to hurt next time, not one bit!

FRENCH DOLL. She does look like a dear child. I'm sure she would be kind to me. Please, Child, can't I be given to you, this Christmas? I want so much to stay with him!

CHILD. (*Calmly.*) Do your clothes button and unbutton?

FRENCH DOLL. Yes. And only see my eyelashes!

CHILD. (*Suspiciously.*) You're not just a new head on an old doll I had last year?

B. B. DOLL. (*Indignantly.*) Indeed, she is not! She came out of the very next box to mine. She's not been in this house two weeks.

CHILD. Oh! Two weeks? Mother has been shutting herself off upstairs for about two weeks, where I couldn't come in, nor talk through the door, nor anything. The last time I knocked, she said if I didn't go away and stay away, she'd tell Santa Claus not to bring me a thing. Oh! Let me tell you something. Come here! I'll tell you a secret. (ALL *crowd about but* UN-KNOWN, *who glowers apart.* CHILD *mysteriously.*) Father and mother are Santa Claus. They don't know that I know. And you mustn't ever tell. It would spoil their Christmas. Promise you won't tell!

(ALL *but* UNKNOWN *take the* CHILD'S *hands.*) We promise!

PLUM PUDDING. 'Ere's ter the spirit of the day!

UNKNOWN. (*Advancing with fury.*) Tr-r-aitors! Not two seconds ago you had all given your word to me, your pr-r-omise. Now, what are you doing? What do you mean?

CHILD. (*Gazing in delight at* UNKNOWN.) Why! If there

isn't my beautiful present that I've always wanted! (*Goes up to him, and touches the yellow flowers.*) Aren't they sweet? I've seen you lots of times in mother's drawer upstairs. I've always wanted you.

(ALL *show astonishment.*)

UNKNOWN. (*Aghast.*) Who? Me? Me beautiful? You—you don't mean you'd really like to have me? Why! What could anyone—what could you do with me?

CHILD. Oh, lots of nice things. You would do beautifully to keep mice in. Or I could cut you all up and plant you for a garden outside my playhouse.

UNKNOWN. A garden! Me a garden! Oh! (*Embracing* CHILD.) You darling! (*Holding her and addressing the others.*) If they'll let me be a garden, I hereby unrevolt!

FRENCH DOLL. Oh, me, too! Me, too! If I can be with him!

B. B. DOLL. Me, too, if I can be with her!

PLUM PUDDING. Hm! W-e-ll—Hi believe Hi'm with yer. Hi never went hin strong for no revylootions. Hi thought them a trifle hextreme.

INDIGESTION. I won't hurt you much, really. And if you don't mind his giving me you, I unrevolt, too.

CHILD. (*Bewildered.*) Unrevolt? Why, what had you all revolted about?

ALL. Against the spirit of the time.

CHILD. (*Shocked.*) Not—not against Christmas?

B. B. DOLL. You bet.

FRENCH DOLL. Yes, indeedy.

PLUM PUDDING. (*Uncertainly.*) W-e-ll, miss, Hi fancy we might call hit that.

INDIGESTION. But it didn't mean anything. Just a passing disagreement.

CHILD. My! What a strange dream I'm having! You really mean no presents; no stomach ache; no secrets; nobody shut upstairs, getting tired?

UNKNOWN. We—we did mean just that, my dear!

PLUM PUDDING. And nobody 'aving ter give nothink 'e didn't want ter give ter nobody 'e didn't want ter give it ter.

FRENCH DOLL. And no one making persons go where they perfectly hated to go.

UNKNOWN. (*Shrieking and throwing himself down at the* CHILD'S *feet.*) Oh! Oh! And no poor, ugly creature, that didn't want to be made, getting made, and sent where he wasn't wanted. Oh! Oh! Oh! (*Sobs.*)

CHILD. (*Puzzled, almost crying.*) Why! Don't people give Christmas presents because they want to? Oh, dear! Didn't mother—I mean Santa Claus—want to give me my white Teddy Bear last Christmas? And my doll that hasn't any head, that I sleep with at night—do you suppose maybe she didn't want to be given to me?

(*Looks appealingly at the* FRENCH DOLL, *who is unhappy, but expects someone to help her out.*)

PLUM PUDDING. Well, my little lydy, of course hit's 'ard hon yer, but think of hour lacerated witals. Think of hours—hand heverybody's self-respects. 'Oo wants ter be givin' hand takin' thinks 'e don't want from folks has don't want ter give hand take them? We got, has hit were, ter mullin' hit hall hover, hand decided, has hit were, ter quit this 'ere Christmas business.

CHILD. Oh, dear, what shall I do? (*Looks sorrowfully from one to another anxious, helpless face. A sound is heard outside.*) Oh! It's mother coming! You mustn't, mustn't do it! I tell you, it would never do! I know father and mother wouldn't like it. Oh, dear! She's coming! Please stand still, and she'll think she's having a dream. Please stand still, till I can get her away!

(*Enter the* WOMAN. *She looks past the* CHILD, *smiling tearfully at her, and sees all the figures standing against the wall. The* CHILD'S *arms are spread out, as if to screen the figures.*)

CHILD. Oh, mother! Mother! Look at me! Don't look anywhere but just at me. I'm having such an interesting dream.

WOMAN. Dream? I had a dream, too. It must have been a dream. I thought—I dreamed—that all the presents had revolted. I thought—I dreamed—that they had all agreed to quit the Christmas business. (*Sees the* CHILD.) Why! There's Baby! She'll get her feet cold. Oh! (*Looks around at the rigid figures.*) Oh! She'll see them, and find out that they've revolted. Oh! That will never do. I mustn't let her find out. (*Moves over to* CHILD, *and puts her arms about her. Speaks tenderly.*) Merry Christmas, you naughty little prowler! Come back to bed and warm your feet, or Santa Claus won't give you anything.

CHILD. (*Looking up at her.*) Oh, mother, tell me!

WOMAN. (*Drawing her gently toward the door, looking around to see that the* CHILD's *eyes are shielded from the figures.*) Tell you what, darling?

CHILD. Tell me, mother, what is Merry Christmas?

WOMAN. Merry Christmas? What a funny question? Why, it's giving things, and getting them, and being happy.

CHILD. (*Mournfully.*) Giving things, and getting them, and being happy? But suppose you aren't happy. Suppose folks don't want to give what they give, nor get what they get; who's going to be happy, mother?

WOMAN. (*Stammering.*) Oh, but honey, not *want* to! How foolish! Everybody wants to give presents and get them.

CHILD. (*Fearfully looking over her shoulder at the figures.*) But, mother, suppose there weren't any presents, what would we do?

WOMAN. (*Looking fearfully around.*) No presents? Why—why—then we'd have to get along, and love each other, and be happy anyway.

CHILD. But can't we be happy both ways, mother?

WOMAN. (*Doubtfully.*) Why, dear—aren't *you* happy?

CHILD. Not if you're tired, and not if you didn't want to give me my white Teddy Bear that Santa Claus brought last year. And not if everybody hates everything, and wishes he wasn't given to people, or giving to people.

(*Great commotion and nodding among figures. Warning gestures from* CHILD *and from* WOMAN.)

WOMAN. (*Drawing* CHILD *gently toward exit.*) Oh, but if we're tired, we love to be tired, and if we give things we don't— just exactly want to, it's because we do want to more than we don't want to. And nobody hates anybody.

CHILD. Really, mother?

WOMAN. Really, dear.

PLUM PUDDING. (*Advancing, in spite of warning from* CHILD.) Hi 'ates 'er. (*Points at* INDIGESTION.)

INDIGESTION. Oh, I hate him!

(WOMAN *gestures frantically.*)

FRENCH DOLL AND B. B. DOLL. We *hate* the Briggses.

UNKNOWN. (*Throwing up his arm.*) Everybody hates me!

(WOMAN *and* CHILD *cling to each other in terror, looking around at last.*)

CHILD. You didn't hear anything, did you, mother?

WOMAN. I—why—did you, dear?

CHILD. I—I'm afraid I did.

WOMAN. Wh-what was it like?

CHILD. It was like a whole world full of tired mothers and greedy children and miserable Christmases.

WOMAN. (*Beginning to cry.*) Oh, yes! That's just it. I am so tired. And I only wanted to make people happy.

CHILD. (*Beginning to cry.*) But I don't want you to be tired making me happy. I don't want you to shut yourself up upstairs, and not let me come in. I don't want anything but you, and—and one other something that I can't have.

WOMAN. (*On her knees.*) Oh, dearest! You always have me. Always! Always! And there's nothing you can't have.

CHILD. (*Cheering up.*) Not even the beautiful red bag, with yellow poppies on it, that nobody likes but me?

(UNKNOWN *steps forward in great excitement.* CHILD *holds up warning finger.*)

WOMAN. What? That awful—that—why, deary! Of course, if you truly want it. But don't you want anything else? Not any dolls, dear? Not even a Buster Brown boy doll?

(DOLLS *tiptoe forward, arm in arm.* CHILD *puts her finger on her lip, and shakes her head.*)

CHILD. Oh, I've so many dolls. I think I don't need any more just now. I'd like to give all the dolls to some nice child who doesn't have any.

WOMAN. (*Reflectively.*) Why! I believe I know the very one! But, dearie, think! Don't you want any plum pudding? Not even a little mouthful?

CHILD. Oh—let's give all the plum pudding to the Briggses.

(PLUM PUDDING *and* INDIGESTION *eye each other, with dawning favor.*)

WOMAN. (*Laughing.*) What a quantity of indigestion we'd be presenting them with!

PLUM PUDDING. Well, my leaves hand 'olly! Hi'd fair hinjoy givin' them Briggs children Hindigestion.

WOMAN. (*Warningly.*) We can do it, dearest, if you really want to. But remember! If we do, there won't be any Merry Christmas at our house!

(*Gets up, beginning to draw* CHILD *out between the figures standing on either side.*)

CHILD. Oh, but yes, there will! You see, the really Christmas part will all be left. I'll have you—and you'll have me. And we'll both have father. And we can all go to see Aunt Lizzie, and take her some of my radishes that I grew in my window garden!

BOTH TOGETHER. (*Laughing, and taking hands and dancing out.*) Oh, won't that be a Merry Christmas!

(*They go out, seeing each other, and not any of the figures who stand looking after them.*)

UNKNOWN. (*Recovering himself, goes about room, from figure to figure, swaggering a trifle, perhaps, and feeling himself.*) What do you think? I'll do beautifully to keep mice in! (*Inspects his poppies with incredulous delight.*) Or I could be cut up and planted in a garden! (*Approaches the door. With sudden burst of enthusiasm.*) She really wants me. I can do something. Hooray! It's Merry Christmas! (*Goes out, leaping and shouting.*)

THE DOLLS. (*Falling into each other's arms.*) Oh, we can stay together always. Down with the revolution! It's Merry Christmas!

(*Dance out, in each other's arms. The stage is left to* PLUM PUDDING *and* INDIGESTION, *who stand as at entering, facing the audience, eying each other.*)

PLUM PUDDING. (*Piously.*) Hi suppose hit's hinevitable that a poor female creeter like yer should foller haround arter a male man. Hit's a lor of nater. So 'oo ham Hi ter blime yer?

INDIGESTION. (*Incredulous.*) Do you mean you don't mind my coming with you to the Briggses?

PLUM PUDDING. (*Quite melting.*) Mind? My dear, Hi may say Hi'm free ter hadmit that the day with the Briggses wouldn't reely be hendoorable without you.

INDIGESTION. (*Straightening up, and holding up her hands.*) Oh, my! Oh, my! I've got to follow him around—and he doesn't mind it! (*Throws herself wildly upon* PLUM PUDDING, *and, as far as possible, embraces him.*) Oh, it's surely Merry Christmas.

PLUM PUDDING. (*Fatly.*) 'Ere's ter the spirit of the day!

CURTAIN

WHAT THE CAMELS BROUGHT
TO MISER CLAUS *

A Puppet Play for Children

By Mary Stewart Sheldon

THE JESTER

(*In Front of Curtain*)

Of all the friends who visit you in story
  Which is the one you love the very most?
Is Peter Pan the best, or Cinderella?
  Does Jack who climbed the beanstalk lead the host?

Ah now I know, I see it in your faces!
  There's one whose place is first in love and song.
His beard is white, his cap and cloak are scarlet,
  His sleigh bells jingle. Yes, we've loved him long!

But oh, my dears, there was a time, believe me,
  When Santa Claus was not at all a friend.
He was a miser, mean and cross and stingy,
  His work-shop camels saw the story end.

They brought him dreams of Christmas joy and blessing,
  He followed them, as we all do today.
The story—oh it is so strange, so lovely,
  You'll see it all right in this little play!

CHARACTERS

Miser Claus. *He has a white beard and long white hair. He wears an old-fashioned frock coat, red cravat, shabby high hat.*

* Where no admission is charged, this play may be produced free. Otherwise, written permission must be secured by sending a fee of $5.00 to Mrs. Raymond Sheldon, Chestnut Ridge Road, Mt. Kisco, N.Y.

POLL, *a poor Irish woman dressed in shabby brown, red shawl over head and shoulders.*

JAKEY, *small ragged boy.*

GRIMES. *Old man, small and bent with a kindly, quizzical look. He is an expert toy maker.*

MELCHIOR, *First King, long beard, gorgeous and dignified, on camel, bearing treasure.*

GASPARD, *Second King, young and magnificent, also on camel, carrying chest of gold.*

BALTHAZAR, *Third King, on camel. Negro, dressed in simple cloak, bearing small Christmas tree.*

ELEPHANT, JACK-IN-THE-BOX, BEAR, SOLDIER.

The toys which "come alive" can easily be made out of cardboard or thin wood if one has a jig saw. They must be painted and their heads or trunk or hand attached to body with wire which is in turn attached to long wire placed behind figure to make it "come alive."

If this play is acted by children they can take the toys parts themselves and for the vision the Three Wise Men can be thrown upon the sheet at back of stage by stereopticon, or else the actors may dispense with large camels and take "Wise Men" parts themselves.

Behold the toy-shop where Miser Claus beheld the Christmas camels!

SCENE: *Interior of a toy-shop. Toy animals, dolls, soldiers, etc., are hanging on wings and standing in front of them. In background, right, is a window through which one sees snow, icicles and a patch of blue sky. At left of background stands a splendid Christmas tree hung with tinsel, colored balls, toys, and upon the top a star. Center right is a desk upon which stand a telephone and money bags. Front, right and left, are toys of large size which later "come alive." On the right* ELEPHANT

and JACK-IN-THE-BOX. *On the left* TEDDY BEAR *and* SOLDIER.
CLAUS *is seated at desk. As he speaks he pores over money bags, occasionally jingling them.*

CLAUS. Well, well, this is Christmas Eve and the year is almost over! A fine pile of money I have made this year. Every dollar has been saved, not a nickel wasted, not a cent given away. I hear that instead of Mr. Claus and Co., I am called Miser Claus, the Skinflint. Ha, ha! What do I care? I care for nothing but money, piles and piles and piles of money until I am called King Claus. And Christmas—what does that day mean to me? Dollars and dollars! This tree now has been sold to the millionaire up town. He sends for it tomorrow morning. He pays me one thousand dollars for it—one thousand! And I paid my work-people less than a hundred for all their work upon it. They will never know, poor fools, starving and slaving in my factory, they will never know what my profits are. No one shall, except my precious money bags. We will keep the secret! But listen—who comes here?
(*Enter* POLL.)
CLAUS. (*Rudely.*) Hullo, what brings you here to see Miser Claus the Skinflint?
POLL. (*Who has been gazing at tree.*) Well, sor, begging your pardon, sor, but you see we're very poor this here Christmas, what with Jim's bein' in France so long and this wee baby havin' been sick and—you see, sor, my Jim he says to me, he says, "Poll, old girl, there'll be nothin' merry about this Christmas for our kids without they have a peep at a toy shop, and there'll be nothin' merry for us without the kids be smilin'." That's what my Jim says. And together we thought that perhaps you having so many new toys, you might let the children have a wee peep at that wonderful tree, and thin, when their eyes are all dazzled and shinin', you might have a few bits of owld broken dolls or soldiers like, that you wouldn't

mind givin' them. Forgive me, sor, if I am too bold, it is for the childher, ye mind—

CLAUS. Mind? Mind? I mind that Miser Claus the Skinflint doesn't give peeps into his workshop unless a large order goes with it. How you got in I can't imagine. Out you go now, fast, you mind that. And don't you come again unless you come in a satin gown with a purse full of money on your arm!

POLL. (*Going out sadly, murmuring.*) The poor childher, the poor, wee childher, not a mite of merriness will there be for us this Christmas Day.

CLAUS. Now let me see, what is there left to do before I close up? That tree stays here until tomorrow morning. The millionaire thinks he has the finest tree in the city! He little knows that shut up in my secret storeroom I have a tree far more splendid! It will bring me fifty thousand dollars next year, at the very least. It is lighted with real stars and will be hung with icicles which cannot melt, powdered with frost of diamond dust, and hung with toys like these. (*He goes to front and touches, timidly, the big toys to left and right.*) Old Grimes who made them says they "come alive"! What on earth does he mean? I'll call him now and ask him! (*Exit* CLAUS.)

(*A music box behind scenes plays and the toys "come alive." The* JACK-IN-THE-BOX *pops up, the* TEDDY BEAR *moves arms and head, the* SOLDIER *salutes, the* ELEPHANT *moves trunk and tail.*)

JACK-IN-THE-BOX. Of course he can't see us come alive! How could an old miser, who doesn't know what Merry Christmas means, see or hear us? We only came alive because dear old Grimes who made us, loved and dreamed about us so much, and if we are sold to any dull old millionaire he won't see us dance, either. But for the children—look now, perhaps there are some children here who love toys and whose hearts are merry! If there are they will see us!

(*To the music of the music box each figure makes its motions.*)

SOLDIER. Hush, I hear someone coming!

(*They all become silent. CLAUS returns.*)

CLAUS. Couldn't find Grimes anywhere. I'll telephone for him. But who is this? (*Enter JAKEY.*) Hullo, what do you want? How all you ragged people get in is beyond me. Clear out now before you have time to steal any of my toys.

JAKEY. Please sir, I'm Jakey, the messenger who carries your toys to your rich customers. And I never stole anything, sir, not even a tin soldier—and I've wanted one all my life too, sir!

CLAUS. Well hurry up, boy, and tell me what you want now. I suppose one of my workmen sent you here with a message. Don't waste my time, speak up and clear out!

JAKEY. No sir, I wasn't exactly sent here, sir. But I have a little sister who is a cripple and it being Christmas Eve I wanted to ask if I could go home a bit earlier so that I could tell her a Christmas story before she goes to sleep. She's never had a doll or a toy in her life, but I tell her stories about the ones here, and that is almost as good as playing with them. To-night I promised to tell her about these wonderful toys. The toys that "come alive," you know, sir.

CLAUS. Come alive indeed! How do you know that? Been spying, have you? Time off you want? No, indeed. You will stay and work after hours to make up for your impertinence. And I'll tell you one thing. You stop telling stories and thinking about toys that "come alive," and make money for your sister. She would rather have that, good jingling money, than any story in the world, wouldn't she now?

JAKEY. Oh, no, sir, you see, money doesn't make Merry Christmas, it's the stories and dreams and stars,—why, even the toys know that. (*He goes to the front of stage and the toys all move gaily for him.*) See, sir, that is the way the toys "come alive." Can't you see them now?

CLAUS. (*Crossly.*) No, I see nothing but a stupid boy who is wasting my time. Go and find old Grimes and send him to me. And you work here until midnight, do you understand?

(JAKEY *salutes the* SOLDIER, *bows to the others and runs off.*)

CLAUS. (*Takes receiver off telephone and speaks.*) Hullo, hullo there! Are my reindeer ready? Put every empty box and sack and basket in the place into my sleigh. I am going to collect my payment for the Christmas toys. No bills or credit allowed from Miser Claus. Bring the reindeer around in half an hour, and someone find old Grimes and send him here with those new camels he has been making. Understand? Sharp now! (*Turning from telephone.*) Reindeer beat all the horses, motors and airplanes ever invented. They go so fast that in this one night I will collect all the money owing me. Thousands and thousands—millions and millions it will be next year when Grimes finishes those strange toys of his. He says the camels are the most wonderful of all. He is a strange chap, Grimes, he could earn a fortune if anyone but I knew how clever he is. As it is—he forgets to eat, the men say, he works so hard. Loves to work,—fool! To love work when it brings you no money! Hullo, (GRIMES *enters.*) that you, Grimes? Didn't hear you come in.

GRIMES. Merry—good evening, sir. I started to say Merry Christmas, sir, but that—

CLAUS. That's nonsense, that's all it is, Grimes. You are the third person who has talked about Merry Christmas in this room today and it has no sense. I don't even know what it means. Money Christmas is all I know about. I make more money this week than all the rest of the year. Money Christmas!—That sounds good, doesn't it?

GRIMES. I don't like the sound, sir. You see the toys and I get so full of merry thoughts around Christmas time that they and I do turn out wonderful bits of work. There are these toys now (*Patting large toys.*) so full of merriment that they come alive every time someone who loves them comes near. It's the Christmas dreams that make them and me so merry. Now pardon me, sir, but did you ever have a dream?

CLAUS. Of course, dreams of money every night! Now how about these camels you have been working on? Are they ready yet?

GRIMES. Yes, sir, they are finished. I don't have to wind or pull or turn. I only call and—here they are!

(*Three camels, about twice as large as the toys which "come alive," enter and walk across the stage. They bear the* THREE KINGS, *like the large ones which come later,* MEL-CHIOR, GASPARD, BALTHAZAR. *Christmas music is heard.*)

CLAUS. Marvelous! Wonderful! They move without any machinery, they come at your bidding! It is beyond belief!

GRIMES. I am glad you are pleased, sir. And now excuse me, but I have an errand of my own and would like to go home a bit early tonight.

CLAUS. Early? No, indeed! You will go down to my stables and help pack my sleigh with empty boxes. I collect payment tonight and nothing else matters. See that my reindeer are brought around in ten minutes.

(GRIMES *stops to pat toys on each side of stage and each in turn answers with its special movement. Facing audience he then speaks to himself.*)

GRIMES. There will be something besides gold in those empty boxes tonight if I mistake not. My camels will not bring their gifts in vain. Dreams and hopes and prayers the camels bring on Christmas Eve. They are bringing a new name to Miser Claus. Will he understand or is his heart a stone? Watch and listen, for strange happenings take place on Christmas Eve!

(*Exit* GRIMES. CLAUS *seats himself behind desk, the stage grows darker.*)

CLAUS. What is this word they all use? Merry—what does it mean? I must be nervous tonight for I am lonely and old and full of a strange longing. What is the trouble with me? I have gold enough to live upon grandly for a hundred years and more, far more, coming to me tonight. And yet—I am miserable. It is the meaning of the word "Merry" which troubles me. Will I ever understand? Could I buy it with gold? I think I would give all I possess to understand its meaning for one moment!

(*The stage grows dark. Under cover of the darkness the foreground is removed and a set of blue which has been placed behind it is revealed. There is a star in this blue background in exactly the same place the star hung upon the tree. Through the star, or from above the background, the light shines, growing gradually brighter until the whole stage is bathed in a silvery, misty light. Christmas music plays during the change.* CLAUS *is apparently asleep in his chair. As* MELCHIOR *enters upon his camel* CLAUS *wakens, stands up slowly, faces* MELCHIOR, *who stops in center, back, while* CLAUS *addresses him in awed wonder.*)

CLAUS. Where are you going with your treasure? Whom do you seek? What payment will you receive for it?

MELCHIOR. (*Intoning answer, as do all the Wise Men.*) I seek the birthplace of a young King to whom I will offer my treasure as a gift, a useless gift, did not my heart go with it! (*He passes on, off the stage, slowly.*)

CLAUS. A gift for a young King! I never gave a gift, I never sought a King! My heart—it has grown cold and lonely. If I found this King I would have nothing but an empty heart to offer him!

(*Seats himself and his head falls forward as in sleep. Enter* GASPARD. CLAUS *sees him, stands, faces the King.*)

CLAUS. Who are you and where are you going with your chest of gold? If you also seek a young King, take me with you, for my heart is filled with a strange longing I cannot understand.

GASPARD. I come from far and I seek a young child, lying in a manger. To him I bring my Christmas gift of gold, precious only because my love goes with it.

(*Exit* GASPARD. CLAUS *again falls into deep thought or slumber and is roused only by the entrance of* BALTHAZAR.)

CLAUS. Where are you going with your tree so green? Do you also seek a young King, a little child? If so, show me the way that I too may worship him.

BALTHAZAR. I seek the children of the world, brothers and sisters of the young King. To them I bring the sign of his love for them, the sign of the joy of his birthday,—the Christmas Tree! (*Exit* BALTHAZAR.)

CLAUS. The children of the world? His little brothers and sisters? (*As* CLAUS *again slumbers the background is changed back to original scene. Gradually the light brightens and* CLAUS *wakens with it.*) Did I dream? Did the camels come? Ah, no, I remember now! I am going to find the brothers and sisters of the young King. In finding them I shall find him! What shall I give them? Shall it be gold and jewels? Oh I know, I know! I can give them all the toys I have, thousands and thousands from my great warehouse. I must start at once for there are so many children and not one must be left out. I'll put on my coat and cap and call for the reindeer! (*He rushes out and light on stage increases until it is brilliant.* CLAUS *re-enters, dressed in scarlet cap and coat trimmed with white fur, the conventional* SANTA CLAUS.) So, so, here I am, ready! Poll and Jim and their kids shall have the marvelous tree, the one with the real stars! Jakey and his sister shall have you, you wonderful toys that come alive! (*Rushes to telephone.*) Hullo, hullo, there! I want old Grimes. That you, Grimes? Please fill my sleigh with thousands of toys, fill every empty box and bag, never mind the payments, I have more important business to-night. What's that? The sleigh is ready now? Full of toys? You thought I would want to follow the camels? Well, you were right! And Grimes—Merry Christmas, Grimes! (CLAUS *turns from telephone and faces audience.*) I begin to understand, I feel so merry! Here, you toys that come alive, can I see you move now? Will you dance for Miser Claus?

(*All the toys "come alive."*)

JACK-IN-THE-BOX. Yes, yes, because you are not Miser Claus any more, you're Santa Claus, the follower of the camels, the giver of Christmas gifts to every child, because—

(*Each toy in turn, in appropriate voices.*) Because you are so merry! (*All dance madly to music.*)

CLAUS. Merry, did they say? Is that what you call it when your heart is bursting with love and joy and you know that to-morrow is Christmas? Then bless your hearts, my dears, I'm off now to carry you all presents and to wish you from the bottom of my heart a very—Merry Christmas!!!!

CURTAIN

THE BLIND BOY OF BETHLEHEM

BY KATHARINE LEE BATES

SCENE: *A dim, curtained alcove, in which may be faintly discerned the outlines of a divan.*

BENONI. (*Calling excitedly from the divan.*)
    Mother! my mother! Mother, come to me!
MOTHER. (*Entering with a soft light, as of a Greek lamp, in her hand.*)
    What is it, my Benoni, son of grief?
BENONI. I cannot sleep because the room—
MOTHER.   Is dark.
    O dear blind eyes, if love could make them see!

BENONI. But mother, mother—

MOTHER. What a trembling leaf
Is this frail hand that clutches mine!

BENONI. O hark!
You do not let me tell you.

MOTHER. Tell me what?

BENONI. I cannot sleep because the room is so—

MOTHER. So dark, my dove?

BENONI. So light! so light! so light!

MOTHER. Alas, again the fever!

BENONI. It is not
The fever. See, O see the splendors glow
Upon the gloom, all radiantly bright!
Sit by me, mother. Hold my hand and look.

MOTHER. (*Seating herself on the side of the divan and strok-
ing the boy's head.*)
Benoni, son of sorrow, full of wild,
Strange fancies, what is there to give you joy?
What should I see within this curtained nook
But hush and shadow and a wayward child,
A sleep-bewildered, mother-missing boy?
There are no splendors here.

BENONI. The gleams! The gleams!

MOTHER. Only this tiny gleam I bear.

BENONI. The stars!

MOTHER. What should you know of stars?

BENONI. The skies! the skies!

MOTHER. O blind from birth, your skies are only dreams,
Child-dreams of seraphs driving golden cars.

VOICE. There is a seeing deeper than the eyes.

(*Into the room, gradually flooded with light, enter in succession, as one after another is summoned by the* VOICE,
*majestic figures clad in hues of gold and amber, pearl and
silver, wearing starry crowns.*)

VOICE.   Come forth to festival, O shining host!
   Ye ministers that do the Holy Will.
   Archer,
  (*Enter* SAGITTARIUS, *bearing bow and arrow.*)
        whose glistening shaft no more shall kill!
   Fierce Hunter,
  (*Enter* ORION, *belted and sworded.*)
       from whose falchion fades the boast!
   Bright Watcher,
  (*Enter, as armed sentinel, the* NORTH STAR.)
       steadfast at thy lonely post,
   Waiting that hour when good shall vanquish ill!
   Fair Pleiades,
  (*Enter six maidens in a sisterly group.*)
       whose hearts of daffodil
   Make spring in winter! Even the furthermost
   Of all Heaven's flaming multitudes,
  (*Enter more* RADIANCES *and more.*)
         come hither
   To chant a song whose music shall not cease,
   To plant a Christmas rose that shall not wither
   Even in the shadow of a Cross, to bring
   A vision for Earth's long remembering,
   To hail the herald of the Prince of Peace!
  (*Enter the* STAR OF BETHLEHEM, *a Golden Child.*)
   Youngest of Stars, our fealty receive.
  (*All the* RADIANCES *bow down and cast their crowns be-for the* STAR OF BETHLEHEM.)
   Teach us the glad new song of Christmas Eve.
STAR OF BETHLEHEM. Glory to Love in the highest,
      And on earth Peace.
ALL THE STARS. Glory to Love in the highest,
      And on earth Peace.
  (*Slowly the* STARS *pass out, chanting the new song, while*

the scene gradually darkens.)

BENONI.   O mother, mother, mother, did you see
The Shining Ones, that bowed themselves before
The Golden Child?

MOTHER.   I saw your face.

BENONI.   High, high
The music mounts. Dear mother, let us be
As glad as angels. More and more and more
Their anthem soars.

MOTHER.   I hear a lullaby.

(*A curtain at one side of the stage is drawn, disclosing the manger tableau.*)

INVISIBLE CHORUS.   Glory to Love in the highest.
And on earth Peace.

O HOLY NIGHT—A PAGEANT

BY C. O. RICHARDSON

In this pageant any number of characters may take part, including shepherds, reader, chorus, angels, Wise Men, soloist, Madonna, and children. The time of presentation for the pageant is about forty minutes.

I—"WHILE SHEPHERDS WATCHED THEIR FLOCKS"

Lights are low to suggest night. Several shepherds are seen sitting or reclining. Soft music is heard in distance.

READER—"And there were in the same country shepherds abiding in the field, keeping watch over their flock by night."

Chorus off stage or in front sings first stanza of "While Shepherds Watched Their Flocks." At the words, "The angel of the Lord came down," the angel appears at one side and is illuminated with a spotlight. The angel sings second, third, and fourth verses and vanishes as the chorus completes the song.

READER—"And it came to pass, as the angels were gone away from them into heaven, the shepherds said one to another, Let us now go even unto Bethlehem, and see this thing which is come to pass, which the Lord hath made known to us. And they came in haste."

The shepherds depart eagerly.

II—"WE THREE KINGS OF ORIENT ARE"

READER—"Now when Jesus was born in Bethlehem of Judaea in the days of Herod the king, behold, there came wise men from the east to Jerusalem, saying, Where is he that is born King of the Jews? for we have seen his star in the east and are come to worship him."

Enter three kings dressed in oriental costumes, each with a gift. The first stanza of the song, "We Three Kings of Orient Are," is sung by the three kings, with everyone assisting on the chorus. The king with the gift of gold sings the second stanza; the king with the frankincense sings the third; the king with the myrrh sings the fourth. Each shows his gift as he sings, and the chorus assists with the refrain. All sing the fifth stanza as the kings walk slowly off stage in search of the Christ Child. The curtain closes.

III—INTERMISSION

A soloist sings "Cantique De Noël" in front of the curtain as preparations for the next scene are being made.

IV—"SILENT NIGHT"

The curtain rises on a stable scene. There is a manger toward front with the Madonna seated by it. Soft light emanates from manger; other lights are low. Two angels hover about the end of manger back of Madonna. The Shepherds stand about in worshipful attitudes. Lights go out as chorus sings "Silent Night."

READER—"Then Herod, when he had privily called the wise men, enquired of them diligently what time the star appeared. And he sent them to Bethlehem, and said, Go and search diligently for the young child. . . . When they had heard the king, they departed; and, lo, the star, which they saw in the east, went before them, till it came and stood over where the young child was. When they saw the star, they rejoiced with exceeding great joy. And when they were come into the house, they saw the young child with Mary his mother, and fell down, and worshipped him: and when they had opened their treasures, they presented unto him gifts; gold, and frankincense, and myrrh."

The Wise Men enter and present their gifts. They kneel while the chorus hums "Silent Night."

READER—"And being warned of God in a dream that they should not return to Herod, they departed into their own country another way."

The three Wise Men depart, while the chorus sings "O Little Town of Bethlehem."

V—"AWAY IN A MANGER"

Several little girls dressed in white gowns enter. They stand around the manger, looking down into it, and sing Luther's cradle hymn, "Away in a Manger." Then they kneel, or seat themselves, at the conclusion of the song.

VI—FINALE

The chorus, singing "O Come All Ye Faithful," enters, half from each side of the stage. They form a semicircle behind the manger. Those on the stage unite with them, except the Madonna and little girls who, with the two angels, form a tableau. All sing "Joy to the World."

A CHRISTMAS-CARD PAGEANT

By Elsie M. Hubachek

This colorful, easily produced pageant is a series of episodes built around the central idea of Christmas cards, thus giving children of varying degrees of talent an opportunity to take part in the Christmas entertainment. Each episode has its own leading characters and supernumeraries, and can therefore be separately rehearsed.

A curtained stage is desirable, but if a curtain is not available, a good suggestion is to have a girl, picturesquely dressed as an artist, "paint in" the scenery, i. e., put into position the properties for each episode. The same girl might announce the title of each card. The background should be a plain, soft green curtain to which the scenery can be pinned.

I—THE CAROLERS

A group of girls is heard singing behind the curtain. When it is parted, they are disclosed grouped in front of the plain green background, wearing choir robes and holding picturesquely large music books. After they have finished singing the first two stanzas of "It Came upon a Midnight Clear," they come down the stage steps in single file and march down the center aisle, singing as they go. The curtain is drawn just as they reach the back of the auditorium. (Children like to walk through the audience, and the audience enjoys a closer view of the children.)

II—THE NIGHT BEFORE CHRISTMAS

For this "card," a fireplace, cut from brick-printed paper, and several real stockings are pinned to the background curtains. Two small chairs stand before the fireplace. When the curtain parts, two small children in pajamas are nodding in the chairs. "Away in a Manger" is played. As the music stops, the children rub their eyes, stand up, and yawn and stretch. Four other children in pajamas run in, and the six children stand in a row and recite " 'Twas the Night before Christmas." The lines are divided among them. When they finish, four run off; the other two seat themselves before the fire so that the "card" is again complete.

III—THE CHRISTMAS TREE

Sleigh bells ring behind the curtain. When it opens, the fireplace is seen again. A small untrimmed Christmas tree stands on a table near the fireplace. A large box stands in the corner. (The box is a large frame covered with heavy paper. The front is a hinged door.) Santa Claus, near the center of the stage, looks as though he had just come in by way of the chimney. He looks at the empty tree and begins to talk to himself about it. He does not find the right things in his bag to trim it with, and is about to give up the search, when he hears a knock. It comes from the big box. He gets up on a chair and looks over the top. He is astonished at what he sees.

"Well, well!" he says, "who are you?"

"I'm the little star for the top of the tree."

"I'll pull you right out."

"Don't do that. You'll break me."

"But how can I get you out?"

"Open the door of the box and I'll walk out."

Santa Claus gets down from the chair very carefully and

opens the front of the box. Out steps a little dancer in white, with a silver star on her head. She gives Santa a big star, and then she dances. As she bows herself back into the box, he puts the star on the top of the tree.

Another knock is heard, and Santa opens the door of the box again. Out step six little girls, each in a different-colored dress. Each carries a shiny ball that matches her dress. They bow and say, "We are bubbles of happiness," and each recites a verse about her Christmas-tree ornament. Santa hangs each ornament on the tree as it is given to him, and the little girls run back into the box. As many other ornaments might be impersonated as there are children to take the parts, and time permits.

The tinsel carriers come out of the box next (as many as desired). The girls are dressed in white, with tinsel in their hair; the boys wear light blouses, and carry ropes of silver tinsel in daisy-chain fashion. They march around and around Santa Claus, giving him the ends of the ropes, and winding the tinsel about him. When they unwind the tinsel, he has it all in his hands. The children sing "Jingle Bells," and run back into the box. There are tiny bells on the tinsel which ring faintly during the drill. After Santa has draped the tree with the tinsel, he stands and admires the result. Then he starts to go up the chimney, and as the curtain closes, "O Tannenbaum" is played.

IV—THE MANGER

For the final episode the carolers enter from the rear, singing "Silent Night" as they march up the aisle. The audience is asked to rise and sing with them. The carolers range themselves at the foot of the stage, and as the curtain parts, the familiar Christmas tableau is disclosed. Mary is seated beside the manger; Joseph, with his staff, is standing back of her; and the three Wise Men kneel in adoration. During the tableau, the carolers very reverently go up the steps to the stage and file out of the picture.

BEFORE DAWN

By Walter De La Mare

Dim-berried is the mistletoe
With globes of sheenless grey,
The holly mid ten thousand thorns
Smoulders its fires away;

And in the manger Jesu sleeps,
This Christmas Day.
Bull unto bull with hollow throat
Makes echo every hill,

Cold sheep in pastures thick with snow
The air with bleatings fill;
While of His Mother's heart this Babe
Takes His sweet will.

All flowers and butterflies lie hid,
The blackbird and the thrush
Pipe but a little as they flit
Restless from bush to bush;

Even to the robin Gabriel hath
Cried softly, "Hush!"
Now night is astir with burning stars
In darkness of the snow;

61

Burdened with frankincense and myrrh
And gold the Strangers go
Into a dusk where one dim lamp
Burns faintly, Lo!

No snowdrop yet its small head nods,
In winds of winter drear;
No lark at casement in the sky
Sings matins shrill and clear;
Yet in this frozen mirk the Dawn
Breathes, Spring is here!

NOW EVERY CHILD

By Eleanor Farjeon

Now every Child that dwells on earth,
  Stand up, stand up and sing!
The passing night has given birth
  Unto the Children's King.
    Sing sweet as the flute,
    Sing clear as the horn,
    Sing joy of the Children
    Come Christmas the morn!
    Little Christ Jesus
    Our Brother is born.

Now every Star that dwells in sky,
  Look down with shining eyes!
The night has dropped in passing by
  A Star from Paradise.
    Sing sweet as the flute,
    Sing clear as the horn,
    Sing joy of the Stars

Come Christmas the morn!
Little Christ Jesus
Our Brother is born.

Now every Beast that crops in field,
   Breathe sweetly and adore!
The night has brought the richest yield
   That ever harvest bore.
      Sing sweet as the flute,
      Sing clear as the horn,
      Sing joy of the Creatures
      Come Christmas the morn!
      Little Christ Jesus
      Our Brother is born.

Now every Bird that flies in air,
   Sing, raven, lark and dove!
The night has brooded on her lair
   And fledged the Bird of Love.
      Sing sweet as the flute,
      Sing clear as the horn,
      Sing joy of the Birds
      Come Christmas the morn!
      Little Christ Jesus
      Our Brother is born.

Now all the Angels of the Lord
   Rise up on Christmas Even!
The passing night will bear the Word
   That is the Voice of Heaven.
      Sing sweet as the flute,
      Sing clear as the horn,
      Sing joy of the Angels
      Come Christmas the morn!

Little Christ Jesus
Our Brother is born.

WHAT IF—

By Robert Haven Schauffler

Somewhere, at this grave hour of dark and danger,
With modern Herods marching on the Manger,
And star-shells laughing older stars to scorn—
What if the modern Christ is being born?
Christmas, 1939.

A CHRISTMAS CAROL

By Gilbert K. Chesterton

The Christ-child lay on Mary's lap,
   His hair was like a light.
(O weary, weary were the world,
   But here is all aright.)

The Christ-child lay on Mary's breast,
   His hair was like a star.
(O stern and cunning are the kings,
   But here the true hearts are.)

The Christ-child lay on Mary's heart,
   His hair was like a fire.
(O weary, weary is the world,
   But here the world's desire.)

The Christ-child stood at Mary's knee,
   His hair was like a crown,
And all the flowers looked up at Him,
   And all the stars looked down.

AT CHRISTMAS

By Edith Lovejoy Pierce

Fall, gentle snow—
As Love divine sinks to forgive and bless.
Under your white forgetfulness
Let the spring grow.

CHRISTMAS

By Ernest Crosby

On the first of the lengthening days,
   When the year's early morn
Gives the first summer pledge with its rays,
   He is born.

Light has conquered the Dark. Did we fear
   As the days shrank and paled
In the trough of the night of the year,
   Light had failed?

And the night's irresistible powers,—
   As the light ebbed away,—
How they swallowed the minutes and hours,
   Day by day!

To the depths of the valley of gloom
   Had the sun to descend.
But today, lo! the cycle of doom
   Has an end!

For the promise of summer reflects
   On the brows of the sky

All the glory creation expects
  By and bye.

Let the winter be cruel and grey!
  We care little who know
That our Christmas hails Easter today
  O'er the snow.

And that Easter brings summer and heat
  And the sunlight of love,
And the kingdom of heaven complete
  From above.

Christmas Day with its greetings and song
  And its brotherly cheer
Is the earnest of days which ere long
  Will be here.

And the Child, whom the manger reveals
  'Twixt the sheep and the kine
Is the earnest of Manhood that feels
  The Divine.

CHILDHOOD CHRISTMAS

By Nancy Byrd Turner

The night was charmed; if any single star
Had swerved, we would have stormed the darkness, all,
And found the dusky stable door ajar,
And crowded trembling to the ox's stall.

CHRISTMAS

By Bliss Carman

Above the weary waiting world,
Asleep in chill despair,
There breaks a sound of joyous bells
Upon the frosted air.
And o'er the humblest rooftree, lo,
A star is dancing on the snow.

What makes the yellow star to dance
Upon the brink of night?
What makes the breaking dawn to glow
So magically bright,—
And all the earth to be renewed
With infinite beatitude?

The singing bells, the throbbing star,
The sunbeams on the snow,
And the awakening heart that leaps
New ecstasy to know,—
They all are dancing in the morn
Because a little child is born.

I'M WISHING THE WHOLE WORLD CHRISTMAS

By Annette Wynne

I'm wishing the whole world Christmas—
The children, the beasts, and the birds;
I'm wishing the whole world Christmas—
And I'd like to have magical words
To wish just the shining wish I would wish

In the Christmas words I would say,
For I'm wishing the whole world Christmas,
And joy on Christmas Day.

O, I'd need a pen to write golden,
The goldenest pen indeed,
To wish the whole world Christmas
For the happy children to read.
I'm wishing the whole world Christmas
And may the dear Lord be kind,
And send blessings down like snowflakes
For all of His children to find. . . .

IN THE MANGER

By Una A. Harsen

A sword shall pierce through thy own soul also. Luke 2:35

In Bethlehem's sheltering stable all is still.
Mary, her darkness and her terror past,
Gazes in wonder on her infant son.
Not for her ears do angel choirs sing
Nor can her eyes behold the natal star.
Only the light from Joseph's lantern shed
Gleams fitfully on the rude walls
And rough-hewn rafters dark
With ancient cobwebs hung,
And in her heart, newsprung,
She feels the first faint tremors of the fear
Which ever has companioned motherhood.

Grotesque in that low room the shadows fall
On drowsy cattle and on manger bed.

Do those dim shapes presage her coming loss,
And in the gloom about her baby's head
Does she discern the shadow of the cross?

ON A SELF-PORTRAIT BY REMBRANDT

By Robert Haven Schauffler

See in this battered face
The radiant hiding-place
Of what a man may borrow
From ugliness and sorrow.

Such eyes need look no higher
For beauty, than the clod;
To Christ, Judaean mire
Was luminous with God.

THE GIFTS

By Odell Shepard

Wise Men, Wise Men,
Riding from afar,
Riding down to Bethlehem
Beneath a steady star;
What have ye in your saddle-bags,
What trinkets do ye bring
To give to Mother Mary
For Heaven's little King?

*Oh, we have brought Him frankincense
And precious myrrh and gold.*
But have ye brought no woollen coat

To wrap Him from the cold?
Wise Men, Wise Men,
Have ye no painted cart
Or bow or top or jumping-jack
To glad His childish heart?

Nay, we have only frankincense
And gold and costly myrrh.
All these are goodly gifts, Wise Men,
But not what boys prefer.
Wise Men, Wise Men,
Had ye been wiser still
Ye would have brought Him a paper kite
To fly on Calvary Hill.

Christmas, 1937.

AGED FOUR

By Mildred Focht

Christmas is a cruel day
  For mothers who are poor;
The wistful eyes of children
  Are daggers to endure.

Though shops are crammed with playthings,
  Enough for every one,
If a mother's purse is empty
  There might as well be none.

My purse is full of money,
  But I cannot buy a toy;
Only a wreath of holly
  For the grave of my little boy.

YULETIDE FIRES

(OLD SONG)

Light with the burning log of oak
The darkness of thy care,
Deck with the scarlet-berried bough
The temple of the fair;
Spread pure white linen for a feast,
Perchance some guest may share.

Give forth thy gold and silver coins,
For they were lent to thee;
Put out to usury thy dross,
One talent gaineth three.
Perchance the hungered and the poor
May pray to God for thee.

Once a pale star arose in the East
For watching herds to see,
And weakness came to Bethlehem,
And strength to Galilee.
Perchance if thou dost keep thy tryst
A star may rise for thee.

THE SENDING OF THE MAGI

BY BLISS CARMAN

In a far Eastern country
It happened long of yore,
Where a lone and level sunrise
Flushes the desert floor,

That three kings sat together
And a spearman kept the door.

Gaspar, whose wealth was counted
By city and caravan;
With Melchior, the seer
Who read the starry plan;
And Balthasar, the blameless,
Who loved his fellow man.

There while they talked, a sudden
Strange rushing sound arose,
And as with startled faces
They thought upon their foes,
Three figures stood before them
In imperial repose.

One in flame-gold and one in blue
And one in scarlet clear,
With the almighty portent
Of sunrise they drew near!
And the kings made obeisance
With hand on breast, in fear.

"Arise," said they, "we bring you
Good tidings of great peace!
Today a power is wakened
Whose working must increase,
Till fear and greed and malice
And violence shall cease."

The messengers were Michael,
By whom all things were wrought
To shape and hue; and Gabriel

Who is the lord of thought;
And Rafael without whose love
All toil must come to nought.

Then Rafael said to Balthasar,
"In a country west from here
A lord is born in lowliness,
In love without a peer.
Take grievances and gifts to him
And prove his kingship clear!

"By this sign ye shall know him;
Within his mother's arm
Among the sweet-breathed cattle
He slumbers without harm,
While wicked hearts are troubled
And tyrants take alarm."

And Gabriel said to Melchior,
"My comrade, I will send
My star to go before you,
That ye may comprehend
Where leads your mystic learning
In a humaner trend."

And Michael said to Gaspar,
"Thou royal builder, go
With tribute to thy riches!
Though time shall overthrow
Thy kingdom, no undoing
His gentle might shall know."

Then while the kings' hearts greatened
And all the chamber shone,

As when the hills at sundown
Take a new glory on
And the air thrills with purple,
Their visitors were gone.

Then straightway up rose Gaspar,
Melchior and Balthasar,
And passed out through the murmur
Of palace and bazar,
To make without misgiving
The journey of the Star.

THE TRAPPER'S CHRISTMAS EVE

By Robert W. Service

It's mighty lonesome-like and drear.
Above the Wild the moon rides high,
And shows up sharp and needle-clear
The emptiness of earth and sky;
No happy homes with love a-glow;
No Santa Claus to make believe:
Just snow and snow, and then more snow;
It's Christmas Eve, it's Christmas Eve.

And here am I where all things end,
And Undesirables are hurled;
A poor old man without a friend,
Forgot and dead to all the world;
Clean out of sight and out of mind. . . .
Well, maybe it is better so;
We all in life our level find,
And mine, I guess, is pretty low.

Yet as I sit with pipe alight
Beside the cabin-fire, it's queer
This mind of mine must take tonight
The backward trail of fifty year.
The school-house and the Christmas tree;
The children with their cheeks a-glow;
Two bright blue eyes that smile on me . . .
Just half a century ago.

Again (it's maybe forty years),
With faith and trust almost divine,
These same blue eyes, abrim with tears,
Through depths of love looked into mine.
A parting, tender, soft and low,
With arms that cling and lips that cleave. . . .
Ah me! it's all so long ago,
Yet seems so sweet this Christmas Eve.

Just thirty years ago, again . . .
We say a bitter, *last* good-bye;
Our lips are white with wrath and pain;
Our little children cling and cry.
Whose was the fault? it matters not,
For man and woman both deceive;
It's buried now and all forgot,
Forgiven, too, this Christmas Eve.

And she (God pity me) is dead;
Our children men and women grown.
I like to think that they are wed,
With little children of their own,
That crowd around their Christmas tree. . . .
I would not ever have them grieve,

Or shed a single tear for me,
To mar their joy this Christmas Eve.

Stripped to the buff and gaunt and still
Lies all the land in grim distress.
Like lost soul wailing, long and shrill,
A wolf-howl cleaves the emptiness.
Then hushed as Death is everything.
The moon rides haggard and forlorn. . . .
"O hark the herald angels sing!"
God bless all men—it's Christmas morn.

A LITTLE CHRISTMAS BASKET

By Paul Laurence Dunbar

De win' is hollahin' "Daih you" to de shuttahs an' de fiah,
    De snow's a-sayin' "Got you" to de groun',
Fu' de wintah weathah's come widout a-askin' ouah desiah,
    An' he's laughin' in his sleeve at whut he foun';
Fu' dey ain't nobody ready wid dey fuel er dey food,
    An' de money bag look timid lak, fu' sho',
So we want ouah Chrismus sermon, but we'd lak it ef you could
    Leave a little Chrismus basket at de do'.

Wha's de use o' tellin' chillen 'bout a Santy er a Nick,
    An' de sto'ies dat a body allus tol'?
When de harf is gray wid ashes an' you hasn't got a stick
    Fu' to warm dem when dey little toes is col'?
Wha's de use o' preachin' 'ligion to a man dat's sta'ved to def,
    An' a-tellin' him de Mastah will pu'vide?
Ef you want to tech his feelin's, save yo' sermons an' yo' bref,
    Tek a little Chrismus basket by yo' side.

'T ain't de time to open Bibles an' to lock yo' cellah do',
  'T ain't de time to talk o' bein' good to men;
Ef you want to preach a sermon ez you nevah preached befo',
  Preach dat sermon wid a shoat er wid er hen;
Bein' good is heap sight bettah den a-dallyin' wid sin,
  An' dey ain't nobody roun' dat knows it mo',
But I t'ink dat 'ligion's sweeter w'en it kind o' mixes in
  Wid a little Chrismus basket at de do'.

THE RANN OF THE CHRISTMAS TREE

By Mary Frances Martin

A little tree in the wood there was,
  O long ago, O long ago.
A little tree that was straight and slim,
There it stood so sturdy and trim,
  In the wood, O long ago.

The steward came from the inn one day,
  O long ago, O long ago.
He saw the little tree standing there,
Graceful, and shapely, and debonaire,
  In the wood, O long ago.

Back to the inn the steward went,
  O long ago, O long ago.
He took with him the little tree,
Sturdy, and trim, and good to see,
  From the wood, O long ago.

There was a cavern at Bethlehem,
  O long ago, O long ago.
With stall, and manger, and doorway wide,

And the little tree was set inside
  The cave, O long ago.

There in the dusk of a wintry day,
  O long ago, O long ago.
Through snow flakes softly sifting down,
Two travellers came to Bethlehem town,
  In the dusk, O long ago.

Two travellers came to the cavern door,
  O long ago, O long ago.
One was Joseph, grave and staid,
And one was Mary, the Holy Maid,
  To Bethlehem long ago.

Into the cavern the travellers went,
  O long ago, O long ago.
And Holy Mary smiled to see,
Three candles a-light on the little tree,
  In the cavern long ago.

The ox and the ass in the stall knelt down,
  O long ago, O long ago.
For the hour of midnight had drawn nigh,
And a heavenly glory filled the sky,
  At Bethlehem long ago.

There was a manger at Bethlehem
  O long ago, O long ago.
Cradled there in fragrant hay,
A child Divinely Holy lay,
  In the manger long ago.

The little tree in the cavern stood,
  O long ago, O long ago.

Its balsam fragrance filled the air,
Incense sweet for the Christ-Child fair,
   In the manger long ago.

The shepherds came from the hillside fold,
   O long ago, O long ago.
They came with songs of praise and prayer,
They came to kneel adoring there,
   Before the Child, O long ago.

With gifts, love prompted, the shepherds came,
   O long ago, O long ago.
They worshiped the Child on His Mother's knee,
They hung their gifts on the little tree,
   In the cavern long ago.

The Christ-Child sleeps in His manger bed,
   As long ago, as long ago.
The years have come, and the years have gone,
And the little Christmas tree lives on,
   Since Bethlehem long ago.

JOSEPH TO MARY
By Sara Henderson Hay

Mary, beloved, if I wounded you
With clumsy silence, or with tardy speech,
It was because my heart was slow to reach
Beyond the limits of its mortal view!
Not that I doubted you, or loved you less,
But it was hard to face the winking town,
And a man's pride is difficult to down,
Whatever faith he may in truth profess!

How many nights I watched you as you lay
With this the Holy Child upon your breast—
What anguish shook my heart from day to day!
Oh little Mary, have you never guessed
That I, who would have died to spare you harm,
So feared to clasp you with an earthly arm?

MARY TO JOSEPH

This fear has sat within me, chilled and numbing—
This dread has been upon me, from the start,
Since first I told you of the Angel's coming,
And of the Child that lay beneath my heart.

It was no easy thing to understand,
And not by word or deed have you reproved me—
But Joseph—Joseph—when you took my hand,
Did you believe me, even as you loved me?

ONE ROMANCE
By THEODORE WATTS-DUNTON

Life still hath one romance that naught can bury—
Not Time himself, who coffins Life's romances—
For still will Christmas gild the year's mischances,
If Childhood comes, as here, to make him merry.

CHRISTMAS CANDLE
By KATHERINE EDELMAN

Tiny little golden flame,
    Symbol burning clear and bright
For the Promised One who came
    On a far-off hallowed night,

Turn our thoughts, show us the way
To Bethlehem this Christmas Day.

THREE CHRISTMAS POEMS

BY ROBERT HAVEN SCHAUFFLER

I

WANTED FROM THE PANTRY OF LIFE:

A pan to frizzle
  Luck's bacon, medium;
A stick to swizzle
  The cup of tedium;

A Hamburg steaker
  To hash anxiety;
A cocktail shaker
  For acid sobriety.

Last, let us borrow,
  And briskly employ,
A sieve for sorrow,
  A bowl for joy.

II

ILLUSIONS

How many a rainbow dream has thinned to air!
  My dooryard crammed with gold—and peacock pie;
    Keats' vision; Hermes' voice, magnetic, mellow;
Small curly-headed climbers on my chair;
  Apollo's body; Leonardo's eye;
    Casals' own touch upon Casals' own 'cello.

Other illusions are more stubborn stuff:
>Hopes that a page of mine may yet survive
>>To give to men unborn joy worth the giving;—
That love and work and friends may be enough
>To keep a quiet happiness alive
>>In one who dreams he knows the art of living.

Dearer than revel, meat, or ingle-blaze,
>My tenuous, rainbow dreams glow on to fill
>>The hours with cheer; and may they dim right slowly!
Though reason cover Christmas with a haze,
>Let me maintain my early vision still:
>>The Wise Men, wise—the starlit manger, holy!

III

Yule Fire in a Slum

Between a garbage pile and a peddler's tray,
I saw pale children circling, hand in hand,
Round a green branch,—their gutter fairyland.
Deep in the slush they froliced, lost in play,
For this was all the Christmas tree they had:
A scrap of wilted pine. They had made it glad
With paper ribbons full of curious holes—
The spoil of broken player-piano rolls:
Festoons of silent music, draped among
The twigs where toys and candy should have hung.

"Let's make it burn!" The tiny blaze leaped higher.
Their Christmas tree was now their Christmas fire.
And, in the sudden glare, I could plainly see,
Printed upon a burning paper's end:
"Johannes Brahms . . . G minor Rhapsody."

I thought how it would please that children's friend
If he could watch his flaming tones achieve
Such radiance for a gutter Christmas Eve,
Though rhapsodies must, phoenix-like, progress
Into another form of loveliness.
How that Pied Piper's coat-tails would grow fat
With sugar toys; how every bright-eyed brat
Would encore "Uncle Bahms" with crow and shout!

.   .   .   .

Children, is there a candy-shop about?

EX ORE INFANTIUM

By Francis Thompson

Little Jesus, wast Thou shy
Once, and just so small as I?
And what did it feel like to be
Out of Heaven, and just like me?
Didst Thou sometimes think of *there,*
And ask where all the angels were?
I should think that I would cry
For my house all made of sky;
I would look about the air,
And wonder where my angels were;
And at waking 'twould distress me—
Not an angel there to dress me!

Hadst Thou ever any toys,
Like us little girls and boys?
And didst Thou play in Heaven with all
The angels, that were not too tall,
With stars for marbles? Did the things

Play *Can you see me?* through their wings?
Didst Thou kneel at night to pray,
And didst Thou join Thy hands, this way?
And did they tire sometimes, being young,
And make the prayer seem very long?
And dost Thou like it best, that we
Should join our hands to pray to Thee?
I used to think, before I knew,
The prayer not said unless we do.
And did Thy Mother at the night
Kiss Thee, and fold the clothes in right?
And didst Thou feel quite good in bed,
Kissed, and sweet, and Thy prayers said?

Thou canst not have forgotten all
That it feels like to be small:
And Thou know'st I cannot pray
To Thee in my father's way—
When Thou wast so little, say,
Couldst Thou talk Thy Father's way?—
So, a little Child, come down
And hear a child's tongue like Thy own;
Take me by the hand and walk,
And listen to my baby-talk.
To Thy Father show my prayer
(He will look, Thou art so fair),
And say: "O Father, I, Thy Son,
Bring the prayer of a little one."

And He will smile, that children's tongue
Has not changed since Thou wast young!

CHRISTMAS PACKAGES

By Wilfred Funk

Her deft and lovely fingers fold
   The silver paper round
The Christmas things, and shining gold
   Will tie and hold them bound.

The little gifts are humble things,
   But in their loving choice
And dress, she gives to each one wings,
   And beauty, and a voice.

SIX GREEN SINGERS

By Eleanor Farjeon

The frost of the moon fell over my floor
And six green singers stood at my door.

"What do ye here that music make?"
"Let us come in for Christ's sweet Sake."

"Long have ye journeyed in coming here?"
"Our Pilgrimage was the length of the year."

"Where do ye make for?" I asked of them.
"Our Shrine is a Stable in Bethlehem."

"What will ye do as ye go along?"
"Sing to the world an ever-green song."

"What will ye sing for the listening earth?"
"One will sing of a brave-souled Mirth,

"One of the Holiest Mystery,
The Glory of glories shall one song be,

"One of the Memory of things,
One of the Child's imaginings,

"One of our songs is the fadeless Faith,
And all are the Life more mighty than death."

"Ere ye be gone that music make,
Give me an alms for Christ's sweet Sake."

"Six green branches we leave with you;
See they be scattered your house-place through.

"The staunch blithe Holly your board shall grace,
Mistletoe bless your chimney place,

"Laurel to crown your lighted hall,
Over your bed let the Yew-bough fall,

"Close by the cradle the Christmas Fir,
For elfin dreams in its branches stir,

"Last and loveliest, high and low,
From ceil to floor let the Ivy go."

From each glad guest I received my gift
And then the latch of my door did lift—

"Green singers, God prosper the song ye make
As ye sing to the world for Christ's sweet Sake."

THE THORN

By Mary Sinton Leitch

Mary, mother Mary,
Crooned her babe to rest.
Fair he was and fragrant
As the rose upon her breast.

Soft she hushed her darling
And watched his eyelids close:
She strained him to her bosom
Forgetful of the rose.

A cry scarce broke his slumber,
But Mary lay till morn
Grieving that her baby's brow
Was pierced by a thorn.

THE THREE KINGS' ROAD

By Anna Blake Mezquida

When all the tinsel has been laid away,
    The tree is stripped, the fevered rush is past—
You still have trees, a hill, a child at play,
    And love, and prayer, and fadeless things that last.
Wear your proud purple underneath your load!
    Touch hand with one who travels lone, afar!
Brave your dark night and walk the Three Kings' road
    To find your Christ beneath his lovely star!

He loves, I know, our pretty baubled trees,
    Our busy shops, our laughter young and gay,

Our ribboned gifts—have we no gifts but these?
  No bright, red wreaths except for Christmas day?
Though broken is some toy beneath your feet,
  Some dear illusion shattered, or grown dim—
The Three Kings' road goes by your dusty street
  That leads up to a star—and Him.

THE SWORDLESS CHRIST

By John Richard Moreland

Cupped in a shell-torn battlefield,
Once spicy with the wind-blown flowers
Of quince and rose, but now whose yield
Is but the fruit of hate's ripe hours,—

Three men are by the moon revealed:
One man has mangled feet, and one
Is deaf, and one's blue eyes are sealed
To Heaven's star-glittering benison.

Above the crimson field of war
How luminous the wonder star!
With shriek of shell are borne along
The words of Love's remembered song
That angels sang when Christ was born,
The King whose hand should pluck war's thorn
From mangled flesh, and heal the wound
With Gilead's balm, till earth abound
In love that daily would increase.
O birthday of the Prince of Peace!

"Look, brother, look! through smoke of war
Still shines the light to lead mankind

To brotherhood . . . the Christmas star!"
One looked in vain, for he was blind.

"O, brother, listen to the song
That sweetens the foul midnight air
And bids truth triumph over wrong."
One answered not . . . he could not hear.

"Up, brother, up! and pray to Him
Whose song is sweet, whose star gleams red,
Ere hope grow faint and faith grow dim."
The man with mangled feet was dead.

Above each war-torn field and hill
The Christmas star is shining still!
And down the years,—O hearts that mourn,—
Listen! upon the air is borne
The Christmas message once again:
"Peace on the earth, good will to men!"
And in a manger keeping tryst
Behold the Virgin's Son, the Christ!
With each new morning starry, dim,
Come, let us kneel adoring Him!

Too long have pruning-hooks and plows
Been beaten into sword and shell;
And manhood's fair and fruitful boughs
Been faggots for the flames of hell!

Too long have hate and wrath conspired
Till truth was scourged and sacrificed;
Too long we wait the day desired:—
The day of Peace: the Swordless Christ!

THE VOICE OF CHRISTMAS

By Harry Kemp

I cannot put the Presence by, of Him, the Crucified,
Who moves men's spirits with His Love as doth the moon the
    tide;
Again I see the Life He lived, the godlike Death He died.

Again I see upon the cross the great Soul-battle fought,
Into the texture of the world the tale of which is wrought
Until it hath become the woof of human deed and thought,—

And, joining with the cadenced bells that all the morning fill,
His cry of agony doth yet my inmost being thrill,
Like some fresh grief from yesterday that tears the heart-
    strings still.

I cannot put His Presence by, I meet Him everywhere;
I meet Him in the country town, the busy market-square;
The Mansion and the Tenement attest His Presence there.

Upon the funneled ships at sea He sets His shining feet;
The Distant Ends of Empire not in vain His Name repeat,—
And, like the presence of a rose, He makes the whole world
    sweet.

He comes to break the barriers down raised up by barren
    creeds;
About the globe from zone to zone like sunlight He proceeds;
He comes to give the World's starved heart the perfect love it
    needs,

The Christ, Whose friends have played Him false, Whom
Dogmas have belied,

Still speaking to the hearts of men—though shamed and crucified,
The Master of the Centuries Who will not be denied!

THE STORKE

A Christmas Ballad

(FROM THE FLY-LEAF OF KING EDWARD VI'S PRAYER-BOOK,
1549.)

The Storke shee rose on Christmas Eve
And sayed unto her broode,
I nowe muste fare to Bethleem
To viewe the Sonne of God.

Shee gave to eche his dole of mete,
Shee stowed them fayrlie in,
And faire shee flew and faste shee flew
And came to Bethleem.

Now where is He of David's lynne?
Shee asked at house and halle.
He is not here, they spake hardlye,
But in the maungier stalle.

Shee found hym in the maungier stalle
With that most Holye Mayde;
The gentyle Storke shee wept to see
The Lord so rudelye layde.

Then from her panntynge brest shee plucked
The fethers whyte and warm;
Shee strawed them in the maungier bed
To kepe the Lorde from harm.

Now blessed bee the gentyle Storke
Forever more quothe Hee
For that shee saw my sadde estate
And showed Pytye.

Full welkum shall shee ever bee
In hamlet and in halle,
And hight henceforth the Blessed Byrd
And friend of babyes all.

A CHRISTMAS SONNET

By Robert Haven Schauffler

Born among beasts, comrade of calf and foal,
  He sang God's fatherhood to king and slave,
And royal lands of heaven within the soul;
  They tore his flesh and sealed it in a cave.
His song rang on. Ages of steel and fire
  Dealt by the haughtiest empire Earth had seen,
Made that victorious music mount the higher,
  Till Rome, too, bent before the Nazarene.
No lordliest power of Earth can overwhelm
  That mortal who, in calm, unweaponed strife,
Waters the gardens of his inner realm
  With tributaries from the stream of life.
    Earthquake may crush and holocaust may bound him,—
    He shall be mightier than the might around him.

CHRISTMAS "GOOD-NIGHT"

By Ethel Robb

Was Jesus just a boy like me
And did He have a Christmas tree?

And was His star the brightest star?
And could you see it very far?

And were the Shepherds good, kind men?
And did they have a dog like Ben,

That stayed and watched the little sheep,
When they found Jesus, fast asleep?

And were the Wisemen very wise?
And did the light blind both their eyes?

Was Mary glad it was a boy,
And not a girl like Baby Joy?

And did the Father know the way
That little children like to play?

And did three cousins stay for tea?
Think He would come and play with me?

And was His Uncle Will like mine?
And did they have a lovely time?

And did it snow, or was it bright?
I'll go to sleep. . . . Good-night. . . . Good-night.

CHRISTMAS TREES

By Irene Wilde

The antlers of the fir are bent
With friendship's glittering favors,

From frosty brackets of the yew
A linnet's carol quavers.

The spruce is twisted to a wreath
Above the window frame,
The holly braids a halo about
The candle's bud of flame.

A star is hung above the cedar
To lift the level eye,
The cypress points a slender finger
Toward the chanting sky.

THE WISE MEN FROM THE EAST

(*A Little Boy's Christmas Lesson*)

By Bliss Carman

Why were the Wise Men three,
Instead of five or seven?
They had to match, you see,
The archangels in Heaven.

God sent them, sure and swift,
By his mysterious presage,
To bear the threefold gift
And take the threefold message.

Thus in their hands were seen
The gold of purest Beauty,
The myrrh of Truth all-clean,
The frankincense of Duty.

And thus they bore away
The loving heart's great treasure,
And knowledge clear as day,
To be our life's new measure.

They went back to the East
To spread the news of gladness.
There one became a priest
To the new word of sadness;

And one a workman, skilled
Beyond the old earth's fashion;
And one a scholar, filled
With learning's endless passion.

God sent them for a sign
He would not change nor alter
His good and fair design,
However man may falter.

He meant that, as He chose
His perfect plan and willed it,
They stood in place of those
Who elsewhere had fulfilled it;

Whoso would mark and reach
The height of man's election,
Must still achieve and teach
The triplicate perfection.

For since the world was made,
One thing was needed ever,
To keep man undismayed
Through failure and endeavor—

A faultless trinity
Of body, mind, and spirit
And each with its own three
Strong angels to be near it;

Strength to arise and go
Wherever dawn is breaking,
Poise like the tides that flow,
Instinct for beauty-making;

Imagination bold
To cross the mystic border,
Reason to seek and hold,
Judgment for law and order;

Joy that makes all things well,
Faith that is all-availing
Each terror to dispel,
And Love, ah, Love unfailing.

These are the flaming Nine
Who walk the world unsleeping,
Sent forth by the Divine
With manhood in their keeping.

These are the seraphs strong
His mighty soul had need of,
When He would right the wrong
And sorrow He took heed of.

And that, I think, is why
The Wise Men knelt before Him,
And put their kingdoms by
To serve Him and adore Him;

So that our Lord, unknown,
Should not be unattended,
When He was here alone
And poor and unbefriended;

That still He might have three
(Rather than five or seven)
To stand in their degree,
Like archangels in Heaven.

TO A SNOWFLAKE

By Francis Thompson

What heart could have thought you?—
Past our devisal
(O filigree petal!)
Fashioned so purely,
Fragilely, surely,
From what Paradisal
Imagineless metal,
Too costly for cost?
Who hammered you, wrought you,
From argentine vapour?—
"God was my shaper.
Passing surmisal,
He hammered, He wrought me,
From curled silver vapour,
To lust of His mind:—
Thou could'st not have thought me!
So purely, so palely,
Tinily, surely,
Mightily, frailly,
Insculped and embossed,

With His hammer of wind,
And His graver of frost."

SOUTHERN CROSS

Christmas Eve in the Indian Ocean

By Leonora Speyer

The unaccustomed eye
Traces it, star by star,
Scant four and wanly far,
Risen to testify.

Nebular, incomplete,
It leans upon its side,
As when the Crucified
Lay fallen in the street.

While scattered wide and bright
About the cross that pales,
Planets like golden nails
Pierce through the tropic night.

CHRISTMAS CAROL

By Helene Mullins

O stricken world look up and see;
The God who died upon a tree
Is born a laughing babe again
To bring new hope to weary men.

Here is a legend never old—
Neither the dark nor the bitter cold

Can stay His coming once a year
To heal the sick and cast out fear.

Bring Him your hunger, bring your thirst,
The blind and crippled shall be first,
The most dejected and forlorn
Shall lie upon His breast this morn.

THE CHRISTMAS STAR

By Nancy Byrd Turner

High in the heavens a single star,
    Of pure, imperishable light;
Out on the desert strange and far
    Dim riders riding through the night:
Above a hilltop sudden song
    Like silver trumpets down the sky—
And all to welcome One so young
    He scarce could lift a cry!

Stars rise and set, that star shines on:
    Songs fail, but still that music beats
Through all the ages come and gone,
    In lane and field and city streets.
And we who catch the Christmas gleam,
    Watching with children on the hill,
We know, we know it is no dream—
    He stands among us still!

BABUSHKA

A Russian Legend

By Edith M. Thomas

Babushka sits before the fire
    Upon a winter's night;
The driving winds heap up the snow,
    Her hut is snug and tight;
The howling winds,—they only make
    Babushka's fire more bright!

She hears a knocking at the door:
    So late—who can it be?
She hastes to lift the wooden latch,
    No thought of fear has she;
The wind-blown candle in her hand
    Shines out on strangers three.

Their beards are white with age, and snow
    That in the darkness flies;
Their floating locks are long and white,
    But kindly are their eyes
That sparkle underneath their brows,
    Like stars in frosty skies.

"Babushka, we have come from far,
    We tarry but to say,
A little Prince is born this night,
    Who all the world shall sway.
Come join the search, come, go with us,
    We go our gifts to pay."

Babushka shivers at the door;
    "I would I might behold

The little Prince who shall be King
    But ah! the night is cold,
The wind so fierce, the snow so deep,
    And I, good sirs, am old."

The strangers three, no word they speak,
    But fade in snowy space!
Babushka sits before her fire,
    And dreams, with wistful face:
"I would that I had questioned them,
    So I the way might trace!"

"When morning comes with blessed light,
    I'll early be awake:
My staff in hand I'll go,—perchance,
    Those strangers I'll o'ertake;
And, for the Child some little toys
    I'll carry, for His sake."

The morning came, and staff in hand,
    She wandered in the snow,
She asked the way of all she met,
    But none the way could show.
"It must be farther yet," she sighed:
    "Then farther will I go."

And still, 'tis said, on Christmas Eve,
    When high the drifts are piled,
With staff, with basket on her arm,
    Babushka seeks the Child:
At every door her face is seen,—
    Her wistful face and mild!

Her gifts at every door she leaves:
    She bends and murmurs low,

Above each little face half-hid
By pillows white as snow:
"And is He here?" Then, softly sighs,
"Nay, farther must I go!"

BETHLEHEM OF JUDAEA

Author Unknown

A little Child,
    A shining star.
A stable rude,
    The door ajar.

Yet in that place,
    So crude, forlorn,
The Hope of all
    The world was born.

OF CHRISTMAS

By Grace L. Schauffler

Sing a song of Christmas,
Of stockings full of toys,
Stuffed by dear old Santa
For all good girls and boys.

Sing a song of Christmas,
Of puddings made with spice;
Of hungry lads and lassies
Who beg a second slice.

Sing a song of Christmas,
Of holly, green and red;

Of crisp and snowy weather,
That calls for skate and sled.

Sing a song of Christmas,
Of carols sweet and gay,
That tell of old Judea,
Where Infant Jesus lay.

Sing a song of Christmas,
May laughter, love and cheer
Possess our hearts this blessed day,
And through the coming year.

THE FOOLISH FIR-TREE

By Henry Van Dyke

A tale that the poet Rückert told
To German children, in days of old;
Disguised in a random, rollicking rhyme
Like a merry mummer of ancient time,
And sent, in its English dress, to please
The little folk of the Christmas trees.

A little fir grew in the midst of the wood
Contented and happy, as young trees should.
His body was straight and his boughs were clean;
And summer and winter the bountiful sheen
Of his needles bedecked him, from top to root,
In a beautiful, all-the-year, evergreen suit.

But a trouble came into his heart one day,
When he saw that the other trees were gay
In the wonderful raiment that summer weaves
Of manifold shapes and kinds of leaves:

He looked at his needles so stiff and small,
And thought that his dress was the poorest of all.
Then jealousy clouded the little tree's mind,
And he said to himself, "It was not very kind
"To give such an ugly old dress to a tree!
"If the fays of the forest would only ask me,
"I'd tell them how I should like to be dressed,—
"In a garment of gold, to bedazzle the rest!"
So he fell asleep, but his dreams were bad.
When he woke in the morning, his heart was glad;
For every leaf that his boughs could hold
Was made of the brightest beaten gold.
I tell you, children, the tree was proud;
He was something above the common crowd;
And he tinkled his leaves, as if he would say
To a pedlar who happened to pass that way,
"Just look at me! Don't you think I am fine?
"And wouldn't you like such a dress as mine?"
"Oh, yes!" said the man, "and I really guess
"I must fill my pack with your beautiful dress."
So he picked the golden leaves with care,
And left the little tree shivering there.

"Oh, why did I wish for golden leaves?"
The fir-tree said, "I forgot that thieves
"Would be sure to rob me in passing by.
"If the fairies would give me another try,
"I'd wish for something that cost much less,
"And be satisfied with glass for my dress!"
Then he fell asleep; and, just as before,
The fairies granted his wish once more.
When the night was gone, and the sun rose clear,
The tree was a crystal chandelier;
And it seemed, as he stood in the morning light,

That his branches were covered with jewels bright.
"Aha!" said the tree. "This is something great!"
And held himself up, very proud and straight;
But a rude young wind through the forest dashed,
In a reckless temper, and quickly smashed
The delicate leaves. With a clashing sound
They broke into pieces and fell on the ground,
Like a silvery, shimmering shower of hail,
And the tree stood naked and bare to the gale.

Then his heart was sad; and he cried, "Alas
"For my beautiful leaves of shining glass!
"Perhaps I have made another mistake
"In choosing a dress so easy to break.
"If the fairies would only hear me again
"I'd ask them for something both pretty and plain:
"It wouldn't cost much to grant my request,—
"In leaves of green lettuce I'd like to be dressed!"
By this time the fairies were laughing, I know;
But they gave him his wish in a second; and so
With leaves of green lettuce, all tender and sweet,
The tree was arrayed, from his head to his feet.
"I knew it!" he cried, "I was sure I could find
"The sort of a suit that would be to my mind.
"There's none of the trees has a prettier dress,
"And none as attractive as I am, I guess."
But a goat, who was taking an afternoon walk,
By chance overheard the fir-tree's talk.
So he came up close for a nearer view;—
"My salad!" he bleated, "I think so too!
"You're the most attractive kind of a tree,
"And I want your leaves for my five-o'clock tea."
So he ate them all without saying grace,
And walked away with a grin on his face;

While the little tree stood in the twilight dim,
With never a leaf on a single limb.

Then he sighed and groaned; but his voice was weak—
He was so ashamed that he could not speak.
He knew at last he had been a fool,
To think of breaking the forest rule,
And choosing a dress himself to please,
Because he envied the other trees.
But it couldn't be helped, it was now too late,
He must make up his mind to a leafless fate!
So he let himself sink in a slumber deep,
But he moaned and he tossed in his troubled sleep,
Till the morning touched him with joyful beam,
And he woke to find it was all a dream.
For there in his evergreen dress he stood,
A pointed fir in the midst of the wood!
His branches were sweet with the balsam smell,
His needles were green when the white snow fell.
And always contented and happy was he,—
The very best kind of a Christmas tree.

THE TWELVE DAYS OF CHRISTMAS

(OLD ENGLISH CAROL)

On the first day of Christmas my true love sent to me
A partridge in a pear tree.
On the second day of Christmas my true love sent to me
Two turtle doves and a partridge in a pear tree.
On the third day of Christmas my true love sent to me
Three French hens, two turtle doves, and a partridge in a pear
    tree.
On the fourth day of Christmas my true love sent to me

Four colly birds, three French hens, two turtle doves, and a
partridge in a pear tree.

On the fifth day of Christmas my true love sent to me

Five gold rings, four colly birds, three French hens, two turtle
doves, and a partridge in a pear tree.

On the sixth day of Christmas my true love sent to me

Six geese a-laying, five gold rings, four colly birds, three French
hens, two turtle doves, and a partridge in a pear tree.

On the seventh day of Christmas my true love sent to me

Seven swans a-swimming, six geese a-laying, five gold rings,
four colly birds, three French hens, two turtle doves, and
a partridge in a pear tree.

On the eighth day of Christmas my true love sent to me

Eight maids a-milking, seven swans a-swimming, six geese
a-laying, five gold rings, four colly birds, three French
hens, two turtle doves, and a partridge in a pear tree.

On the ninth day of Christmas my true love sent to me

Nine ladies dancing, eight maids a-milking, seven swans
a-swimming, six geese a-laying, five gold rings, four colly
birds, three French hens, two turtle doves, and a partridge
in a pear tree.

On the tenth day of Christmas my true love sent to me

Ten lords a-leaping, nine ladies dancing, eight maids a-milking,
seven swans a-swimming, six geese a-laying, five gold
rings, four colly birds, three French hens, two turtle doves,
and a partridge in a pear tree.

On the eleventh day of Christmas my true love sent to me

Eleven drummers drumming, ten lords a-leaping, nine ladies
dancing, eight maids a-milking, seven swans a-swimming,
six geese a-laying, five gold rings, four colly birds, three
French hens, two turtle doves and a partridge in a pear
tree.

On the twelfth day of Christmas my true love sent to me

Twelve pipers piping, eleven drummers drumming, ten lords

a-leaping, nine ladies dancing, eight maids a-milking, seven swans a-swimming, six geese a-laying, five gold rings, four colly birds, three French hens, two turtle doves, and a partridge in a pear tree.

TO A CHRISTMAS TREE

By Mona Dale

Heaven twinkles where you stand
With the snow-drift in your hand
Interweaving myriad charms
As you cradle in your arms,—
Here a bauble—there a gem—
Little stars of Bethlehem!
Wistful now, and wonder-wise,
Children stand with lifted eyes,
Gazing on your fair festoons
Of gossamer and magic moons,
Singing birds and swaying bells,
Marshmallows and caramels,
And every kind of fairy thing
That ornaments imagining.

Yuletide must be bare indeed
For him who feels no inner need,
When Christmas comes, when Christmas comes,
Of elfin dreams and elfin drums.
He hears no goblin trumpets blow.
For him in vain the baubles glow
Who is so blind he cannot see
Beauty in a Christmas tree.

A CHRISTMAS CAROL

By GILBERT K. CHESTERTON

The Chief Constable has issued a statement declaring that carol singing in the streets by children is illegal, and morally and physically injurious. He appeals to the public to discourage the practice.
—Daily Paper

God rest you merry gentlemen,
Let nothing you dismay;
The Herald Angels cannot sing,
The cops arrest them on the wing,
And warn them of the docketing
Of anything they say.

God rest you merry gentlemen,
May nothing you dismay:
On your reposeful cities lie
Deep silence, broken only by
The motor horn's melodious cry,
The hooter's happy bray.

So, when the song of children ceased
And Herod was obeyed,
In his high hall Corinthian
With purple and with peacock fan,
Rested that merry gentleman;
And nothing him dismayed.

SANTA CLAUS

By LEIGH HANES

Now this is the thing I'd like to know:
How Santa Claus can step in snow

With a world of toys upon his back
And leave not the slightest hint of a track;
How one so big and round and fat
Can slip through a hole that would choke a rat
And smoke so thick it can hide the trees,
And never even cough, nor sneeze!

Well, my son, it does seem queer,
But it's just like this: you're standing here
Thinking of things you cannot see
And wondering how such things can be. . . .
The fact is, son, nobody knows
What Santa looks like nor where he goes,
For Santa Claus is a sprite that lives
In the heart that loves, in the heart that gives;
He may be here and he may be there,
You are likely to find him anywhere.
But really, folk are so very blind
They can't see sprites in the heart or mind;
They can't see the spirit that gives and loves,
So we picture a thing in coat and gloves
Like a jolly old man who is round and fat,
And we love the thing, and we look at that;
And being a spirit, through and through,
Of course, he can do what a spirit can do.

But the Santa himself we never see,
The Santa in you, the Santa in me.

HARROWING REFLECTIONS

By Julia Boynton Green

'Twas the night after Christmas, and all through the flat
Not a creature was stirring, not even the cat;

When close at my side there arose such a wailing
I leaped from my dreams and with words unavailing
Endeavored to fathom my Mary's distress;
At last she was forced the weird truth to confess:
"O Jack! I am ruined forever, I fear,
I sent Aunt the workbag she sent *me* last year!"

THE AFTERMATH—DECEMBER TWENTY-SIXTH

BY JULIA BOYNTON GREEN

'Twas the night after Christmas, and all through the house
We were paying each one for our Yuletide carouse.
I felt in my tummy a burden like lead
And visions of tumors careered through my head.
Martha tumbled and tossed, at last breathed with a sob,
"I've got 'pendicitis—I'm sure of it, Bob."

But it was not for long we could nurse our own aches,
Tumult rose on the air—Martha cried, "Goodness sakes!"
It was mouthing and screeching that made my flesh creep—
Brother Henry was spouting a toast in his sleep.

I hustled to shake him; 'twas cold as the dickens,
Then skipped back to blankets and bed, frozen stiff.
But the respite was brief for we heard in a jiff
The sound a hyena in fits might have made—
Like the howl of a Banshee— Quoth I, "The plot thickens.
That's nightmare—poor Grandma!" I flew to her aid.

Coming back I saw Martha was ready to cry.
Then to add the last straw to our nocturnal cares
A small spook in pajamas stole stealthily by—
Little Ted, our somnambulist, trotting down stairs.

I need only add that from midnight till two
We were hushing a juvenile hullabaloo.
Papa in his prowler, mamma in her cap,
Sat each with a suffering kiddie in lap.
*Some*thing they had swallowed that didn't agree,
And we very near drowned them in hot ginger tea.

I swore, about sunrise, "It's not worth the price.
Believe me, *next* Christmas we dine on boiled rice!"

ESSAYS

NOTHING EVER HAPPENS

By Velma West Sykes

It was a great throng that had come to Bethlehem for enrollment at the command of Caesar. David, the stable-boy at the inn, had never been so busy, nor so eager to get away to the great world outside, where such marvelous things happened. It had been wonderful hearing all these travelers, who had come back to their own city to register, telling tales of life in larger and far-away places.

David was very young and suffered from the feeling of disdain that almost all young people have for their native environment. Bethlehem was a quiet little town and the people in it lived, for the most part, meager, uneventful lives. The boy longed restlessly for change—adventure—excitement—anything but the monotony that seemed a part of the placid atmosphere of the town.

Then came what seemed to be the great opportunity—the chance to slip away with a merchant who needed another boy to help with the camels. David's father had apprenticed him to the inn-keeper and the lad knew it might go hard with him if he were caught and brought back, but his spirit was ready to take chances in the hope of escaping from the dullness of his existence.

So he had gone, and was even now looking back from the hills outside of town. An unusually large, bright star stood almost directly over the crude old stable where David had been in the habit of sleeping in one of the mangers at night, to be with the beasts under his care. The star gave a strange luster to the rude shelter. He remembered with some chagrin that only that morning he had put fresh straw in his bed, not realizing he would be gone before the night.

Well, some other stable-boy would doubtless be glad to find clean, fresh straw in the manger. As for David, he turned away, glad to be leaving stodgy old Bethlehem, where nothing important ever happened.

CHRISTMAS CONSERVATIVE

By Virginia Scott Miner

This is being a conservative at Christmas time: To think that a green tree, with its multi-coloured decorations saved from year to year and lovingly added to, is more beautiful than any artfully prepared at the florist's. To think that even a simple dinner, cooked at home and shared either with those dearly loved or with those desperately in need of love, is better than the rarest foods any hotel on earth ever served. To feel that for even one week out of the year no symphony, no aria, is quite so precious as the carols of the Christ Child's coming. To feel that, however disillusioned we may have become, there is at least for this small space a Way, a Message, and a Light—

This is being a conservative at Christmas— *But Oh, it's being happy, too!*

THE PALACE AND THE STABLE

By Hendrik Willem Van Loon

It was the seven hundred and fifty-third year since the founding of Rome. Gaius Julius Caesar Octavianus Augustus was living in the palace of the Palatine Hill, busily engaged upon the task of ruling his empire.

In a little village of distant Syria, Mary, the wife of Joseph the Carpenter, was tending her little boy, born in a stable of Bethlehem.

This is a strange world.

Before long, the palace and the stable were to meet in open combat.

And the stable was to emerge victorious.

CHRISTMAS

By Dorothy Canfield Fisher

Do you know anyone who is really satisfied with Christmas as we observe it now? I don't. I could not count the people I have heard speak mournfully of the way Christmas has been "spoiled," nor the number of guesses I have heard as to the reason why, against our wills, we have allowed it to be so spoiled. My guess is that we have been helpless to defend Christmas because of our muddle-headedness. Certainly not from lack of good intentions. Perhaps if we took the trouble to do some thinking about what Christmas is, and to use our imaginations a little about what it might be, we could direct with more effectiveness our efforts to keep it from being an orgy of "give and grab" as someone has sadly dubbed the day that should be hallowed.

Look with me for a moment at the history of the festival, which is of the greatest antiquity. From the dawn of time, before history, all peoples have celebrated the winter solstice with thanksgiving. North, south, east, west,—the Jewish Feast of Lights, the Druid Mother-night, the Roman Feast of Saturn, the Scandinavian Yule ceremonies, everywhere there have been ceremonies to express the emotional relief felt by humanity over the day which marks the turn of the year, the day when the sun, giver of life, after having for months grown steadily weaker and feebler, turns back from death and begins to grow stronger and warmer. From this primitive rejoicing over the annual rebirth of the sun come all those of our Christmas usages that have to do with fire—lighted candles and lamps, the Yule log, the cheerfully illuminated home and street. After about four hundred years, the Christian Church, trying to simplify the transition from paganism to Christianity, wisely decreed that the celebration of the birthday of its Founder should coincide with the date on which this older and universal folk festival was held, thus uniting into one, two mighty currents of human feeling.

Our Christmas customs come from the strangely varied ways in which men have celebrated this old feast. The bountiful Christmas dinner is a reminiscence of the Roman banquets at this time, in honor of ancient gods and goddesses, in whose name cheerful hymns, the originals of our carols, were sung in the streets. In ancient Rome also, people exchanged presents along with the lighted tapers which symbolized the relighted sun. Our decorations of holly and mistletoe come from an entirely different direction, straight down from our pre-Christian Druid ancestors, to whom these were sacred leaves. The Christmas tree is infinitely more modern, starting in a corner of Germany (probably from dim memories of the Scandinavian sacred tree) only three centuries ago, taking two hundred years to spread over all of Germany, and another century to reach England and America. The Christmas card is the most recent of all, not starting till 1862. So you see that of all our Christmas program, the crèche and going to church are the only ones to express our joy in celebrating the birthday of the Founder of the religion we profess.

Now, examine the variegated items in this old, old folk-festival from another standpoint, that of the person who is looking for chances to make money, and in an instant you will see why the giving of presents, and the exchange of Christmas cards have received such an enormous amount of skilled, commercial publicity as practically to make us forget all the many other beautiful and significant aspects of the day. And isn't it considerably easier to resist commercial propaganda when you see clearly where and how you are being exploited?

The festival of Christmas is a part of the universal history of our race, unimaginably rich with old meanings. There is something awe-inspiring in the thought that, as with our children we light the candles on the tree, we are one with our prehistoric ancestors, poetically and symbolically rejoicing over the rebirth of the sun. A usage as old as that, as beautiful, based on such a fundamental human instinct should not be hurriedly passed over as a mere preliminary to getting something for nothing. It should be explained to the children whose naturally fresh and poetic imaginations are always apt to understand and appreciate folk-ways; it should be considered a dignified part of one of our finest old traditions. And the Christmas greens—! Give its true, strange, thought-provoking flavor to what is now a thin, meaningless gesture, remind yourself and tell the children of the curious origin of that custom, give a thought to our prehistoric Druid forefathers, still living on in our homes with every branch of holly and mistletoe we hang. It is good for the children, good for us, it gives a new and shapely perspective to life, to realize that the poorest and humblest of us have grandfathers, aeons of them, living, fearing, rejoicing, passing on to us their driving impulse to try to understand and to beautify life.

And don't forget, every time you focus the attention of your family on one of these age-old, profoundly human aspects of this grand old feast day, you lessen the strangle-hold on their minds of the acquisitive instinct so poisonously bloated by the commercial overemphasis on present-giving. For it is only overemphasis that is hurtful. Present-giving and present-receiving are not bad in themselves. To give well, generously, thoughtfully, to receive with pleasure, delicacy and gratitude—those are beautiful arts which every child should learn by practice. But it stands to reason that he has an infinitely better chance to learn them well, and not badly, if his attention is not solely concentrated on this part of his Christmas Day.

And of course, strangest and most incredible result of the modern distortion of Christmas, is our forgetfulness of what should be its dearest and most sacred meaning, its celebration of the birth of Christ, even to think of which, once, truly, brings tears of thankfulness to our eyes.

There is the day as we inherit it from our life-loving, deep-hearted ancestors, radiant with associations, evocative of emotions that run the gamut from simple light-hearted gaiety through the sweet poetry of symbolic old customs, to religious awe that shakes the heart and purifies the soul. If we do not open the door and let our boys and girls into all of these riches, rightfully theirs, we are cheating them. The child for whom we begin to prepare the Christmas festivals is, literally, the heir to all the ages. We steal the best of his birthright from him if, on Christmas Day, we give him nothing but presents.

SHARE YOUR CHRISTMAS

By Mrs. Thomas A. Edison

Of the National Women's Committee of the 1934 Mobilization
for Human Needs

Louisa May Alcott in her world-famous book, "Little Women," gives us an account of Christmas in the sixties, in the New England home of the March family. The war between the States was then raging. Mr. March had answered the call and was miles away. Mrs. March and her four daughters, Meg,

Jo, Amy and Beth, were carrying on as best they could, in the weatherbeaten, shabby, but much-beloved home that was theirs. Meals were scanty, clothes were turned and mended, and then mended some more.

Yet Christmas was Christmas and must be observed. One small present to each girl—but a precious one—was Mrs. March's contribution to her "little women." The girls in turn, somehow or other, contrived presents for their courageous mother. Small gifts they were but so weighted with love and sacrifice that they were to Mrs. March very wonderful gifts indeed.

And, as for Christmas itself, if the March family had been the wealthiest in all the land there could not have been greater anticipation of the day. It was to start with a marvelous breakfast —marvelous, that is, for the March family with its scanty resources. Muffins and delicious, hot buckwheat cakes, and real cream, after months of bread and milk. It was a gala occasion.

But just as the family was about to sit down to this Christmas feast, someone came to the door to announce that a family not far away was without food. Mrs. March put the question up to the children. Would they be willing to give their Christmas breakfast to these neighbors? Just a minute's hesitation, a glance at their mother's face, and each of the "little women," stifling her disappointment as best she could, ran to get baskets in which to pack away the good things they had been looking forward to for so long. With their mother they trudged to the home where there was no-Christmas-at-all.

Miss Alcott, writing of this venture in neighborliness, said: "It was a very happy breakfast though they did not get any of it, and when they went away, leaving comfort behind, I think there were not in all the city four merrier people than the hungry little girls who gave away their breakfast and contented themselves with bread and milk on Christmas morning."

Today we do not do our neighboring in this way. Our cities

and towns have grown so large that it has been necessary to establish welfare organizations to do the "neighboring" which our parents and grandparents formerly did one for another. These organizations do the work a great deal better than many of us could do it, with all the good intentions in the world. And yet, there is one weakness in the plan. We give our money, but we no longer come in contact with those to whom it goes, for we have learned today that it is often a source of pain to a family to be visited by its benefactor. But there are other ways to know what becomes of our gifts, if we will only follow them through.

If I were bringing up children, I would want them to know a great deal about their community's "good neighbor" organizations. I should consider a knowledge and sympathetic understanding of people as important a part of their education as "schooling." I should wish them to get the feeling early of sharing what they have. I should want them to know the joy of giving.

It seems to me at this time that half of the troubles of the world have come because we have forgotten that a "good neighbor" gives where there is no possible chance of return, and gives at a sacrifice of some of the things he himself wants.

The success of children in later years does not depend, after all, upon the amount of money parents have to invest in their education, but rather on the intelligent thought they put into the guidance of this early training. As part of this daily-guidance plan, I should like to recommend that parents consider bringing their children into closer acquaintance with the Community Chest agencies or the other welfare organizations of their community. Take them to visit the organizations you think will interest them. Explain these new forms of neighborliness. Make them understand early that poverty is no disgrace, but that selfishness and greed are. Train them while they are young so that the true spirit of Christmas will abide in their lives not just one day in the year but every day.

I WISH YOU ALL A MERRY CHRISTMAS

BY JEAN AUSTIN

Every Christian nation has made of Christmas time something beautiful, made of the Christmas festivities something especially its own. And in every country except ours, Christmas is a strictly religious festival—as indeed it should be. Scandinavians scour their houses and hang paper streamers, let the children seek out their little hidden gifts, go to church through starlit fields of snow at midnight, and scatter grain for the birds' Christmas. An Italian Christmas is not complete without the revered praesipio, and Spaniards go to midnight mass on the "noche buena." Bavarian children look forward to painted toys and gingerbread menageries. In Holland they carry the great Star of Bethlehem on a pole through the streets. French children find lucky coins in the big Christmas cake and little cakes with a sugared Christmas child on top. In Tyrolese villages they sing lustily and happily on Christmas Eve. South of the Danube there is feasting, all seated on a straw-strewn floor, and on Christmas day great oak trees are felled and children sing to cows in their stalls for milk to bathe a new-born Babe on the birthnight of "The Little God."

And here, in America? We exchange washing machines, checks, and mink coats; our pianos are silent and the radio sings our Christmas carols for us; no fragrant scents come from our kitchens days before Christmas—we are too "emancipated" for that—and our children give us Christmas lists, instead of cherishing what we might give them of our own volition. They, and we, are poor indeed. We Americans have lost the art of simple happiness. We have forgotten what the true spirit of Christmas really signifies.

When I wish you all a Merry Christmas, it is the simple joy

and the spiritual beauty of a peasant Christmas that I am wishing for you. May your "presents" be less and your happiness greater. From my house to your house—a kindly, sincere hope that this Christmas may more nearly approach the lovely, holy thing it should be—in your house and in my house.

THE SPIRIT OF GIVING

(Editorial in The Woman's Home Companion.)

By Anne Bryan McCall

Thanksgiving the festival of receiving or of gratitude for what we have received; Christmas the festival of giving!

Of giving and receiving, receiving is the more ancient in man's experience.

It seems rather happily appropriate then that in our calendar, as by a kind of lovely and unpremeditated logic, Thanksgiving comes earlier than Christmas.

These two festivals, growing out of man's old urge for thankfulness and his deep ineradicable desire to give, have very ancient psychological laws underlying them. They are founded on man's oldest and most permanent behaviors and ideals and hopes.

"Freely ye have received; freely give"; most of us think of that as an ancient command and obligation; but in the light of man's history and modern psychology it seems almost more like a prophecy, as though one were to say, "Having received so bountifully, man is by his very nature destined to give." And it is true that as far back as you can go in man's race experience you will find him Man the Receiver-giver; humbly thankful for the gifts he has received from the world in which he lives and from the mighty powers of life, comprehended or uncomprehended, which surround him; but also, out of the pride and dignity and aspiration of his own nature, rising to bring gifts and offerings in his own right, in his own hands.

Nothing in fact is more ancient and fundamental in man than this mingled humility and pride. David, so magnificently humble and proud himself, sums it up beautifully and memorably: "What is man, that thou art mindful of him; and the son of man, that thou visitest him?" There, you see, is the ancient humility, as of old; then follow the proud assertions: "For thou hast made him a little lower than the angels, and hast crowned him with glory and honor."

This sense of the dignity of man, the Giver, this vision, dim at times but permanent, of the individual doing his part, being equal to life, not being merely a pensioner on life's bounties, or on the bounties of others; not only receiving but giving gifts—all this, like any of the fundamentals of human nature, you will find reiterated again and again, in race-history, in art, in science, in legend and folklore.

But nowhere else will you find it more beautifully, floweringly evident than in Christmas story, Christmas legend, Christmas practice. Here are receiving and giving at the height of their loveliness and at the depth of all their deepest meaning.

Examine the Christmas story and the Christmas symbols as some of the greatest of the painters have represented them. Here is the Christ child, the "Son of Man," bringing the greatest of all gifts; royal, yet lying in the humblest of man's shelters. And over this shelter bend herald angels royally attendant on Him. And below in the foreground—" a little lower than the angels" —stand or kneel the shepherds and the Wise Men, receiving devoutly the gift that has been given them, but bringing, also, gifts and offerings in their own hands.

This is the essence of the Christmas story. This is the spirit of giving; giving not from a sense of duty, not as a return for receiving, but from a glad sense of recognition, and awareness that in a world where such gifts are given to man it is fitting and appropriate that man too should himself give gifts.

And you will find this spirit appearing and reappearing all through man's history, whether in his early days he threaded the deep jungle at certain times of the year to bring offerings of the fruits of his hands, in recognition and awareness of the earth's dark bounty to him; or whether in Greece at the height of her glory he joined at a certain recurring season with men and women as we know them on the frieze of the Parthenon, as they brought gifts and offerings to Athena, the goddess of wisdom, in awareness of the gifts of judgment and safety and order which wisdom had vouchsafed them; or whether he came as he still does with the Wise Men, more endeared, offering gifts, and giving gifts nobly out of the abundance of his heart and his experience.

And always, *always,* it is true that the best and most generous giver is the one who is most aware, who is the most awake to what he himself has received from life; precisely as the most grudging, the miserly, and those who would even rob others of the gifts that are by right theirs, are those who hardly know what you mean when you speak of the gifts that life is forever bestowing on us.

And here also you will find the lovely and ancient Christmas symbols true to the ancient facts. For there were those in Bethlehem that night of long-ago who slept soundly and were unmindful, were unaware; who did not see the light of the star, nor hear the angels' song. And there were those like Herod bent, for their own gain and selfish purposes, on robbing others; people who could not realize or understand what gift was being given. And these gave no gifts and brought no offerings; and because of the very laws of life and human nature they could know no gladness of that night.

Then in contrast to these turn once more to those others whom each year we love to remember, the "shepherds abiding in the fields, keeping watch over their flocks by night." These saw and heard. These were aware. These accepted the gift of that first Christmas with thankfulness and amaze. And the Wise Men, the "Kings of Tarshish and of the Isles," these for long years had been wakefully aware, eagerly ready and expectant of the gift. And these bent low with the shepherds, offering devoutly their rich gifts of long garnering—jewels, myrrh, frankincense and gold.

There was in the Companion years ago a story which I do not remember at all exactly, but whose title has stayed with me. It was called "The Stingy Receiver." I believe in the story the stingy receiver was someone who had not the grace to receive graciously; but what a striking summing-up that title is, too, of the person without the grace or awareness to receive graciously the gifts that life is forever offering.

I believe one of the loveliest gifts that life offers to us this year is the fact that as time goes on there are among us fewer and fewer stingy receivers.

Modern times and modern science and modern psychology are giving us a better understanding of man, his history, his hopes and aspirations; and with this we are gaining a better awareness of our own rich human inheritance and possibilities.

One woman writes me, "In the August 'Tower Room' you wrote an article about the home, 'A Place of Encouragement.' In that article you pointed out that we inherit man's ancient and fundamental need and ideals of home, as men inherit rich legacies. Since then I think I understand human nature and myself better. I begin to realize that I have these gifts within myself, to give: peace, shelter, comfort and encouragement; and I am giving them now in my own home."

Among us, and on all sides of us, there is a growing awareness of the human gifts and riches that are ours; not ours in a general way only, but personally, individually ours; an awareness in the individual of the riches bestowed on him by life to be garnered and cherished and given and bestowed richly, like gifts of the Magi.

There are new forces at work in the world which are daily making man more conscious of the richness of his own gifts. We are giving a greater respect for human beings; a deeper respect for ourselves and others; better ideals for the home; better understanding of little children, of youth and of each other. An understanding of psychology is changing and broadening our thoughts, our conduct, our aspirations, our estimates of ourselves and others. We are learning what Robinson calls "the importance of psychology for life at large."

Each Christmas is, I believe, to the fully aware, a better Christmas than the last because of the new gifts which man himself brings to the festival. This Christmas, among many other precious gifts is this gift of man's growing understanding of himself and his fellow men. There is a greater awareness concerning it in our homes, our schools. It is talked about, thought about everywhere.

And out of this better understanding of ourselves and others there are developing greater tolerance, kindness, patience, wisdom and an infinitely richer spirit of giving; gifts of the Magi.

THE HEART OF CHRISTMAS

By HENRY C. LINK

Christmas commemorates the birth of a great Personality. We celebrate this occasion more widely than any other because his personality stands out above all others.

What is the greatness in the personality of Jesus? The fact that he loved all men regardless of race, creed, or social status. He hated the intellectual smugness of the Pharisees, the indifference of the rich, the avarice of the tax collectors, and the incompetence of the poor. Yet he loved the better man beneath, and it was to this higher self that he appealed. All people were God's children to him. He made a friend of Nicodemus, of the woman at the well, of Zacchaeus the publican, of the rich young ruler. Wherever he went, the multitudes followed him.

He so loved the goodness in people that he gave his time, his talents, his comfort, and his life in their behalf. He was so interested in others that he forgot himself. Even in death, his last thought was for his enemies: Father, forgive them, for they know not what they do. He forgot himself so completely that the world can never forget him.

We see around us today hatred, greed, and violence where only love can succeed. We see grandiose schemes said to be for the betterment of the human race without the elements of love in their administration. We see billions spent for the needy, but very little love. We find it easier to contribute dollars than to contribute acts of kindness. We are full of the new social consciousness, but it is of the mind rather than of the heart. Our interest in the mailman, the milkman, the elevator operator, or the society right around us is as mechanical as before.

The secret of personality lies in forgetting oneself in the service of others. Christmas, with its unique custom of giving gifts, is the symbol of this fact. Yet, like all symbolic customs, it tends to become an empty routine. It degenerates into an exchange of gifts, a mere system of bookkeeping, a last minute shopping rush. Instead of inspiring us with a love of mankind, it threatens to turn us sour on the human race.

To celebrate the heart of Christmas is to forget ourselves in the service of others.

Many children stumble through the social relationships of life because they have never practised the skills of serving other people. Giving children money with which to buy gifts does little to teach them to give themselves. Doing the work of Christmas for one's children may be easier on the parents but tends to confirm the selfishness and awkwardness of their children.

Here is an occasion to inspire children with the thought of their fellow men, and with an awareness of who their fellow men are. Not merely their relatives and friends, but the garbage man, the milkman, the grocery boy, the mailman, and a dozen others who represent families and elements of society. Impersonal gifts do not reach the hearts of people, but the garbage man may have a little daughter, or the mailman a young son. A child may share his possessions with these. In order to do so he must first talk with his parents and find out what will be acceptable. Adults might well help their children in making the acquaintance of these parents. Even if no gifts are given, the range of human contacts is expanded. We discover men where we had accepted machines.

Here is a lesson not in the social sciences but in the arts of social intercourse. Here is society not in the abstract but at our very doors. Here is the simple and the obvious, yet that which for many of us is most obscure. Here is the homely road by which our children may yet achieve what their elders have lost, Peace on Earth and Good Will to Men.

KEEPING CHRISTMAS

By Willard L. Sperry

General William Booth's wife once asked her oldest daughter, "Kate, why is it that God can't keep a thing pure for more than a generation?" That is the sort of question we are all asking about Christmas. How did it become impure and what can we do to restore its purity?

We have made a start. We are slowly teaching our children that they must make Christmas a happy day for the postman and the shop-girl and the delivery boy. For our children have no right to get their happiness at the cost of the unhappiness of all those who have to serve them.

But can we go beyond this? What are our own beliefs about this day? Each age creates for itself its own particular religious difficulties and our age is no exception. Being products of the new psychology we are haunted by the suspicion that all religion, our own included, is a sentimental flight from reality, the escape mechanism of timid and defeated natures. There is, thus, the haunting fear that the more religiously we try to keep Christmas for our children the less real it becomes.

I doubt it. You cannot send your child out into the maelstrom of modern life with the advance assurance that everything he meets there is real. For there are times when the doings of the world around you seem like nothing so much as a corporate insanity. Dr. Alexis Carrel has just written a book about *Man, the Unknown,* who is, he tells us, unhappy and slowly degenerating. The trouble is, he says, that in our cities we have not taken the trouble to "create islands of solitude where meditation would be possible."

You have to fight every day of the year to make and keep your home a tranquil little island in the midst of the storm. You have to fight every day of the year for the quiet of a genuine Christmas day. But it is worth fighting for, one of the few things that really is worth it. You owe your child this mature conviction which has come to you. He may not understand it now; he will later.

Furthermore we should not fail to tell our children from the first that whatever may be meant by God and religion we learn our first lessons about these from what is right at hand. In one of his books Phillips Brooks compares the worship of the Sphinx with the Christian adoration of the Virgin and Child. He discerns the "eternal feminine" in both religions. He feels the mysterious power of the Sphinx but turns finally to the Nativity. "A father, a mother, a child are there. No religion which began like that could ever lose its character." Christmas recalls us who are older, and given to speculation, to the immediacies of life. It makes us realize that if the near relations of life lose their character, religion is lost also.

And then the day challenges us to draw the line truly between childishness and childlikeness. Childishness is something which ought to be outgrown and to pass away; childlikeness is something to be kept to the last. What is that elusive quality? Perhaps you may learn it watching your own child at his Christmas play. I have read the Gospels many times to try to identify and isolate that quality without which—we have it on the word of Jesus—we shall never get into God's Kingdom, and in the end it always seems to come down to one thing—trust. To trust life, to trust one another, to trust God—that is what faith meant to Jesus. Alas, the world in its entirety is not trustworthy, as we learn to our sorrow. But so long as there is in it that which can be trusted, religion is possible. You cannot look on the trustfulness of a little child without being rebuked and then reassured. For you see there, whatever your own imperfections, the intimation of all religion. And the observance of Christmas becomes thus your attempt to create and to reaffirm a trustworthy world around the next generation. What you learn about religion from your own child you return to him with the sober meditative approval of your longer experience of life. This is your holy day communicating its spirit to his holiday.

SIGNS, SYMBOLS AND PSYCHOLOGY

A Christmas Talk

By ANNE BRYAN McCALL

Are you stubbornly opinionated and literal-minded or are you, instead, tolerant and imaginative? Do signs and symbols mean little or much to you?

Answer me these questions and I can tell you fairly well what your life and fortune are likely to be. For man has been from the beginning not stubbornly opinionated but imaginative; not boasting that he calls a spade a spade; but, rather, reading in every object many meanings and giving those meanings many names. In short, from the beginning man has been an inveterate maker and reader of signs and symbols. And all this for very good reason: he has found it unsafe, dangerous, to be otherwise.

Always man has valued life and so has gone seeking safety. In other words he has sought to retain the right to keep on living; and it is precisely in trying to retain that right that he has developed through the ages his magnificent use of symbols, and his inveterate liking for them. His alertness, his watchfulness, his observations, his ability to see that a spade might very well be something else, or something more, than a spade, protected him again and again from danger, and at the same time enriched his life immeasurably by giving him the use of symbols.

For a symbol is based on the observation of likenesses and analogies; and usually is something that suggests or stands for or stands in the place of, something else—sometimes many things else—than itself.

Primitive man must have discovered early the danger of being stubbornly opinionated and literal, and the usefulness and value of symbols. He must have learned early that appearances are often misleading and things are not always what they seem; that keen observation is needed in these matters; that a slight sound for instance, which he could have sworn was only the sign of a pleasant and welcome stirring of the wind in the leaves, might prove to be instead a symbol of danger—a sign of the stealthy approach of a beast of prey or the near presence of a dreaded enemy. So he became as time went on more and more observant, more and more watchful of likenesses and signs; and symbols became of vital and fundamental importance to him.

They still are. The fundamentals of human behavior do not

change. Signs and symbols, whether we realize it or not, are a vital and important part of the daily lives of all of us. It is, I believe, vitally important that you and I should know something about them as they relate to us and to those with whom life calls us to deal.

What then are signs and symbols?

They are, generally speaking, guides and safeguards; but they are much more than that and have many and multiple uses: They are, for instance, abbreviations; condensations; conveniences; time savers; sorrow savers; calamity savers; reminders; omens; warnings; symptoms; explanations; informers; records; condensed histories; evidence; tokens. They are always full of truth and significance. Our very word "significance"—the strongest synonym we have for "meaning"—is based, as its first four letters show, on the word "sign."

Break open a symbol and you will always find that its kernel or heart is a truth or a fact. "Saint George for England," the British soldiers' cry for victory in the darkest hour of the battle, has at the heart of it the fact that very long ago a hero, later called Saint George, really did fight and win and bring deliverance against terrific odds (in the story the symbol used for the terrific odds is a dragon) and at the heart of it is the fact too that men cherish and value and honor and remember courage and valor.

The symbolic phrase "the sun rose" has as its kernel of truth that men in the long unscientific ages really did believe that the sun "rose," got up in the morning in the same literal sense that they did.

Our symbolic terms "good morning," "good day," "good evening," "good night," are records of the fact of the many and varied dangers by day and night which have long beset man; and a record too of the friendliness of man in wishing that his fellow man might escape these dangers, that he might have *good* mornings, *good* days, *good* evenings, *good* nights.

"Good-by," our abbreviation of "God be with you," is a symbolic record and reminder of the perils of the road and the longing of the human heart for the guidance and protection of those it loves.

The act of offering your hand in greeting has back of it whole ages of man's insecurity and his fear for his life, and so of his habit of carrying weapons; and it testifies no less to his willingness to give up carrying weapons if it be safe for him to do so. Indeed the symbolic meaning of hands meeting in greeting might be said to be the original agreement of disarmament. For each hand outstretched says by that outstretching, "It is safe to deal with me. I bear no weapons." This was the ancient first meaning of handshaking.

Thousands of examples could be given, if there were space, of similar deep truths hid in symbols. But perhaps enough has been said to show that the ability to read and understand symbols is one of the most enriching opportunities that life offers us.

And along these lines richer opportunities than ever before are being offered us: Students of psychology for a long time undervalued or neglected the study and the science of symbols. Today that is no longer true; and it is today mainly through the efforts of psychologists that it has become generally known that practically all our human behaviors are not literal but highly symbolic; that they too are not always what they seem; and that if men would live safely with themselves and others, they must learn to read and interpret these in the simple or difficult daily human matters and human relations with which they are obliged to deal.

Most of us used to think very literally and rather stubbornly of anger as merely anger, jealousy as jealousy, love as love, hate as hate, awkwardness as awkwardness, bullying as bullying, and so on to the end of the chapter. Today many of us know that these behaviors represent and stand for other things than themselves and that by understanding their symbolic character we can remedy and mend them.

There is not space here to go fully into so large a subject, but I quote this from a chapter on symbolic behaviors in my book, *You Yourself:*

"Shyness and blushing are not fear or timidity; they are signs or symbols of timidity. Jealousy is a sign of self-mistrust; temper is a sign or symbol of insecurity . . . malice—malicious gossip, for instance—is a sign or symbol, or symptom, if you like, of envy; and envy is in turn a sign (like jealousy) of self-mistrust. . . . The behavior of the man who 'takes to drink' is also highly symbolic. It is . . . a sign of flight, escape. Escape from what? That depends on what his experience has been. . . .

"It is only when we begin to understand the deep race law of symbols and the ancient race habit of symbolizing that we begin to understand what such common daily behaviors really mean, symbolize, stand for and are signs of. It is only then that we begin really to understand ourselves and others."

And all of this is in turn not merely and literally psychology. It is a symbol of a more thoughtful understanding of each other and so a sign of better brotherhood.

And this brings it close to that great and lovely symbol which we celebrate yearly at Christmas time.

For Christmas is one of the loveliest and profoundest of symbols; suggesting and standing for the richness and wonder of life, and the depth and richness of life's meanings. It holds within it the story of man's struggles and his hopes, his longings and his attainment, his patience, his dignity, his reverence, his simplicity. The sign of a star is set in the heavens. The Kings of Tarshish and the Isles come bringing gifts out of the ages. Herod, a dark symbol of envy and denial, tries to stop them but they arrive despite him at the place of their intention. Shepherds and their simple sheep assemble from near-by pastures.

Heavenly ministers lead and guide them to a little child whom, for more than two thousand years, men have called "Hope of the World," "Light of the World," "Son of Man."

And you? Are you in step with all this, or are you apart from it? How much do you really know of human nature? How rich and faithful are your determination and intent to deal with it, in yourself and others like wise men, wisely; like simple men, kindly and devotedly; how resolved are you to bring with you out of the ages that richest of all human gifts—human understanding?

LIGHTING THE YULE LOG

(FROM THE LITERARY DIGEST, DEC. 26, 1931)

Commonplace coal or oil in the cellar has displaced the great hearths of old.

Electricity and gas have all but put out the candle.

And the old Yule log, too, once a central feature of Christmas custom, is little more than a memory.

But it is not altogether gone. In some parts of the world the custom of drawing in and lighting the Christmas log is still observed, and elsewhere logs of sorts and varied lengths to fit smaller hearths serve as in the ancient way. Candles still appear in the window to light the wayfarer home and invite the passing stranger in. Old custom does rise occasionally to tease this age of the machine.

In the old days, F. M. Verrall reminds us in *The Catholic World* (New York), the special Christmas fuel must be of good wood. Oak logs served in the north of England, the birch-tree in Scotland, while in Cornwall and Devon the Christmas wood was an ash fagot, because, according to tradition, the first Christmas fire was lit in the Bethlehem stable by a shepherd boy, who, seeing that the Holy Family was suffering from the cold, ran out, gathered ash wood—the only wood which burns freely in a green state—and soon made a glorious blaze.

But whatever the wood, it was not brought into the house until Christmas Eve, when everyone lent a hand hauling on the ropes. Many superstitions, we are told, surrounded the ceremony. Maids must not touch the log with dirty hands, children must not sit on it, and in medieval England so great respect was paid to the log that people who passed as it was being drawn to some house touched their hats to it, or, presumably, what it stood for.

Since the days of the Tudor Kings, the writer tells us, Yule log festivities in England have been merely a merry diversion, whereas in Catholic Brittany, Normandy, and Provence, a certain amount of religious ceremony is associated with the *trefoir*, the French Yule log.

"In Provence, for example, the wood must be cut from a healthy fruit-tree in full bearing.

"On Christmas Eve, the whole family, singing carols, go out to fetch it in. The log is then put on the hearth, on a bed of shavings and easily combustible wood.

"All the lights in the room are extinguished, and the head of the household says a prayer, first for the living members of the family who are present, then for those who are absent, then for the souls of all dead relatives, who are, by both Provençal and Breton, thought to attend these intimate domestic ceremonies.

"The 'Our Father' is recited in unison, then the head of the house takes a sprig of box or olive which had been kept from Palm Sunday for the purpose, dips it into the vessel of holy water held by the youngest child, and with a wide Sign of the Cross, blesses the *trefoir* in the Name of the Most Holy Trinity. The child holds two lighted candle ends which have been preserved from last year's Christmas Eve, and with them kindles the brand of last year's log and the *trefoir* of this.

"Occasionally the ceremony varies a little—wine is sprinkled on the log, a practice so old in France that it was mentioned by Saint Martin of Braga in the sixth century."

In practically every country, we read, it is held essential that the special wood burn until Twelfth-night, even if it means taking the log off the fire every evening and smothering or extinguishing the flame. In both France and England, it is said, belief still lingers that the ashes bring fertility to crops and cattle, cure childish complaints, and alleviate toothache.

In the Balkan countries the ceremony of bringing in the Christmas log is accompanied by quaint and rather superstitious customs. The fuel is cut and carried into the house before dawn on Christmas morning between two rows of people holding lighted candles. The head of the house brings the log in himself, and as he enters the door, corn and wine are sprinkled both on him and on it. When the wood is kindled the first visitor to the house brings wheat hidden in his glove. This is thrown on the threshold, with the words, "Christ is born." One of the children of the house responds with the answer, "He is born indeed," and at the same time throws corn on the visitor, who stirs up the log to make it burn brightly, and wishes good luck to household and farm.

In medieval England the star of Bethlehem was remembered by putting a great Yuletide or Christmas candle up in church, and setting one on the supper-table of every home on Christmas Eve, and relighting it every night until Twelfth-day closed the Christmas season.

A candle was lit in court and college as well as in the cottage, being once as popular in England as it still is in the rural parts of Ireland today. And, we read:

"Saint John's College, Oxford, still possesses the great stone candlestick with an *Agnus Dei* carved on it, in which was set the Yuletide candle for the fellows' and undergraduates' feasting.

"Though the use of it in church and court probably died out

soon after the 'Reformation,' large Christmas candles were seen in the homes of middle-class and poorer people until recently, for, until gas and electric light became the universal means of domestic lighting, grocers gave their customers large packets of special Yuletide candles. And even in the nineteenth century, village children in Lancashire presented their schoolmaster with one candle each on the last day of the term.

"Another curious candle custom was prevalent in a Shropshire mining village until well into the nineteenth century, when, on Christmas Eve, miners carried about the streets small boards in which were fixt a number of small lighted candles."

A memory of candles lighting altars and crib at Midnight Mass seems to have lingered on among the country people of some Protestant lands long after the memory of the Mass itself had faded, says the writer, and he goes on:

"In Wales, which is on the whole a strictly Protestant country, until the middle or end of the nineteenth century a service called Dawn (Plygain) was held in many Welsh Episcopal churches about 4 o'clock on Christmas morning. Young men carrying lighted torches accompanied the minister from his house to the church, brilliantly lit up for the occasion with numerous colored candles. The service itself might be a celebration of Holy Communion, or it might be chiefly of carol singing.

"In the Isle of Man, too, on Christmas Eve—called Mary's Eve, as in some other Celtic districts—was a carol service in which each singer, as he or she sang, held a lighted candle. When the candle went out the carol stopt.

"Scandinavia also has similar customs of churches brilliantly lit up by candles for services held on Christmas Eve. Domestic candles of great size are lit in the farmstead, but appear to symbolize nothing except a superstitious foretelling of the length of the master's or mistress's life.

"But in Ireland—where, by the way, the Yule log was never seen—the Christmas candle shines brightly from every window in the country (and also in the Irish working-class districts of many English and Welsh towns), proclaiming to the world that this is Christmas Eve, and in this house is welcome for Our Lady and her Child."

THE DAY BEFORE

Christmas Traditions of One Kentucky Family

By Mary Lindsay Hoffman

Even better than Christmas Day itself, at our house, is The Day Before. Indeed we think it is the best day of the whole year. It is better than Thanksgiving, which is after all nothing much but an eating day, and liable to leave one with an uncomfortable stuffed-animal feeling. It is better than Halloween, even counting carrying in our crop of one pumpkin and carving it into a Jack. Fourth of July, of course, was ruined long ago by careful parents, and April Fool's Day and Valentine's Day are the kind of days that are nice, if you like them. But no one would compare them with Christmas Day, and, as I said, The Day Before outshines even that.

At our house The Day Before Christmas begins long before The Day Before Christmas. The hunt for the Christmas tree comes first. It is a joyous day! With two other families we go, on a Sunday afternoon, to the quiet winter woods. There we wander happily around for hours, trying almost vainly to find three perfect trees. One must be quite small and bushy, one must be medium sized and bushy, and one must be as large and glorious as it is possible to get into a room, and yet also bushy. This last tree is ours. Now, if you have ever engaged in the search for the perfect Christmas tree, you will know just how hard a quest it is. But every member of each family finds one that is just right for his family or for one of the other two, and then every member of each group within hailing distance must come to see and to pass judgment. For we think it no small matter to cut a cedar, even though we live in a part of the country where they are often considered pestiferous weeds. At last the early winter twilight warns us that we positively must decide between this shorter bushy one and that taller, lovelier, feathery one. Then come the sounds of three axes and away we all trudge, following the three fathers who bear our treasures. Will you ever forget the year when a soft feathery snow glorified the whole scene and made the three very small persons in the crowd look like darling little gnomes in their leggings and woolly caps, trudging bravely behind all the long way? Then the end of the trail every year is home, and in one of the three is a blazing fire and hot soup for us all.

Then there are other preliminaries. The other greens must be ready, piled on the porch ready for The Day Before. Holly we use sparingly, as all good patriots now do. Ground pine too is scarce and hard to get, but it adds a flavor all its own to the Christmas house.

Tall red candles there must be. If none came as gifts the year before, they must be bought, and laid away, ready to be placed on either side of a bowl of bright red apples.

Time would fail us to tell of all the baking that has been done before the dawn of The Day Before. We long ago gave up cakes. They are too sweet. Nobody wants a big squashy piece of cake at Christmas time, but how everyone does love the crisp cookies and small cakes. There are gingerbread boys and girls for the tree, in quite original shapes, due to being carved out with a knife; crisp little fig cookies, nut cookies, big white cookies stuck all over with pretty candies; and cup cakes with red, green and white frosting. All these must be ready and packed away in tin boxes.

From year to year our candy making varies. We always make chocolate-covered raisins and peanuts, and brown sugar fudge poured over Puffed Wheat, and stuffed dates, and sometimes we specialize on fondant of all colors and flavors. Then, there must be popcorn balls, and strings of it for the birds' tree. The popcorn has an interest of its own because its final appearance in the glory of balls, is the culmination of planting, hoeing and reaping by The Little Girl and her "Dud."

Somewhere earlier, along in December, after Christmas can be felt in the air, we say "each to t'other"—the Little Girl and I—"We must be getting the dolls to the repair shop." So we set a night for us to work. I used to do it alone as a grand surprise, and have been known to be frantically sewing on a leg as the clock struck twelve on Christmas Eve. But as the Little Girl grew and the doll family grew too, it seemed more common sense, and more fun too, to do it together. I say we set a night, but it has often taken several. In the good old days before the dolls went into semi-retirement, they lived a strenuous life, and by the end of the year there were a mighty lot of arms and legs and heads to sew on, new heads or new hair, or new paint on old faces. Our two greatest triumphs were the healing of an enormous gap in the head of Bob, by means of liberal quantities of adhesive tape, gracefully concealed under two coats of house paint; and the construction of a wooden forearm and hand from a clothes pin, this last being "Dud's" invention. But every year every doll—seventeen at the last count—is gone over and in some way renewed or dressed up for Christmas. They are not really all dolls, but those who are not dolls are "creatures." One year the forty-year-old brown cotton flannel elephant, Bim, went all the way from North Carolina to South Dakota, to his creator, Grandma, for a new coat. He came back funnier than ever, with red buttons for eyes!

A little nearer the end of the month we begin to say we must get out the tree trimmings, for though each has been carefully wrapped and put away on the day after New Year's, that is a long time ago, and we have forgotten how many were broken,— and, anyway, it is a part of our Christmas procedure to look them over ahead of time. It makes Christmas so much longer! If they were only colored balls it would not be so much fun, but our tree trimmings have an infinite variety. There is the Santa "Dud" that I got the very first Christmas, when we were only dreaming of a boy and a girl. He is faded and decrepit, but still holds the place of honor on the tree, just below the Star. Then there is the pheasant's feather from Manchuria sent by "Dud" in war time, and the tiny brown jug made by a Chautauqua lecturer for The Big Boy, when he was a little one. And so on through the years, we have saved cunning little things that we like, until the trimming of the tree is an adventure in family history.

At last we come to The Day Before. Where to begin! How to crowd it all in! Morning clean-up is restricted almost entirely to the living room. Other rooms must fend for themselves or close their doors in shame. While these inevitable preliminaries go on above stairs, from the lower regions of the basement comes the sound of hammering and of much talk. The Tree is being set up. It is a job; for the lovely feathery branches of the cedar have a most beastly scratchiness to them.

It is nearly noon by the time these jobs are done, but we try to get the greens ready for the outside of the house before we stop. The Little Girl runs to get the wreath bases from the attic, that are cardboard, colored green by herself. Soon this tough little job is over and the lovely things are ready to adorn the windows. Then long branches of cedar or pine frame the door, the outside light has a lining of red, and a cap of greenery, until the whole looks like the pictures in the Christmas magazines. The very last thing is the birds' Christmas tree. The little cedar growing near the door holds our strings of popcorn, bits of suet, with nuts and oatmeal underneath. The Big Boy rigs up colored lights for the pleasure of passers-by at night. This we feel the birds will not resent, even if they do not care for lights themselves.

After a nondescript meal—just any old thing will do—we scatter to our own affairs for a few hours. There are always last-minute errands, finishing touches on a present. Somewhere during this free time, Mother and everyone else who happens to be free, wrap the little gifts for our neighbors and dearest friends. These are very small indeed, involving little or no expense, but are a very dear part of our Christmas. Sometimes it is flower seed. Last year The Little Girl and I made tiny three-cornered envelopes in three colors, to hold pink, white and blue moon flower seeds saved from our vines. That meant that away back in October we were making Christmas plans. Or it may be home-salted nuts, or popcorn balls. We try always to find something whose chief virtue is its originality or the loving effort involved. These jolly-looking little packages are piled on trays and put on a high shelf till mid-morning of Christmas Day, when one or both children deliver them.

At four o'clock we assemble again for the grand finale of The Day Before. We are now washed and clothed for the evening, as there is not a minute free until bed time. Christmas has begun. Our box of trimmings is brought from the attic and the motley collection finds places on the tree. Each is greeted with, "Oh, do you remember?" or, "I had forgotten all about that," or, "Don't you just love this?" The discussion of where each should go makes the process a long and exciting one. Of course, there is the inevitable crash of a fragile ball now and then, as a fastener breaks or fingers slip, and it is sure to be somebody's "favorite one." With due consideration of fire warnings and the most careful precautions, we still put candles on the tree. Somehow "candles on a Christmas tree" has a sound and a flavor that we cannot resist. They add the final touch of beauty and mystery to what was once just a cedar tree. Well, finally, it is done. Everything has found a place, from the brand new star to the crazy old pheasant's feather from Manchuria. Now come the dolls from their clothes basket upstairs.

How excited they are as they find their places at the base of the tree! With their arrival the whole corner comes alive, and we all say, "Let's always have the dolls." The greatest care is taken to have them cunningly placed. Someone must hold the babies. The bears are always sitting at some rakish angle, while the ancient and honorable elephant has the place of prominence in front. Santa is sure to leave some candy and a few trinkets for them.

While a light but good supper is being made ready to be eaten in front of the fire, "Dud" and the Boy and Girl get out the goodies. The cupboard shelves are full of them. Much discussion follows as to which looks better in this dish or that bowl or basket. Nuts in the wooden bowl, of course, and red apples in the old-fashioned tall fruit dish, brown sugar candy in a blue bowl, and so on till each has the best setting possible. No tasting either! Not a nibble! The array looks positively greedy as we look almost vainly for places to put it all. But we have no qualms of conscience when we remember how many friends will drop in on the morrow, and especially the horde of students staying over for the holidays. Their capacity is as unlimited as is our pleasure in seeing them devour our goodies.

Now we are ready to sit down in a house just overflowing with Christmas, to our fire-side supper of hot soup and fruit salad, with carol-singing after it. We will never forget the remark of The Big Boy a few years ago, when we were trying to decide whether to go to a Sunday School entertainment that had been scheduled for Christmas Eve. "Why, mother," he said, "I think it is positively sacrilegious to have anything on Christmas Eve." We did not go to the entertainment, and our little family ceremony has been doubly sacred ever since. It really is hardly a ceremony, except that we repeat it each year. We just sit in the firelight after supper and sing the old carols, ending with Silent Night. One which we found in a magazine years ago, is reserved for the processional on Christmas morning, but must always be practised the night before lest we forget the words. It is called The Holly and the Ivy, and we love it for its quaintness.

The candle for the Christ Child is always put in the window right after carol singing. It seems the right time for it somehow. We use a long one so it will burn all evening. It sits in a holly candlestick—one of those gifts that the sender thought, despairingly, we would never care about or use!

The last act before the arrival of Santa, is the placing of our gifts to each other. They are seldom wrapped till the last minute, so involve much scurrying about for paper and string and greeting cards, and much shouting of "You can tell mine from the shape," or "Don't you look!" But at last, at length, and finally, they are all under the tree—always much later than we intend. The stockings are then "hung by the chimney with care,"—in our family just two, the grown-ups having taken pity on Santa in this regard.

Just as on that busy Night Before we keep thinking this is the last thing, and then thinking of something more, so after mentioning the last thing, I recall two more, each most important: the "Christmas cocktail." It consists of a good substantial dose of soda in sour lemonade for all hands. It is a very good preparation for the sweets of the next day. Then, too, Santa must have a plate of cakes. He always eats them and leaves a hurried note of thanks.

"And so to bed," with many happy calls back and forth about the possibility and even the probability of Santa actually coming again. These conversations about the Christmas saint we enjoy almost as much as we did when all my declarations were received with round-eyed wonder and complete faith. The transition to the grown-up state of pretending, just the same, has been gradual and based on the solid fact that The Christmas Spirit always does come to our house.

During this interval, while we wait for the conditions above stairs to warrant the arrival of Santa Claus, we clear up a little and set out the breakfast things. Then we help Santa down the chimney, brush him off, and assist him to unload a share of his pack. With the help of Dog Bear we also dispose of his cakes! The note he always writes himself, though! "Dud" is always amazed and a trifle scandalized over the number of things that emerge from various hidden places, but to me there are never enough. It is not so much that I want them to have the things as that I simply adore playing Santa Claus, and arranging them under the tree till they look like a picture book Christmas. Only once did I feel perfectly satisfied, and then "Dud" was in Manchuria, so it was only half nice. That year there was a big red and black wooden train of five cars, and stone blocks like the German ones I used to have, a woolly Teddy, and just the right books.

Now that neither of them can by any stretch of even my imagination be called little children, it is not so easy to make it look like a story book. But we manage pretty well, even yet. So that against the background of the tree and the doll family, with the flickering light of a smoldering fire on it, we still have a catch in our throats as we take a long last look from the stairs, and know that another Day Before Christmas is gone.

THE BOY IN NAZARETH

A Story That Might Have Happened

By Emilie E. King

Simon, the crippled child, often leaned out of his window to see the Boy pass. The street was narrow and flooded with the clear light of the Nazarene sun, except where the shadows of houses threw arabesques of shade across the way. The Boy was going down the street now. Simon looked down, and the Boy, feeling his gaze, looked up and smiled.

"Peace be with you!" he called gaily, giving the customary greeting.

"Peace be with you," returned Simon, seriously, but he wished the Boy would stop, open the wide door leading to his house, and come up and talk to him. He had so few friends among children, and while his father was a well-to-do merchant and gave him everything his heart desired, he longed for a lively companion of his own age.

For weeks now he had watched the Boy come and go in the street beneath his window. There was something about the Boy that fascinated and attracted him. His appearance was not unusual, save for a strangely beautiful expression of his face. He ran and laughed, and shouted, with the other boys, yet there was something about him that caused him to stand out in Simon's mind. Simon, himself, could not say what it was.

One day Simon remembered hearing a great shouting and

laughing going on in the street below. On looking out he had seen a crowd of boys chasing a wounded bird that hopped awkwardly about in a terrified endeavor to escape them. One of its wings had evidently been broken and it cried out pitifully, "Peep, peep! Peep, peep!"

The more the bird fluttered and cried, the more eager the boys became to catch it. Just as one of them seized it the Boy had come running up. Making a frantic effort, the bird escaped from his captor's fingers and half-fell, half-fluttered to the ground at the Boy's feet.

"There! Catch him! Now we've got him. Here, he's mine, I saw him first. Quick now, don't let him get away again!" shouted the boys, and quarreling and yelling they surrounded the Boy.

Simon had a wonderful view from his window and he watched intently as the Boy, paying no attention to the clamoring children, reached down and picked up the bird. He held it between his two palms for a moment and spoke softly to it. Simon had not been able to catch his words above the tumult.

But, as the angry children surged about the Boy, demanding the bird as their rightful prey, Simon saw the Boy open his hands and free the bird that, miraculously, spread its wings and flew away.

For a moment the crowd of children were dumb with surprise, then one of the boys, evidently the leader, shouted:

"He let the bird go! It was none of his business. He is always doing those things, the sissy! Here, let him have it!" Seizing a stone he hurled it at the Boy, who only laughed, and turned and ran on his swift, strong legs, down the street.

Perhaps if Simon had himself been able to run and catch birds he would not have been so impressed by what he had seen, but as it was he had never forgotten it. The memory came back to him clearly today, as the Boy stood smiling up at him. Then, as though the Boy had read Simon's thoughts he said,

"I will come back and visit with you on my way home if you want. I have to go on an errand now."

"Oh, please do stop," cried Simon delighted. "I have wanted to talk to you for a long time."

So the Boy went on his way whistling.

Now it happened that this was a feast day and Simon's father came to him, after their noon-day meal, and said, "My son, soon you will be twelve years old, and today is a sacred day, so your mother and I would like to get you a present, something you most desire." The merchant smiled, and laid his hand on Simon's thin shoulder caressingly.

Simon looked up quickly into his father's face, and remembering how the Boy's strong legs had looked running down the street, he said, "Oh, Father, there is nothing in all the world I want except to run, to run down the street through the sunshine and out into the hills I can see from my window!"

The merchant turned his head away, and for a moment he could not speak, and when he did there was bitterness in his voice.

"And that wish, my son, is the one thing I cannot grant you," he said sadly.

Meanwhile, the Boy hurried on down the street, so that he would have time to visit with Simon awhile before his mother expected him back home. He remembered now that he had felt Simon watching him the day he had rescued the bird from the crowd of children. He had almost forgotten that experience. It did not seem strange to him that the bird had been able to fly away after he had picked it up. Things like that were always happening to him. He never tried to explain them—they all seemed natural enough. Still, he had never seen things like that happen to his playmates. He walked on.

He had passed through the town now and was out in the beautiful countryside. His errand was with a shepherd, so he climbed up the steep hillside to find him. As he climbed, he breathed in the sweet, warm air. How beautiful the world was —how glad and happy he felt! He reached down and picked up a lamb that lay in the grass near its mother. Neither the ewe nor the lamb protested. The Boy petted the pretty creature and laid his cheek against its soft head.

"Little brother," he whispered, "dear little brother!"

Then, feeling a little breathless from his climb, he threw himself down on the soft hillside to rest. He let the lamb go, but it made no effort to return to its mother; instead, it lay peacefully beside him.

He looked down at the steep pathway where he had just ascended; violets bloomed in the path. The Boy was surprised; they had not bloomed there a few moments before. Well, no matter, things like that were always happening to him.

He looked about him at the splendid view he loved so well. To the east lay Mount Tabor and Mount Gilboa, where the mighty King Saul was slain in a great battle with the Philistines —he knew the story well. It was one of his favorites of all those his mother told him.

To the west rose Mount Carmel, beautiful and green. The Boy remembered that it was on this mountain that Elijah contended with the priests of Baal and called down fire from Heaven.

And to the south, far beyond the mountains and across the plains, lay the Holy City of Jerusalem.

Something stirred in his heart and urged him on. A kind of restlessness passed over him and was gone, as though someone was urging him to do something—something that lay half-sleeping in his memory, something that he had once known and forgot. It was often so lately; he meant to ask his mother about this strange feeling one day.

Suddenly his attention was arrested by the sight of one of those desperate struggles with which nature is replete. A ferret ran almost across his feet in pursuit of a fat young rabbit. The chase was almost over; the rabbit, wild with fright, had lost all sense of direction and instinct, and, at the sight of the Boy, doubled in its tracks and ran full into the ferret who immediately laid hold upon the little rabbit and began his kill.

The Boy jumped up and ran to the two struggling little creatures. He laid his hand upon the ferret who immediately released the rabbit and ran up the Boy's arm to perch like a squirrel upon his shoulder; while the rabbit, bleeding and quivering, crept into the Boy's shirt and lay there panting.

After playing with the two animals for a few minutes, the Boy placed them on the ground. In a minute the ferret disappeared to continue his hunt by night, and the rabbit hopped away into the underbrush, leaving no trail of blood behind him. The Boy laughed happily and ran on to find the shepherd to whom he had been told to deliver a message from his father, the carpenter.

The afternoon sun was low as the Boy started down the hill, and he knew it would soon slip out of sight behind Mount Carmel. He had stayed, talking with the shepherd longer than he should, so he hurried; for he had not forgotten his promise to stop and visit awhile with Simon, the crippled boy. He wondered vaguely why people called Simon "crippled"; he appeared to him to look as any other boy in Nazareth.

In his arms the Boy carried the little lamb he had played with on the hillside; the shepherd had given it to him to take home to his father in payment of a debt. The Boy meant to ask his father if he could have the lamb for his own pet.

At last he reached Simon's house and opening the street door, he called out, "Hello, Simon, I have come to talk to you. See what I have brought down from the hills!"

"Hello!" called Simon joyously. "Come on up the stairs; I have been waiting for you all afternoon."

So the Boy ran up the stairs and entered the room where the little cripple sat among his silk cushions on a couch.

Once inside the room the Boy stopped and stared, overcome by its richness and splendor. For his own house was plain and dark, with barely enough for his parents and brothers. But as he stood still looking at Simon, sitting helpless amidst all this beauty, compassion swept over him like a great wave and his heart was full.

He looked deep into Simon's face; then he said, "Come, and see what I have brought; it is a little lamb from the hills."

Simon looked at the Boy in wonder and some embarrassment. "But I cannot walk," he said quietly.

Then the Boy put the lamb down, and running across the room he said, "Come, arise, I will help you walk."

And slowly, awkwardly, moving as in a trance, and holding fast to the Boy's strong brown hand, Simon rose from his couch and together the two boys walked across the room to where the little lamb stood bleating faintly.

"But I cannot walk," repeated Simon, dazedly.

The Boy laughed, and a great warmth entered into Simon. "Of course you can walk," said the Boy, "you can walk and run as any other boy in Nazareth! You can see, as I see, the hill and the plains and the violets springing up in the paths. It is spring, Simon, and tomorrow we shall go up into the hills together." The Boy stopped and turned his radiant face toward the opening door.

The merchant entered the room. At first he did not seem to see Simon standing near the Boy, and when he did he stood dumb with surprise. Could this be Simon, his only son, crippled since birth?

Simon, himself, answered his father.

"Look, oh, look! Father, I can walk, I can run! He made me so!" And Simon ran across the room and threw himself, sobbing with joy, into his father's arms.

Quietly the Boy passed them and went down the stairs and out into the street. The swift dusk had already fallen. As he hurried toward his home he felt again that strange urging, that strange pulling at something sleeping in his mind. "Soon I will be twelve," he told himself. "And then I shall go with Mother and Father to celebrate the Feast of the Passover in Jerusalem, the Holy City."

Softly he passed out of the dusk into the quiet comfort of his home. Already his mother and father and brothers were gathered about the table for the evening meal.

His mother looked up and smiled. "I am so glad you have come," she said. "I was worried."

The Boy smiled, too, but he made a strange answer.

"Soon I must be upon my way," he said.

In Simon's home the merchant was beside himself with joy and surprise. Carefully he questioned Simon concerning the Boy. But Simon knew little, save that the Boy was the son of a humble carpenter, and that he frequently saw him run down the street and out in the direction of the hills.

"But what is his name?" persisted the merchant.

Simon thought a moment, then he said, "His name is Jesus."

CHRISTMAS ADVENTURE

By Edith Mason Armstrong

Lonny looked out of the kitchen window and shouted for joy. "Oh, Edie! The milk bottles have got ice caps on! There will be snow for Christmas!"

Edie came and looked at the bottles. The frozen contents had pushed up their caps so that they stuck out an inch or so. George and Fred and Marjory came, too; and they all shouted when they noticed a few snowflakes falling out of the overcast sky.

The children were not going to have Christmas Day at home this year. Their mother was visiting one of their older brothers, and their father had decided to take them over to their Grandfather Mason's. Right after church on Christmas morning he loaded them into carriages—in those days there were no automobiles—and they drove across the city to the other house.

Lonny, who was only six at this time, and Edie, who was not yet eight, were a little confused, when they arrived, by the sight of so many relatives. It seemed to them as if there were cousins and aunts and uncles of all ages and sizes.

"It's dreadfully hard," Edie said to her little brother after three cousins she had never seen before got through hugging her, "to tell whether you ought to kiss them or shake hands with them. And I never know what to call them. If I say 'cousin' it's sure to be 'aunt,' and if I say 'aunt' it's sure to be 'cousin.' "

"I don't call 'em anything," replied Lonny. "I just let 'em hug."

The children's grandparents, Colonel and Mrs. Mason, entered the big drawing-room. Lonny and Edie ran to their grandfather, a merry-faced old gentleman with apple cheeks and a long snowy beard. He wore his new smoking jacket and a cap of quilted red silk.

"Oh, Grandpa," exclaimed Lonny as he was caught up and tossed in the air, "you look just like Santa Claus!"

"I know why you say that, young man. You want me to hurry up and give out some more Christmas presents! As if you hadn't had enough in your stocking at home!" He laughed and set his grandson down.

Lonny laughed, too, and turned to join his sister, who was standing by her grandmother's knee.

Mrs. Mason was a majestic-looking old lady in silk and rare lace, with towering white hair and snapping black eyes. She spent so much time visiting her older sons and daughters in their homes in distant cities, and she had so many grandsons and granddaughters, that she had not seen a great deal of the younger ones. Edie and Lonny were very much in awe of her, and they twisted about and kept their eyes down when she spoke to them.

"I hope you will try to be good children today and not make too much noise," she told them austerely.

They nodded, trying to think of something polite to say. When she turned from them to some of the older ones, they felt relieved.

"C'mon, Lon!" said Edie. "Let's find the others and play tag in the hall."

It did not take long to collect half a dozen young cousins and as many brothers and sisters. The hall was an excellent place to play tag. The front part of it was large and square like a room, and the part next to the staircase was long and narrow with window niches to dodge into! Just at the height of the fun the folding doors into the drawing-room were opened suddenly and a tall spare man looked out, with a frown. It was one of the children's uncles.

"You mustn't make so much noise," he said. "Your grandmother doesn't like noise."

Lonny drew a long breath. "I wish she did. It doesn't seem like Christmas if we have to be still."

A game of "Puss-in-the-Corner" was started next, in the hope that it would be quieter. But they had not been playing long before the folding doors opened again, and a young lady cousin came out. She had her fingers on her lips.

"You're making too much noise," Cousin Hattie told them. "It disturbs Grandmother, so she can't enjoy the other guests. Come in the library and I'll help you cut out pictures. Dinner will be ready soon."

The children cheered up. They did not feel like sitting still, but the thought of the turkey helped.

At last the feast was ready and everyone trooped into the dining-room and stood behind their chairs while Grandfather asked the blessing. Grandmother knew what an old-fashioned

Christmas dinner should be like and it was late when the guests rose, sighing. The older ones said they were going to take naps and the younger ones were shooed up to the big roomy attic, where they were told they could romp as much as they liked.

But this did not prove to be the case. Right in the midst of a vigorous game of "I Spy" when everyone was screaming and shouting and having a really good time, a cousin they did not know—a tall, black-haired woman in a plum-colored dress— opened the door of the huge, high-ceilinged attic.

"This is Cousin Emma," she announced severely. "I came up to say you were making such a dreadful noise nobody can sleep. You shake the whole house running around wild, like that!"

"Don't see how we can play 'I Spy' standing still," muttered Lonny.

The lady ignored him. "Come down to my room and I'll get out the tiddly-winks set," she suggested.

Tiddly-winks for fourteen children!

That was an idea! They managed to make it sound respect- ful, but they all laughed.

Cousin Emma flushed. "You don't seem to understand that Grandmother isn't used to noise. The house must be kept quiet when she's taking a nap."

The children were discouraged but fortunately kind Cousin Hattie appeared and invited them down to the old-fashioned kitchen in the back of the house for a candy pull. The dinner things had been put away and the maids had gone out, so they could have it all to themselves.

For almost an hour the various nappers, stretched upon beds upstairs and sofas downstairs, were undisturbed by any sound from the youngsters.

Then came a terrific hubbub!

While Cousin Hattie's back was turned one of the boys had pushed the candy over the red part of the big coal range to make it cook faster and it had boiled over. A tremendous hissing sound mingled with the cries of the children. Cousin Hattie was unable to quiet the disturbance before several nappers put their heads in the door to protest.

"Just as if it weren't hard enough," the young girl said indignantly, "to keep fourteen children quiet on any day, let alone Christmas!"

When the candy was finished she took it and her charges up the back stairs into a large second floor sitting-room. She got out some of their new toys and put them on a table, then cut the plate of the warm taffy and gave each one a huge piece.

"There," she said laughingly, "perhaps that will keep you quiet for a little while!" And she left them.

The truce lasted for perhaps an hour. Then the restless spirits of those two irresponsibles, Lonny and Edie, broke loose again. They had tiptoed out of the sitting-room without being noticed and were sitting at the head of the back stairs. It was a very long, steep staircase, polished and worn and uncarpeted.

"I know what let's do," said Lonny. "You know that big black tea tray the maids used to pile dishes on after dinner?"

"Yes," said Edie.

"Well, let's get it and slide down the stairs. I bet it would go like a streak!"

"Oh e-eee! Lonny Mason, how'd you think of it?" his sister exclaimed.

"Well," said Lonny modestly, "there isn't any toboggan slide at this old house like the one we have in our yard at home. If we can't slide outside we might's well try it indoors!"

The tray which their grandmother kept for family reunion dinners was unusually large, and when the children placed it at the head of the stairs, it covered the first two steps. Chuckling, the children got on it, sitting Turk fashion, Lonny in front and Edie behind. They kept it in position until they were ready to start, by clutching the banisters.

"Clear the way!" Edie's shout was carefully subdued but

nothing could disguise the terrific clatter made by the descent of the tea tray as it bumped from wooden step to wooden step.

It was marvelous how the children stayed on. So it was not to be wondered at that the final bump of landing on the floor brought loud screams of pain as well as joy! It also brought again the irate grown-ups who, roused from their naps, threw open the doors leading into the front hall and the library.

"Good heavens, what's the matter?" asked Cousin Edwin, rubbing his eyes.

"Of all the dreadful children!" began Cousin Emma, and various other exclamations of alarm and reproof followed.

The children's father, humiliated that these two blatant disturbers of the peace should be children of his, seized Lonny by the ear and Edie by the shoulder.

"If you don't stop making such a racket," he said, "I don't know what I shall do!"

There was a rustle of rich silk and the crowd in the doorway made room for another arrival. It was Grandmother.

"It seems strange that we have to have so much noise. It woke me up!"

"There now, children," said their mortified father, "see what you've done!"

"Never mind, Edward," said the old lady, with resigned expression, "I daresay it is too much to expect my grandchildren to let me have a nap. Besides it's nearly time to dress for tea. You know there will be Christmas callers."

Lonny and Edie were taken up into the sitting-room again in disgrace. Here another relative, looking very severe, brushed their hair and clothes, and washed their faces. Then she sat them on two tall chairs side by side and left them with a "Now be good."

"This is the funniest Christmas we have ever had," remarked Lonny, swinging his short legs and looking very forlorn.

"Yes," agreed Edie. "It's been the longest day!"

"Well," said Lonny with a sudden expression of heavenly goodness, "I've been thinkin' it's because we don't try to do something for somebody else. You know what the minister said in church this morning about tryin' to make others happy if you want to be happy yourself?"

Edie nodded admiringly.

"I wish I knew someone we could make happy," continued Lonny. "I'd give him all the presents we got today, and invite him to tea and everything!"

He was gazing in rapt fashion straight ahead of him. Suddenly he realized that he was staring right at a large photograph of his grandfather, who at one time had been fire commissioner of the city, standing with a helmeted battalion chief, while their hands rested on the necks of three large white horses. These were the hook and ladder horses, Nelly and Joe and Whitey. His grandfather had told Lonny stories about them many a time.

"I know!" exclaimed Lonny, suddenly inspired, "let's ring the fire alarm and get the firemen here so we can give them some presents and invite them to tea! Grandmother said there was goin' to be lots of good things to eat! I don't believe anyone ever thinks of doing anything for them on Christmas!" He turned to his sister with misty eyes and glowing cheeks.

Edie was overcome with the splendor of the idea. Accustomed as she was to her brother's creative genius, this surpassed anything he had ever thought of before—even sliding downstairs on a tea tray.

She and Lonny were so carried away by the Christmas spirit that they did not stop to think that they had no right to ring the fire alarm unless in case of need. The only drawback to the plan seemed to Edie to be the courage required actually to perform the deed.

"Do you dare, Lonny?" she asked breathlessly.

Lonny puffed out his chest manfully. "Yep," he told her, "I

dare. And while I'm ringin' the alarm you get some of the presents ready to give to them."

Throwing his leg over the front hall banister he flashed to the foot of the stairs, rummaged in the coat closet for his plaid reefer and the next moment slipped out of the big front door. Edie, watching from one of the hall windows, saw him strain up on tiptoe in the snow and turn on the old-fashioned alarm which required no breaking of glass, only the twist of a big brass key.

It was certainly unfortunate that the children's grandmother had declared for a noiseless Christmas. She was just arranging her lace cap as the final touch to her afternoon costume, when the sound of fire engines startled her—the raucous shriek of whistles, the clang of bells and the screech of brakes! She rushed to the window.

To her amazement she saw that a hook and ladder, and engine and hosecart had stopped at her door, as well as the fire marshal's red-wheeled buggy. Helmeted firemen were unwinding the hose in a workmanlike manner, while a rain of blows sounded on the front door. At the same time shouts of "Fire!" resounded through the house, and there was a rush of feet.

Surprised and frightened by the noise, the elderly lady hurried down the front stairway to find the hall below filled with firemen and excited guests. In the midst of the group her husband was talking to the fire marshal.

"There isn't any fire, Harriet," he said, turning to her, "but the chief says an alarm was turned in for this address. I would like to know who did it!"

There was a pause. Then a boy in a white serge sailor suit stepped forward. It was Lonny. He was a little pale but composed.

"I did. I thought the poor firemen ought to come to our Christmas tea party. Nobody ever thinks of 'em." His voice quivered, but he went on bravely. "Edie an' I wanted to give 'em some of our presents, too—the silver dollars we had in the toe of our stockings, and some other things."

He held out a dollar to the fire chief and Edie, very much frightened but loyal, held out her skirt filled with toys: jumping jacks, popcorn balls and tin soldiers.

There was an astonished silence. Then everyone began to talk at once.

"You called the fire department just to invite them to tea?"

"Whoever heard of such a thing!"

"You naughty boy!"

Lonny's lips quivered but he held the dollar out steadily. "Here, Chief," he said, "this is for you. Please take it."

The tears began to come then, but before many had fallen his father gathered him up in his arms.

"I won't explain just now," he said, "why little boys must never call the fire department unless there is need, because I know you were only thinking of Christmas."

The fire chief patted Lonny.

"Never you mind, old fellow," he said. "The boys down at the fire house were all saying they never did have any fun on Christmas. But, of course, you mustn't *ever* do a thing like that again."

Then, wonder of wonders, through his tears Lonny saw his grandmother, elegant in black velvet and old lace, come forward and shake hands with the fire chief.

"I think Lonny is quite right," she said. "If anyone deserves eggnog and cake and doughnuts on this cold Christmas Day, it's the firemen who guard our homes."

She led the abashed men into the drawing-room, where a blaze of pine logs and a tea table, laden with good things, welcomed them. When they had eaten their fill of the tea that she graciously served them, they rose to go.

"Good-by, Colonel," said the fire chief, who had known the children's grandfather when he had been fire commissioner.

"The boys and I are much obliged."

When the firemen had gone Lonny ran to his grandmother and threw his arms around her.

"S'cuse me, Grandma," he said. "At first, I thought you weren't like a real grandma, because you didn't like noise on Christmas. Now I know you're the grandest grandmother in the world, because you gave those brave firemen such a nice Christmas party!"

THE DOLLS' CHRISTMAS TREE

BY REBECCA DEMING MOORE

Two playmates, Judy and Janet, had said cross words to each other. Judy did not know just how it had happened. They had been playing at Janet's home. Janet had noticed a tear in the dress Judy's doll, Maisie, was wearing.

"Maisie ought to have a new dress for the Christmas-tree party," Janet had said, pointing to the tear.

"Maisie has *plenty* of dresses," snapped Judy.

"I should think she would wear something else then," Janet snapped back. "I wouldn't let my Polly be seen in a torn old dress like that."

Then the cross words came faster and faster. Both little girls grew very angry. Judy took her doll and marched home.

The next day Judy was sorry. She wished she could take back the cross words. She sat by a window and wondered what to do. The day had seemed very long with no Janet to play with.

Judy had mended the tear in Maisie's dress. She had dressed and undressed her half a dozen times and combed her hair in new ways.

Then she looked at the tiny flowerpot Christmas tree that she and Janet had planned to trim for the two dolls. At last she put it away. It would be no fun to trim it for Maisie alone. What a pity that the dolls' Christmas would be spoiled!

Judy looked over to the next house. She was almost sure she could see Janet behind the curtain in the living-room window. Judy set Maisie up in her window. Pretty soon she saw Polly at the window next door.

She looked out a minute later. Surely, Polly was waving her hand.

"You may wave back to Polly, if you like," said Judy to Maisie.

PRIMARY STORIES FOR CHRISTMAS TIME

By Juanita Cunningham

The Tiny Christmas Tree

Bobby and Betty went with Father to get a Christmas tree. A friend of Father's had said they could get one from his farm. Father cut a cedar tree and fastened it to the automobile. Then Betty saw a tiny cedar tree.

"Oh," she said, "it looks lonesome."

Father's friend laughed and cut down the tiny tree for Betty. Soon they were home again. They put the big tree in the living room. Mother and Betty decorated it.

"Where are you going to put your tiny Christmas tree?" asked Father.

Betty thought and thought. "Outside in the window box," she said. "Then it can look inside and see the big tree, and it won't be lonesome."

Bobby and Betty put the tree in the window box, and trimmed it with strings of pop corn.

On Christmas morning the children hurried downstairs to find their presents on the tree. Suddenly Betty exclaimed, "Oh, look at the tiny Christmas tree!"

There sat two redbirds, trying to eat the pop corn on the tree!
"Let's make it the birds' Christmas tree," said Betty.

So the children put cracked nuts, grain, and bread crumbs
in the box around the tiny tree. Then all day Bobby and Betty
enjoyed watching the redbirds, blue jays, chickadees, and
snowbirds who came to the feast.

Reading Tests

Fill the blanks in the following.

Bobby and Betty decorated the tiny tree with _____ ____.

On Christmas morning two _____ were sitting on the tiny
tree.

The children put _____ _____, _____, and _____
_____ near the tree for the birds.

Write T *after the sentence if it is true. Write* F *if it is false.*

Father bought the Christmas trees at the market.

They were cedar trees.

The big tree was put in the dining room.

The tiny tree was put in the window box, and trimmed with
pop corn.

Activities

Find out what kinds of trees are used for Christmas trees
where you live.

Find out what kinds of birds spend the winter where you live.

Decorate a tree for the birds.

THE SLED RACE

"Hurry, Jack, hurry, Julia!" called three happy children after
breakfast. Jack and Julia hurried. Soon they had on their warm
wraps and were off.

Jack was pulling his new sled. Two of the other children had their sleds, also. They were going to a big hill to coast. It was nearly half a mile to the big hill. Every winter the children had fun coasting there.

They reached the hill. They climbed slowly to the top, and then all three sleds went whizzing down the hill. How the children laughed!

Down the hill they coasted, again and again. What fun it was! "Isn't it time to go home?" asked Jack at last. "I'm hungry."

"Let's have a race before we go," said one of the children. The three sleds were placed evenly at the top of the hill.

"Go!" called Julia. Away went the sleds. Jack's sled was ahead. Suddenly it hit a bump at the foot of the hill. Over went the sled, and over went Jack in a snowdrift. The children and Jack laughed as he got up.

"You won!" they shouted. "Your sled went the farthest."

Then they started home, to tell their mothers what fun they had had.

Reading Tests

Fill the blanks in the following.

The name of the story is _____ _____ _____.

There were _____ children in the story.

Every _____ they went coasting.

_____ won the sled race.

Draw a line under the word or group of words in parenthesis that makes the sentence correct.

The children had (two, three, four) sleds with them.

It was nearly (one mile, two miles, half a mile) to the big hill.

They went coasting in the (morning, afternoon).

Jack's sled turned over because (it broke, it hit a bump).

A GIFT FOR SANTA CLAUS

By Theda Pearson Hedden

It was the day before Christmas, and Micky, Nicky, and Dicky, the three fat elves, were writing letters to Santa Claus. "How do you spell 'ball'?" asked Micky.

"Everyone knows that," said Nicky. "It's b-a-l-l, of course."

Scritch, scritch, scritch went three little pencils. Rustle, rustle, rustle went the letters to Santa Claus.

"I'm not writing a regular letter," said Dicky, "for there are a number of words I can't spell. I'm just making a list of the things I want Santa to leave in my stocking."

"My list is as long as my stocking," said Micky. "Do you suppose Santa Claus will mind?"

"Of course not," cried Nicky. "Santa loves to fill stockings for everyone."

Micky jumped to his feet excitedly.

"Oh, I say!" he cried. "I've just thought of something. Who fills Santa's stocking? Who trims Santa's tree? Who cooks his Christmas dinner?"

The three elves looked at one another in astonishment.

"Well," said Micky, as he pinned his Christmas list to his stocking, "perhaps Santa has never had a Christmas dinner. I'm going right into the kitchen and cook one and pack it in a basket. I'll leave it here for him to take with him when he comes tonight."

He went to the clothes closet and put on a cook's tall white cap and a clean white apron.

"Well," said Nicky, as he pinned his list to his stocking, "perhaps Santa Claus has never had a Christmas tree. I'm going right out to the Green Woodlands and hunt for a Christmas tree. I'll trim it and leave it here for Santa."

He went to the clothes closet and began putting on his out-door things—two sweaters and a leather jacket, a red wool stock-ing cap and muffler, a pair of gloves and a pair of mittens, and a pair of high four-buckled galoshes!

"Well," said Dicky, as he pinned his list to his stocking, "perhaps Santa Claus never hangs up his stocking. I'm going to take our red pocketbook and buy some presents at the store. I'll put them in a stocking for him here by ours."

He went to the clothes closet and put on his very best clothes—his sky-blue slipover sweater, his very best muffler with red pin stripes, his green overcoat with black velvet lapels, his high silk hat with fur ear muffs, his brown leather gloves, and his shiny black rubbers.

Bang! went the kitchen door, and Micky began murmuring to himself as he stirred up the fire.

"I'll roast the little gray goose and stuff some celery and bake some cookies and . . ."

Bang! went the side door, and Nicky began murmuring to himself as he went through the Green Woodlands.

"I'll hunt for the tallest, greenest, straightest, prettiest fir tree. I'll trim it with tinsel and candles and popcorn and . . ."

Bang! went the front door, and Dicky began murmuring to himself as he entered the Green Woodlands' store.

"I'll buy some books and neckties and shirts and . . ."

"Woo-oo-oo!" shrieked the North Wind as it chased the snowflakes across the fields. "Woo-oo-oo!"

It was much, much later, and 'way past the little elves' bed-time when they came again to the big living room.

"Well, well," cried a deep voice. "I thought you were in bed and fast asleep."

The elves turned quickly from the fire, and there at the door was Santa himself!

"Oh dear! Oh dear!" cried the three little elves. "How can we ever explain to Santa Claus!"

"Go ahead and explain," said Santa. "I promise not to be cross."

Micky began bravely. "Today we just happened to think that there was no one to cook your Christmas dinner, trim your Christmas tree, or fill your stocking. So we decided to do it. I went into the kitchen and cooked a very good dinner. Then a man came along and said his family would have no Christmas dinner, so I gave him yours!"

Nicky spoke up. "I found a Christmas tree for you, Santa, but as I was bringing it home to trim, the little birds told me that the snow had covered their food. So I trimmed the tree with popcorn, suet, corn, and nuts, and left it in the forest for the birds' Christmas tree!"

Dicky's story was much like that of his brothers. He said, "I went to the store to buy presents to put in your stocking, Santa, but I bought toys for a family of children who had none."

The elves sat down and began to cry.

"Come! Come!" cried Santa. "I want to thank you for the dinner and tree and other gifts."

"But we gave them away!" cried the elves, wiping their eyes vigorously.

"Surely," said Santa, "you've heard this rhyme:

> 'To make a gift for Santa Claus
> Is plain as one and one;
> You make a gift for someone
> Who'd otherwise have none.' "

"Do you really mean it?" cried the elves.

"Certainly, I do," Santa replied. "Now skip off to bed and don't peep to see what I'm putting in your stockings!"

The three elves squinched their eyes tight shut and skipped off to bed.

GAMES AND OTHER ACTIVITIES

CHRISTMAS GAMES

By Alice Crowell Hoffman

The Christmas Stocking.—Stuff an old stocking with numerous wads of paper to make it knobby-looking. The players stand in two lines of equal number against opposite walls, facing each other. The Christmas stocking is placed halfway between the lines. The first player in one line and the last in the other come out into the open space between the lines when the leader cries, "Snatch the Christmas stocking!" Each tries to get possession of the stocking without being tagged by the other. If a player snatches the stocking and takes it back to his line without being tagged by his opponent, his side scores a point. If he is tagged before reaching his line, the other side scores. Thus the game goes on until all members of both sides have participated. The side having scored the most points is the winner of the game.

"Holly Reds"; "Ever Greens."—The players stand in two groups of equal number, facing each other. One side is known as the "Holly Reds" and the other as the "Ever Greens." The leader in each row is given a hoop. When the signal "Go" is given, each leader holds the hoop over his head, and drops it so that it will fall over his body to the floor. As soon as he steps out of the hoop, the player next to him picks it up, holds it over his head, and drops it in like manner. Thus the game goes on simultaneously down both the lines. The line which finishes first is the winner.

To add a holiday touch to the game, the hoops could be wound with paper, one in red, one in green.

Christmas Bells.—All players except one who is "It" stand in a row, close together, with back to the wall. Two of them have been given small bells. They pass the bells from hand to hand behind them while "It" tries to locate one of them by either the sound or the expression on the face of the one who has it. When "It" locates a Christmas bell, he exchanges places with the one who had it.

Santa Lost His Christmas Pack.—Santa tells the rest of the players that he has lost his pack. They express keen interest and regret. They ask him questions in an effort to find out where the loss occurred. To all their questions he answers "Yes" or "No." Someone might ask him if he lost his pack in North America. If he should answer "Yes," another player might say, "Did you lose it in the United States?" Should the answer again be affirmative, someone might say, "Did you lose your pack in the eastern states?" Thus the questioning goes on until some player finds the exact place. That one is the winner and becomes Santa for the next round.

CHRISTMAS PARTY GAMES

By Alice Crowell Hoffman

An Opening Game. Provide as many headbands as there are to be guests. Each headband should be lettered with the name of something which has to do with the Christmas season, as holly, Christmas tree, carol, mistletoe, greeting card, toy, gift, and so on. There may be several headbands with the same word, if desired. As the guests arrive, each is fitted with a headband, with the name concealed from his sight. Each guest tries to guess from the remarks which are addressed to him what word is on his headband. Sometimes the guessing is difficult; and even after a guest knows the answer, the fun may be prolonged by playing the assigned part.

Christmas-Tree Nuts. Into paper bags of different sizes put nuts. Some bags should have more than others, and some should be empty. Inflate all the bags and tie them to confine the air. Tie the bags on the Christmas tree. Form two lines of players. The first in line on each side goes to the tree, removes a bag, returns, and pours the contents in a pile at some designated spot. Thus the game goes on down the line until all bags have been emptied. The side having the largest pile of nuts is the winner. Much fun results from the deceptive appearance of the bags.

Christmas Pantomime. One player stands before the rest and pantomimes something relative to the Yuletide season, as trimming a Christmas tree, or the like. The first one to guess the action exchanges places with the first player, and performs another suitable pantomime. The game goes on as long as interest is maintained.

A variation might be to have one player leave the room. The others decide who or what the player is to represent. When he returns, they suit their actions to the idea which they have in mind. If the player is to be a Christmas candle, they might pretend to light it or to blow it out; if a Christmas tree, they might pretend to decorate it, and so on. When the player guesses what he represents, he chooses another player to take his place, and rejoins the group.

Mrs. Santa Lost One of Her Children. A player is chosen to be Mrs. Santa Claus. She leaves the room. Another player is chosen to be the lost child, who hides, while the rest of the group change seats. Mrs. Santa Claus is then called in, and tries to tell which of her children is missing. If she guesses correctly, she takes her place in the group, and names another Mrs. Santa Claus. If she cannot discover which of her children is missing, she has another turn.

This is a good game in many ways. It is well adapted to indoor playing; it keeps all the children interested all the time; and it is a suitable closing game for the Christmas party.

SEASONAL GAMES FOR DECEMBER

By Harvey Haeberle

Holly Wreath Toss

Players, divided into sides called "Holly" and "Mistletoe," are to toss a small, soft ball through a paper holly wreath suspended in the doorway. They are allowed three throws. Success at the first throw counts fifteen points; at the second throw, ten points; and at the third throw, five points. The team having the highest score wins.

Passing the Bell

The players sit in a circle. All but one are given a small cardboard bell. At a given signal each player passes his bell to the right, and also those which he receives, until another signal is given. The one who is empty-handed at that time drops out of the game. The bells are distributed again in the same manner as before, and the passing is repeated. The player who remains in the circle the longest is the winner.

Star Base

Large stars cut from yellow paper are placed on the floor near the walls. There should be a few less stars than players. The players form a circle and march around. At a signal, each rushes to a star base and stands on it. If he fails to reach a base, he is charged with one point. At a second signal, the circle is formed again, and the procedure repeated. The player having the lowest number of points at the end of the game is the winner.

GIFTS CHILDREN CAN MAKE

By Erma M. Stockwell

Children of five or six years of age can make these Christmas gifts, cutting them and doing all of the work.

For a needlebook, cut three pieces of outing or other flannel about three by seven inches. Cut a piece of bright silk one-fourth inch larger all around than the flannel pieces. Place the flannel and silk together, with the silk underneath, and either sew through the middle of the four layers or pin them together with a small safety pin.

Use two or three circles of chamois or heavy cloth, about three inches in diameter, to make a penwiper. Fasten them together with a brass paper fastener. The circles may graduate in size, with the largest one placed on the bottom.

The most interesting parts of last year's Christmas cards may be cut into squares, triangles, or diamond shapes, and one pasted at the top of each of a set of twelve correspondence cards. These cards may be appropriately used in acknowledging gifts.

To make a set of place cards, cut bright envelope linings into tree, bell, or other simple shapes, and paste each one on a white or colored card about two by three inches.

Flowerpots and bowls may be decorated with triangular-shaped pieces of bright envelope linings. The corners must be well pasted. When the paste is dry, shellac the entire surface.

Older children can make candle sconces of construction paper. The part of the sconce directly back of the candlewick may be cut out and a piece of bright envelope lining pasted in.

A NOVEL UNIT OF WORK

By Jack Hoskins

Often children hear discussed at home plans for making Christmas fruit cake. This may be made the subject of an interesting unit of work. Ask the children to collect pictures of, and recipes for, fruit cake. Study the recipes, decide upon one, list on the blackboard the ingredients required for this recipe, and discuss their food value.

For drill in arithmetic, let the class find out the cost of fruitcake ingredients. Estimate the cost of the ingredients for one cake and the cost of a slice for each pupil.

A study of these ingredients may form the subject of interesting work in geography. The new words encountered may be included in the spelling lesson; and in the making of booklets, which may conclude the activity, rules previously learned in drawing class may be carried out.

PRACTICAL HANDWORK FOR CHRISTMAS

By Dorothy B. Hansen

Children like to see a gift that they have made used by its recipient. Therefore all Christmas handwork should be practical.

Inexpensive brushes of different sizes may be purchased, and the backs of the brushes enameled and then decorated with a simple design. These may be used for nail, vegetable, or scouring brushes.

Bags may be made from filet curtain material or net dishcloths, and original designs woven or darned into them with yarn. Handles of the same material as the bag, and a bright lining, give a finishing touch to these useful gifts.

Button, marble, or bean bags are easily made, and may be

decorated with stick-printing or with potato prints. These decorations may also be applied to hot-dish pads or chair covers.

Macaroni beads make fascinating gifts for little girls. Break straight macaroni into the desired lengths, enamel them in bright colors, and string them alternately with small pieces of cardboard enameled in contrasting colors.

Dolls and animals made from corks or spools delight very young children. The finished toys should be enameled.

Stuffed toys may be made from outing flannel and colored with crayon. A large pattern should be provided for the pupils to use as a guide in cutting.

CHRISTMAS-CANDLE CANDY

By FRANCES L. SHARPE

Christmas-candle candy makes a novel and inexpensive treat for the children from their teacher. Wrap penny sticks of candy with red crêpe paper cut an inch longer than the candy. Let the paper extend above the candy at the top, and twist into it two pointed flame shapes cut from orange and yellow crêpe paper. From black construction paper cut two circles and the candle holder. (See diagram.) Glue the upper part of the holder around the bottom of the candle. Be sure that the edges of the handles meet. Glue the two circles together, to make a firm base for the candle; then glue the bottom of the candle in its holder to the center of the circles. This completes the gift.

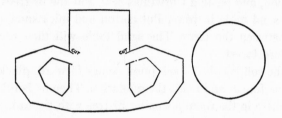

MAKING CHRISTMAS GIFTS

By Louise Broadbent

Many school children cannot buy Christmas presents but they will enjoy spending their drawing and free periods in making simple gifts. The following gifts are easy to make and inexpensive.

Oatmeal boxes may be covered and made into baskets or flowerpot holders, in which flower seeds or slips may be planted. These boxes may also be made into attractive hat stands. A satisfactory doll's cradle may be made by covering an oatmeal box and painting or pasting a decoration on each end. Turn the box on its side and cut out an oblong section.

Paper dolls cut from magazines may be mounted. Attractive pictures may be mounted and cut into puzzles. Bean bags may be made from pieces of gay print or oilcloth. Scrapbooks may be made of cut-out pictures, stories, or recipes.

If there is a domestic science department in your school, boxes of homemake cookies and candy may be prepared.

CHRISTMAS ROLL CALL

By Juanita Cunningham

From green construction paper cut a pointed fir tree for each pupil. On the back of each tree write a number and a Christmas quotation, and paste a Christmas seal. Put the fir trees upright in the sand table in rows. Put cotton and mica snow over the sand between the trees. The sand table will then resemble a miniature forest.

As the roll is called, each pupil comes forward, plucks a tree from the forest, and reads the quotation. Then he is told to find somewhere in the room a smaller fir tree with the same number as is on the tree from the table. These smaller trees are attached to long red cords which wind in and out and over and under furnishings in the room to the place where the gifts are concealed. The gifts should have a sprig of fir tied in with the ribbon on each package, if possible.

The teacher may wish to use the Christmas roll call as the final event of the entertainment, so that the miniature forest may remain in the sand table during the program or other activities. The gifts to which the cords lead may be inexpensive favors, the fun being increased if each favor is hidden in a different place.

CHRISTMAS SYMBOLS

By Alberta Johnson

In the days preceding the Christmas holidays, when girls and boys are full of the Christmas spirit, let them learn the significance of the Christmas symbols. This will make an interesting lesson in language or reading. The pupils may be given the responsibility for finding the information themselves under the guidance of the teacher. It may be gleaned from encyclopaedias, story-books, class readers, poems, and magazines. The pupils may also be encouraged to express their own ideas concerning the emblems which help make the Christmas season one of the most enjoyable of the year. The study may include Santa Claus, the Christmas tree, bells, holly, mistletoe, candles, and poinsettia.

The following is a brief outline to aid in studying the Christmas symbols.

1. Have each pupil list the Christmas symbols which he has observed in use at Christmas time.

2. From the individual lists, a class list is compiled and placed on the blackboard.

3. Each pupil selects the symbol which he wants to find out about.

4. Oral and written reports of the findings are presented.

5. In art class, designs may be made for booklets, or the symbols may be used in decorating Christmas gifts. Pupils may also have a part in decorating the classroom with Christmas emblems.

Other related activities may be developed. The Christmas greetings used in various countries, the story of Christmas cards, and the history of Christmas giving are topics which naturally present themselves for attention.

The information gained may well be organized for presentation to the school as an auditorium program.

AN ARITHMETIC CHRISTMAS TREE

By Marian Elder Jones

In December we added interest to our routine work in arithmetic by using an arithmetic Christmas tree. This was cut from cloth, and was hung up in the room on the first of December. The tree was three feet high, and at the top was a gold star.

The first problem to be solved was: The teacher paid 10 cents for one yard of green cambric for the tree; 17 cents for white cloth mounting; and 5 cents for a sheet of gold paper. Her street-car fare was 7 cents each way. How much did the arithmetic tree cost?

The next day, during the seat-work period, the class cut out candles and bells for the tree. The children were seated in rows of six. The first row was to make three red candles each; the second row, four yellow candles each; the third row, six blue candles each. We calculated how many candles of each color there would be. Each time I asked, "Will that be more or less than a dozen?" Then we found the total number of candles.

The fourth and fifth rows were to make tiny red bells. The next problems, therefore, were: "If each child makes 2 bells, how many bells will we have?" and "Suppose we had bought the bells, and had paid 5 cents each for them. What would they have cost?"

The children brought pictures of playthings to class. A few were pasted on the tree each day, and then were used as the subject of problems involving each of the four arithmetical operations.

A CHRISTMAS TOYSHOP

By ALICE M. CORSON

This unit of work was carried out by a first grade during the month preceding the Christmas vacation. The details of the unit were planned with a twofold purpose. First, it was to provide many opportunities for growth in social habits and in correct mental attitudes. The children were to learn the joy of working together for a common end, of assuming responsibility, and of making and carrying out plans. Second, it was to be a vehicle not only for the motivation of the tool subjects, but for certain definite gains in knowledges and skills in reading, arithmetic, language, writing, handwork, music, and physical education.

The children were most enthusiastic when the idea of the toyshop was suggested. They decided that they would make the toys during the weeks remaining before the vacation, that the pupils of the other two first grades in the building should be invited to be the purchasers, and that the sale would be held just before school closed. The question of what toys to make evoked much discussion. We listed on the blackboard the toys which we might expect to find in a toyshop. Which of them could we make? Who could bring materials? Even the most timid child forgot himself in the excitement of offering a suggestion.

The children collected all kinds of pictures, spools, and empty boxes. The spools and boxes we converted into doll furniture during free work periods before school. From small shoe boxes and stationery boxes we made doll beds by painting them red or green and gluing four spools to the bottom of each, for legs. Other rectangular boxes, when painted and supplied with four bottle caps each for wheels, and strings for pulling, served as carts. Round oatmeal boxes were used to make old-fashioned cradles. One little girl brought a long, narrow box, which she transformed into a grandfather's clock by painting it black and pasting on one side, near the top, a clockface, and cutting a long, narrow door at the bottom.

We spent several seatwork periods making scrapbooks containing magazine pictures mounted on sheets of gray drawing paper. During another seatwork period we made rocking ducks by cutting two ducks from oak tag, coloring them, and using the curve of the breast and wing for rockers, fastening a seat between them. Another day we made stencils from oak tag and envelopes of colored instruction paper to hold them. Each envelope contained five or six stencils.

Among the most popular toys were black oilcloth animals stuffed with cotton. We used commercial patterns, making each animal about twelve inches tall. The features were outlined with colored floss and the edges were overcast with yarn.

In spare minutes several children made dolls' rugs, using cardboard looms and weaving in the colored carpet warp with their fingers.

We secured sets of spool pets, containing pictures of the front and back of several familiar animals. We completed the animals by cutting out the pictures and gluing them to opposite ends of spools.

One directed handwork period was spent making turtles. We filled halves of walnut shells with plastic clay, and then stuck in a clove with the large end showing for the head; another, reversed, for the tail; and four for the legs. The shells were painted green.

The work of making the toys was scarcely begun when it was suggested that fathers and mothers might like to know about our toyshop; and couldn't we make a book which would tell what we were doing? The children contributed items of interest, which were written on the blackboard by the teacher, criticized by the class, and organized into little stories. These were mimeographed, illustrated by the children, and pasted into notebooks.

During the story hour we discovered that there were many interesting poems about toys and pets. Some of these we enjoyed hearing and a few we memorized. These included "The Little Turtle," by Vachel Lindsay, and the nursery rhyme, "I Love Little Pussy." Poems read included "The Animal Store," "The Cuckoo Clock Shop," and "The General Store," by Rachel Field; "The Duck," by E. L. M. King; and "Furry Bear," by A. A. Milne.

Animal riddles were such fun that no one recognized them as drill in oral language. A child described an animal in three sentences and called upon another child to guess the animal described. The one who guessed correctly gave the next riddle.

After the toys were nearly completed we made a book for our primary supervisor. Each child in turn came to the front of the room, held up the toy which he had made, and told how he did it. The best of the stories were typewritten by the teacher and illustrated by the children. Later, when they had learned to write their names, they added a personal touch to the stories by signing them. The sheets were assembled into a book with covers of construction paper tied with yarn.

As the time drew near for the sale of the toys, the matter of assigning various duties was brought up. Someone must sell the toys. What name was given to that person in a real store? No one knew. The word, "clerk," was added to the children's vocabularies. Who took the money? A boy proudly gave the word, "cashier." What did we call the people who bought articles in stores? What sort of clerks and customers did we want to be? What would polite clerks and customers say? Our ideas were written on the blackboard, organized, and printed on charts.

We correlated reading and language throughout the month. The children learned to recognize the names of the toys when they saw them written. For one seatwork lesson large sheets of paper each with a drawing of a Christmas tree were distributed. On the branches of the tree were written the names of toys. The children drew the pictures above the words. For supplementary reading they read from the blackboard, by location, the stories which they had given, and enjoyed finding the words and phrases which they knew, and learning others. Most opportunely, we were presented by our primary supervisor with a pre-primer, *Christmas Time,* a story of the visit of a girl and boy to a toyshop.

The class had already begun formal writing. Since many of the toys made were animals, an animal book was planned. During the seatwork period the children drew the animal chosen for the day, colored it, cut it out, and mounted it on drawing paper. In writing period they practiced writing on the blackboard the name of the animal. Then they wrote it with black crayon on the drawing paper. When six or eight pages had been completed, a cover was made and the pages fastened together in book form. A toy book was made in the same way.

Toward the end of the month the children made from large sheets of newsprint three sets of advertising posters to be sent to the other first-grade rooms, one each day for the three days before the sale. Since not all the children could work on the posters, each day we chose, to represent the class, those who did the neatest handwork. The first set of posters showed a wreath of holly surrounding a huge interrogation point. The second bore several pictures of toys and the words, "Toys, Toys, Toys," written by the children who were acclaimed the best writers. On the third set were more pictures of toys and the invitation, "Come to Our Toyshop," with the place and time added by the teacher.

When the posters were finished, the children practiced writing the signs, "Toys for Boys," "Toys for Girls," "Toys for Baby"; and the words, "Clerk," "Cashier," and "Information," for arm bands. These were copied with crayon on paper by the best writers.

During the activity we found *The Music Hour* a treasure house of songs about rabbits, dogs, dolls, stores, and shops.

According to our outline in physical training, much of our work during December and January takes the form of imitating Christmas toys. This coincided excellently with our toyshop activity, and we proceeded to adapt the suggestions to our program.

Being jumping jacks and jacks-in-boxes was very popular and was an excellent recreation exercise for just a moment or two. The jumping jack stood in the aisle with feet together and hands at sides. When the teacher made the motion of jerking the string, the children jumped into the air, at the same time throwing their arms out shoulder high and spreading their feet apart; coming down, they assumed the original position. The jacks-in-boxes stooped low until the teacher made the motion of raising the lids of the boxes. Then all jumped up and stood erect.

To music, the children marched like tin soldiers, with elbows stiffly bent, raising legs high at each step. They imitated the motion of toy airplanes by running around the room on their toes, arms shoulder high, and swaying from side to side while running. They walked around the room with stiff knees, like jointed dolls. They became dancing dolls, taking tiny steps in circles. They hopped around the room like bunnies. They used the song, "Ducks," from *Songs to Sing,* by Edna Shaw, as they imitated the waddle of toy ducks by stooping, clasping hands around knees, and keeping bodies low as they stepped in time to the music.

Two stunts which were in keeping with our unit of work were Puppy Dogs and Pussy Cats. For puppy dogs, the children walked on all fours, with feet in stride position and hands the width of the shoulders apart. They kept the knees straight and the back as high as possible. For pussy cats, they took the same position as for puppy dogs, but with knees bent, for greater speed, and with longer steps.

As the work of making the toys progressed, questions arose as to the prices to charge and what to use for money. The teachers felt that the children would gain much more from handling actual coins than from using representations.

Several dimes, nickels, and pennies were brought into the classroom one morning. The children learned the name and value of each. The question was asked, "What other pieces of money could be used instead of a dime to make ten cents?"

After discussing the problem, each child made a chart showing two nickels, ten pennies, and one nickel and five pennies. We also played a money-guessing game. A child took two or more of the coins from the teacher's desk and, holding them behind his back, said, "I have — cents. What pieces of money have I?" The class guessed in turn until the correct coins were named.

We decided to limit the purchases of each customer to two toys, in order to keep the arithmetic involved simple enough for the children to grasp. The maximum price for a toy was five cents.

It was evident to the children that both customers and cashiers must be able to find out the cost of two toys when given the price of each. Again we used our money, counted out the correct amounts, and recorded the number combinations on the blackboard for reference.

It occurred to us that our customers might have the same difficulty in computing the cost of their purchases that we had, so we cut Christmas trees from green construction paper, wrote the combinations on them, and pasted them at the top of the blackboard.

We played games of buying. Pictures of the toys were drawn on the blackboard, with the price of each written beneath it. One child chose the two toys which he would like to buy. We drew the two on another piece of paper and wrote the combined cost under the pictures. Later we dispensed with the pictures and used only the figures, writing the combination used.

The day of the sale found everything in readiness. Three clerks were assigned to each counter. Cashiers and information people were chosen. Four children had brought toy cash registers and these were placed conveniently in the four corners of the room. From printing outfits we borrowed stamp pads and the letter P, which the cashiers stamped on the sales slips as they were paid.

Business was brisk from the first, and soon the counters were bare. One by one the pupils from the other rooms, with their treasures clasped tightly in their arms, reluctantly departed.

Surely there had been no dearth of joy from the moment that the sale was suggested until the last toy was sold. What of the rest of our two-fold purpose? Had we succeeded as well in satisfying its demands? We believe that the answer will be found in a study of the review of the work accomplished, given on page 186.

BIBLIOGRAPHY

Barrows, Marjorie: *One Hundred Best Poems for Boys and Girls* (Racine, Wis.: Whitman Publishing Co.).

Field, Rachel: *Taxis and Toadstools* (Garden City, N.Y.: Doubleday, Doran & Co., Inc.).

McConathy, Osbourne, and others: *The Music Hour* (New York: Silver, Burdett & Co., 1932).

Milne, A. A.: *Now We Are Six* (New York: E. P. Dutton & Co., Inc., 1927).

Schenk, Esther M.: *Christmas Time* (Chicago: Lyons & Carnahan).

Shaw, Edna: *Songs to Sing* (Buffalo, N.Y.: Simcoe Publishing Co.).

Thompson, Blanche Jennings: *Silver Pennies* (New York: The Macmillan Co.).

RESULTS OF TOYSHOP UNIT

I. Opportunities for growth in social habits and mental attitudes.

   1. Making and carrying out plans.

     a) Giving suggestions about toys.

     b) Asking and answering questions.

     c) Discussing problems.

   2. Co-operation.

     a) Sharing materials brought.

     b) Contributing toys made.

     c) Working together to keep the room neat.

     d) Combining effort in making posters.

     e) Waiting on customers.

   3. Courtesy.

     a) Working quietly.

     b) Not interrupting others.

     c) Being polite to customers.

   4. Assuming responsibility.

     a) Bringing materials.

     b) Getting toys done on time.

     c) Arranging counters.

     d) Attending to details of sale.

   5. Joy of work well done.

     a) Competing with classmates for privilege of working on posters.

     b) Voting on best handwork.

   c) Making toys good enough to sell.

   d) Making books worth keeping.

II. Motivation of tool subjects and gains in knowledges and skills.

  1. Reading.

    a) Increased interest.

    b) Enlarged reading vocabulary.

    c) One pre-primer read.

  2. Language.

    a) Ability and inclination to enter into class discussions.

    b) Ability to tell simple stories and riddles.

    c) Appreciation of audience situation.

    d) Increased interest in poetry.

    e) Enlarged vocabulary.

  3. Arithmetic.

    a) Recognition of dime, nickel, and penny.

    b) Knowledge of what coins make ten cents.

    c) Introduction to number combinations, sum not to exceed ten.

    d) Ability to read and write figures through 10.

  4. Writing.

    a) Ability to write simple words and figures legibly.

  5. Music.

    a) Added interest in singing.

    b) Several new songs learned.

  6. Handwork.

    a) Manual skills developed.

    b) Need for careful work recognized.

  7. Physical Education.

    a) Increased skill in rhythmic responses.

    b) Improvement in motor co-ordination.

A CHRISTMAS SAND TABLE

By FLORENCE I. WILLIAMSON

For the Christmas season the sixth-grade geography class made a Holy Land scene on the sand table. The Mediterranean Sea, Nile River, Egypt, Red Sea, Arabia, Jerusalem, Bethlehem, and Nazareth were shown. Pyramids, sphinx, sheep, shepherds, and so on, were made from cardboard, plastic clay, and sand.

In the English class the children composed Christmas stories. In the drawing class the children made illustrations of camels, palms, pyramids, desert life, sphinx, shepherds, flocks of sheep, the Wise Men, stables, oases, flag of Egypt, and other subjects. Pictures of the Holy Land were mounted. Christmas stories, carols, and hymns were collected.

HOLIDAY CANDLESTICKS

By KATHRYN MIHM

The wooden plugs from rolls of wrapping paper make attractive candlesticks for Christmas gifts.

Cut crêpe paper into strips from three to five inches wide, according to the height of the plug, and a yard long. Stitch in the center the length of the strip by machine or by hand, and gather the strip fully and evenly.

Paste a piece of cardboard to the bottom of the plug to cover the hole. Cover the remainder of the plug with crêpe paper, leaving an opening at the top to insert the candle. Paste the center of the strip around and around the plug. Pull and crinkle the edges. Make a ribbon of the crêpe paper to tie over the stitching.

AN ORIGINAL CHRISTMAS SCENE

By Kathleen Carmichael Dietz

A low table covered with cotton which had been sprinkled with artificial snow was the base for an original Christmas table in the fourth grade.

Some of the children chose to make houses from cardboard, colored with crayon. Others brought branches from evergreens and set them in small blocks of wood for the trees. One boy brought his treasured reindeer, and a little girl came with a papier-mâché Santa Claus carrying his pack on his back. The boys and girls made tiny packages for his sled.

But more figures were needed. Ingenious pupils fashioned children and animals from soap and dressed them in bits of fur. Among the figures were a dog harnessed to a sled, and children coasting down a hill, which was an inverted bowl covered with cotton.

The background, drawn with colored chalk, showed mountains, trees, houses in the distance, and some animals.

A LIVING CHRISTMAS TREE

By Louise Boelte

The following is an effective way of closing a Christmas program. Any number of pupils may participate, depending on the amount of space that can be used.

For each child the older pupils make an evergreen tree shape of newspaper, long enough to reach from the neck to the bottom of the child's dress or suit.

They paste a green crêpe-paper tree over the one of newspaper. On each tree are pasted various ornaments, such as balls, horns, candy canes, and so on, cut from colored paper or from white paper and then colored. The smaller children make these ornaments and also colored paper chains. The trees are pinned on the children at the shoulders.

To assemble the living tree, about fifteen of the smallest children kneel on the floor at the front of the stage. The next row, about twelve children, stands behind those kneeling. The third row, about eight pupils, stands on boxes. The fourth row, about five pupils, stands on tables. For the top of the tree, there is only one child, who wears a star crown. He stands higher than the fourth row of pupils.

When all the pupils are in place, the paper chains are draped about the "tree." The children sing Christmas carols. One rehearsal will be all that is needed in order to give each child his place on the stage.

CHRISTMAS TREE ORNAMENTS

By ALICE CROWELL HOFFMAN

The children of a rural school had a happy time making Christmas tree ornaments covered with silver paper which comes wrapped around chocolate bars, camera film, and the like. Stars of varying sizes were cut from the tablet backs and covered with the paper. Bells were cut out and covered. Some of the children covered eggshells from which the contents had been blown. Others covered acorns and various other kinds of nuts. Even small apples were turned into silver. The ornaments were fastened to the tree with thin wire, which comes in short lengths for this purpose.

From the strips of silver paper that were left the children cut narrow stringlike pieces, which were thrown promiscuously over the tree after the other trimmings had been put on. These narrow silver strips gleamed brightly.

Celebrations for
St. Valentine's Day

PLAYS

IN BEHALF OF SAINT VALENTINE *

BY RUTH RENO SMITH

CHARACTERS

JOAN

NAN

DICK

SAINT VALENTINE, *a very old man*

ARGUS, *his secretary*

JULIUS CAESAR

MARK ANTONY

MARCUS ⎫
QUINTUS ⎭ *Roman Soldiers*

CHILDREN, *as pretty valentines*

CHILDREN, *as "comic" valentines*

SETTING:

Scene 1. *A modern living room. Table and easy chairs at right. Divan at left. At rear left, doorways with draperies, to be drawn back from off stage.*

Scene 2. *Divan replaced by dais, draped. Right stage same as in Scene 1. Spot light to flood left stage, shield to darken right.*

Scene 3. *Same as Scene 1.*

Entrances right and left.

---

* For permission to produce, apply to the author, Fort Myers, Florida.

Costumes:

Joan, Nan *and* Dick, *modern school clothes.*

Saint Valentine, *flowing white hair and beard; Roman toga of blue; sandals, long staff.*

Argus, *tunic of green, sleeveless; wide red belt or scarf, bare legs, black half-hose or sandals; a large scroll and quill pen.*

Julius Caesar, *white toga with gilt paper border, multi-colored sash or scarf, fillet of red or wreath of green leaves about head. Sandals.*

Mark Antony, *sleeveless tunic of red, wide gilt belt, small sword, sandals, etc.*

Marcus *and* Quintus, *short tunics of gray, sleeveless; vest of gilt paper to represent armor; bare legs, sandals; belt, head-dress and half-hose of black oilcloth; spears, small round shields and daggers of gilt paper.*

Pretty Valentines, *little girls in fluffy white or pastel-tinted gowns, silver crowns, large red paper hearts in evidence.*

"Comic" Valentines, *the more grotesque the better.*

Scene 1

As curtain rises, Joan *and* Nan, *seated at table, are busy with envelopes and valentines.* Dick *upon divan is studying.*

Joan. (*Laying aside pen.*) There, that's the last. Every valentine safe in its envelope and ready for tomorrow.

Nan. (*Enthusiastically.*) And they are beautiful, too. Oh, I think it is splendid of Miss Cramer to let us celebrate and have the box and take time off to open all the valentines at school.

Joan. I think so too. (*Suddenly to* Dick.) Oh, Dick, aren't you through with that history lesson yet?

Dick. (*After a moment.*) Who? Me?

Nan. Yes, aren't you through?

DICK. (*Crossly.*) Through? Gosh, no. I'll never get through all this. (*Turning to book and apparently trying to concentrate.*) "Caius Julius Caesar, now dictator of Rome, was offered the crown by Mark Antony, but—" (*Tosses book aside.*) Aw, shucks, what do I care about these old fellows? If it wasn't for Miss Cramer and that pesky test tomorrow (*Saunters toward girls.*)—Say, when you going to make that fudge?

JOAN. As soon as you have your lesson—oh, do hurry.

NAN. Yes, do. Finish your lesson and get your valentines ready for the school box tomorrow!—Oh, our valentines are SO pretty. You should have seen them. (*Displays envelopes proudly.*)

DICK. (*Scornfully.*) Pretty! Aw, heck! Who wants a pretty valentine? Valentines are silly, anyway—'cept, of course, the comic ones! (*Confidentially.*) Say, you ought to see the ones I'm going to send! They're sure lolli-pops! (*Draws papers from pocket.*) See, I'm going to send this one to Fatty Brown (*Displays.*) and this to Gertie Graham (*Girls view the valentines with dismay.*) and this to Messie Phillips! And—oh, ho, ho, this goes to Miss Cramer! (*He laughs gleefully.*)

NAN. (*In distress.*) Oh, Dick, you are not.

DICK. (*Laughing.*) Ha, ha, 'deed I am. Isn't this a lulu? Looks just like old Cramer.

JOAN. (*Indignantly.*) I think that's perfectly horrid.

NAN. (*Severely.*) Dick Travis, you're not going to send that to Miss Cramer.

JOAN. And after she's let us have the school box, too?

DICK. You bet I am. Ho, ho, won't she be mad?

JOAN. (*Sternly.*) Richard Travis, you ought to be ashamed.

DICK. (*Stoutly.*) Well, I'm not. It's just a joke, anyway.

NAN. A joke!

JOAN. I think it's the meanest, horridest kind of trick. That's what I think!

DICK. Say, what's the fun of Valentine Day if you got to send out such silly, wishy-washy stuff as yours? (*Nods toward table.*) All silly lace and paper and red hearts and mushy verses! Gosh! (*Mimics.*) "Roses are red, vi'lets are blue, I love potatoes and so do you." Ho, ho.

JOAN. (*Indignantly.*) Our valentines don't read that way one single bit, and you know it.

NAN. Most certainly they don't. (*With dignity.*) Our valentines and all decent respectable valentines express love, love and respect, every single one.

DICK. (*Scornfully.*) Yes, love and respect!—Valentines are silly just as I said,—except, of course, the funny ones.

JOAN. The "funny ones" are the only silly ones there are; and I hope you don't get a single pretty one—not a single one; but heaps and heaps of the very horridest, old comic ones, so there.

DICK. Pshaw, I wouldn't care.

NAN. (*Reproachfully.*) And after all Miss Cramer told us about Saint Valentine, too, and how he lived. Why, these silly, comic ones aren't a bit in keeping with him—the way he went about being kind and always doing good!

JOAN. Yes, and when he was too old, staying at home to *write* folks letters, loving, kindly letters! Oh, I think he was a great and very good man.

DICK. Aw, shucks, for all we know maybe he never lived.

NAN. I'm sure he lived, just as truly as Mark Antony or Caesar, or any of the rest we read about in History.

DICK. Well, even if he did, he's History, and I hate History. What do we care about these old ginks that lived ages ago?

JOAN. Well, you ought to care. Miss Cramer says they gave us our civilization!

NAN. Yes, and you will care too, if you don't get back to your lessons! (*Glances at watch.*) Oh, dear, it's nearly eight o'clock. We'll have to hurry about the fudge if we get it done. (*Hastily gathers up letters.*) Come on, Joan.

JOAN. (*To* DICK *coaxingly.*) And—and Dick, please—please

don't send those horrid pictures to Miss Cramer and Gertie and the rest. It would hurt their feelings, and—and I don't think it's carrying on Saint Valentine's work, as Miss Cramer said we should.

DICK. Oh, bother! What do I care? I'm going to send 'em— and you just watch Miss Cramer's face (*Girls are moving toward right.*) and Fatty's and the rest when they get 'em. (*Laughs.*) Ho, ho, ho.

(*Exeunt girls right.*)

DICK. (*Regarding his valentines gleefully.*) Huh, girls are the goofiest. They never can see any fun! (*Sits in chair beside table, slowly opens book.*) I reckon I'll *have* to study some more, or that test— (*Yawns, stretches; then slowly, as though vainly trying to recall his lesson.*) Let's see—what did it say?—"Mark Antony, now dictator of Rome was offered the crown—by Caesar?" (*Thoughtfully and trying to find place in book.*) Was that it? (*Stretches, yawns, then adjusts himself comfortably.*) History is such a bore— Ho, ho, won't Miss Cramer—and Messie and Fatty and the rest—be—mad.—I wonder—when that —fudge—will be done. (*Slight pause.*) Gee, I'm getting—sleepy. (*Slides down more comfortably into chair, nods, nods again, and sleeps. Lights slowly dim and Curtain falls.*)

SCENE 2

Curtain rises to show spot-light directed on dais at left. Indistinctly DICK *is to be seen asleep in the shadow of right stage. Enter left,* SAINT VALENTINE *and* ARGUS. VALENTINE *walks very slowly and leans heavily upon his staff. He is supported by* ARGUS.

VALENTINE. I grow old, feeble, Argus.

ARGUS. Thou art over-weary, master. Thou hast had a difficult fortnight.

VALENTINE. True, but I am old, very old, Argus. Methinks I shall not tarry here many birthdays longer.

(ARGUS *seats* VALENTINE *carefully upon the bench of dais, and sits at his feet.*)

ARGUS. Say not so, master.

VALENTINE. And tomorrow is the day, and (*Wearily.*) there are so many missives yet to fashion.

ARGUS. Less than a score remain, sir. We can easily attend to them.

VALENTINE. And didst direct the rest by courier, as I bade thee?

ARGUS. Aye, sire, most carefully.

VALENTINE. And the portraits— They are all completed?

ARGUS. Most assuredly, master.

VALENTINE. Then let us at once to the remainder. Art ready?

(ARGUS *nods. He has partially unrolled the scroll, and with quill in hand sits ready.*)

ARGUS. Ready, sir?

VALENTINE. (*Thoughtfully.*) Let me see. We did the one to Fatty Brown, Argus?

ARGUS. Yes, master.

VALENTINE. And the one to Gertie Graham?

ARGUS. Yes, and to Messie Phillips and Pig-eye Sutton.

VALENTINE. Aye, true, I remember now.

ARGUS. (*Consulting the scroll.*) The next, sire, is to Nan.

VALENTINE. Ah—to Nan. (*Thinking a moment, then dictates.*)

"To Nan:

    Roses are red, but your eyes are blue.

    You make excellent fudge and 'divinity' too;

    You've a gift for translating

    My prose into rhyme,

    And the way you straighten my tie is sublime."

(*Pauses as* ARGUS *writes.*) Now read it, Argus, I pray you.

(ARGUS *reads dramatically.*)

VALENTINE. (*Pleased.*) Ah! Think you the sweet young lady will be pleased?

ARGUS. (*Enthusiastically.*) Most assuredly, honored master. 'Tis a beautiful sentiment and perfect rhythm.

VALENTINE. Aye, yes, perfect rhythm!—And now to the other sister. It is the other sister, eh, Argus?

ARGUS. (*Consulting scroll.*) Yea, the other sister, Joan, sire.

VALENTINE. True. Then write thus, Argus, in your best flourishes (*Pauses thoughtfully.*)

ARGUS. Aye, sire.

VALENTINE. (*Slowly dictating.*)

"To Joan:

Oh, you are so dandy,

As sweet as your candy,

Your taffy and puffs are so swell,

That if I were a count, or a prince or a king,

Or consul or bishop or any such thing,

I'd buy you a crown

And a lovely sport-gown,

And a Pekinese sweet, to lead by a string!"

(ARGUS *nods approvingly as he completes writing.*) You like it, Argus? Think you the metric beats co-ordinate properly?

ARGUS. Most symmetrically, sire.

VALENTINE. And you think Sister Joan will approve, my son?

ARGUS. Most emphatically, honored master.

VALENTINE. (*Anxiously.*) And that I grow not less versatile as time advances?

ARGUS. Thy verses grow more delightful every day, more classical, good father, even now as the Iliad or Odyssey.

VALENTINE. (*Pleased.*) Ah, that is well. And now, son, one more. Take you special pains with this, I entreat you.

ARGUS. Most certainly, sire.

VALENTINE. She is a special friend of mine! She understands

me—my aims, my desires.

ARGUS. Aye, sire.

VALENTINE. (*After a moment's thought.*) Write thus, my son—

> "Oh, Mistress Cramer, bright and fair,
> With ruby cheeks and curly hair,
> If you were eight instead of twenty,
> Besiege your heart I would aplenty.
> I'd tote your books, I'd take you home,
> I'd call you up by telephone,
> I'd give you lollipops and taffy,
> You'd be my girl, 'bout whom I'm daffy."

ARGUS. (*Enthusiastically as he finishes writing.*) The best yet, sire, the very best.

VALENTINE. You like it? Think you she will like it?

ARGUS. Like it? Why sire, of course she'll like it. How could it fail to please her?

VALENTINE. Then to the portraits to accompany our missives! They must be the finest, handsomest we can make. (*Commotion off-stage left. Loud knocking.*) Hist! Who comes?

CAESAR. (*Without.*) Open! Open at once, I command it.

VALENTINE. To the portal, Argus. (ARGUS *starts forward; but* JULIUS CAESAR *strides in followed by* MARK ANTONY, MARCUS *and* QUINTUS.) Ah, Caesar, the mighty consul, the Dictator!

CAESAR. (*Sternly.*) Sire, what mean these charges against you?

VALENTINE. (*Puzzled.*) Charges?

CAESAR. Aye, that and more. (*Growing more stern.*) What knavery is this reported of you on the streets of Rome?

VALENTINE. Sire, I know not of what you speak. (*To* ARGUS *who is standing.*) What does he mean? (*To* CAESAR.) Speak, speak, sire. What do you mean?

CAESAR. (*Haughtily.*) What do I mean? Would you evade my question?

VALENTINE. Nay, sire, but—

M. ANTONY. (*Interrupting. To* CAESAR.) Great Caesar, would it not be well to state the charges, confront this rogue with his crime?

VALENTINE. Crime?

ARGUS. Crime, sire?

CAESAR. Aye, crime! (*Severely to* VALENTINE.) Sire, you are accused of defaming the character, decrying the deeds of right-eous citizens, defiling the fair names of the populace.

VALENTINE. Sire, I know not what you mean.

CAESAR. Scoundrel, villain!

ANTONY. Aye, scoundrel, villain, indeed!

(MARCUS *and* QUINTUS *show uneasiness.*)

VALENTINE. I have done no wrong.

CAESAR. (*Scornfully.*) No wrong! You who have committed deeds such as no soldier in all my legions would have dared commit.

ANTONY. Aye, and surely such crime as his demands im-mediate punishment.

MARCUS. Aye, down with him!

QUINTUS. Away with him!

(*They push forward as if to take* VALENTINE.)

ANTONY. No punishment too great, no penalty too severe, friend Caesar. To do away with such as he would indeed free Rome of a veritable monster.

CAESAR. Aye—he must be brought to trial.

MARCUS. To the hippodrome! The arena!

VALENTINE. To trial—the hippodrome?—For what?

ARGUS. Aye, sir Dictator—for what crime accuse you this good man here?

ANTONY. Good man, indeed!

CAESAR. (*Severely.*) You write missives, epistles—and send them?

VALENTINE. Aye, sire, but surely no harm—

ANTONY. No harm, say you?

(MARCUS *and* QUINTUS *push forward but are restrained by a gesture of* CAESAR.)

CAESAR. You are accused of writing, disclosing, missives, epistles—such as were displayed yesternight—

MARCUS. (*Interrupting.*) Away with him! Away with him!

VALENTINE. I write only kindly, loving messages, sire, and with suitable pictures and decoration.

ANTONY. (*Scornfully.*) Aye, suitable? (*To* CAESAR.) You heard, great Caesar?

ARGUS. Aye, sire, and always as beautiful as we can make them.

ANTONY. Confront him with his misdeeds, sir. Display the evidence.

CAESAR. Aye, the evidence. (*Glances about.*) Produce the evidence!

ANTONY. (*Motions to door with draperies, which are drawn back and the first "comic" valentine is disclosed. It is conspicuously lettered, "Fatty Brown."*)

VALENTINE. (*Bewildered.*) I know no Fatty Brown. I never saw such a portrait before.

(*Draperies are closed.*)

ANTONY. Knave—villain!

CAESAR. What do these in thy house? (VALENTINE *shakes head slowly. He is both puzzled and distressed.*) The next, friend Antony.

ARGUS. (*With a groan.*) Another.

ANTONY. (*Draperies open to disclose a second "comic" labeled "To Gertie Graham."* ARGUS *covers face with hands.* VALENTINE *draws back in horror. To* CAESAR.) These are identical, sire, with those displayed in the streets yesterday. They are here, in his house—what further evidence of wickedness, vileness could be offered?

VALENTINE. (*Weakly.*) I cannot understand.

CAESAR. For these—and those displayed upon the streets of Rome are you arrested, tried!

QUINTUS. Away with him.

VALENTINE. (*Mystified.*) How came they here?

CAESAR. You deserve no trial, you who have thus so grossly insulted, defamed the fair names of our most worthy citizens. You know the penalty for such a crime.

VALENTINE. (*Brokenly.*) Sire, I am innocent. I have done no wrong. I have sent only lovely missives—beautiful portraits—Argus, show him the other portraits.

(*Draperies are closed.*)

QUINTUS. Away with him—to the hippodrome.

MARCUS. To the lions with him. To the wild beasts!

ANTONY. Aye, to the hippodrome, the lions. Let him pay the penalty.

CAESAR. Aye, let him pay the penalty. (*Quickly to* MARCUS *and* QUINTUS.) Seize him! Away with him! To the hippodrome, the lions.

(MARCUS *and* QUINTUS *seize* VALENTINE *and drag him from dais.*)

VALENTINE. (*Dismayed.*) To the hippodrome? The lions? (*Brokenly.*) Ah, have I not one friend? Not one? After all these years? Argus, hast thou also deserted me? Forsaken me?

ARGUS. (*On knees before* CAESAR.) Have mercy, have mercy, oh great and noble Caesar!

CAESAR. (*Coldly.*) To the hippodrome, the lions, and at once. To death with him.

(MARCUS *and* QUINTUS *drag* VALENTINE *toward exit.*)

DICK. (*Rushing forward and greatly excited.*) No, NO, they shall NOT give you to the lions. (ARGUS *has sprung up. All register great astonishment.*) See, it is really all my fault. (*To* CAESAR.) Sire, I—I am to blame. I bought them. I sent them. (*He has caught* CAESAR's *arm.*)

CAESAR. What—what means this? Who are you?

DICK. (*Still greatly excited.*) He did no wrong, I say. Those (*Pointing to draperies.*) are my valentines. I got them for the school box. I don't know how they came upon his wall.

CAESAR. You—you sent—them?

(DICK *nods. He is frightened but very much in earnest.*)

VALENTINE. (*Weakly.*) Lad—who—who are you?

DICK. I'm Dick—Dick Travis, and—and I thought I liked "comic" valentines; but—but—if it's going to make you trouble —(*Suddenly to* CAESAR.) Oh, you must not give him to the lions, or send him to the hippodrome—I heard what he and Argus wrote for Nan and Joan—and, yes—for Miss Cramer!

(*Curtains again open and "comics" are displayed.*)

CAESAR. (*Puzzled.*) For Nan? For Joan—and Miss Cramer? You mean—those are yours—those vile—hideous—

DICK. (*Hastily.*) I'm sorry, sir. Oh, I'm dreadfully sorry— but you must not blame him. Oh— (*Suddenly with surprised glance toward doorway. The "comics" stand aside.*) Look, look! There are St. Valentine's valentines!

(*All turn, and from door, the "pretty" valentines dance out gayly.* CAESAR *and M.* ANTONY *start back. Soldiers release* VALENTINE, *etc. Girls dance to soft music. Lights slowly diminish as dance closes, music grows softer, dancers exeunt doorway, and*

CURTAIN FALLS

SCENE 3

Music continues softly until curtain rises. Spot-light and shield are removed and stage is same as Scene 1, except the "comic valentines" have fallen from DICK'S *hands and are scattered about the floor.* DICK *is fast asleep. He stirs slightly as* NAN *and* JOAN *enter with platter.*

NAN. (*Gayly.*) Here's the fudge, Dick, and I do hope you will be a good boy and not send those horrid— (*To* JOAN.) Sh, look, he's asleep.

JOAN. He fell asleep over that old History. (*Surprised.*) And his valentines are scattered all over the floor. (*Starts to pick them up.*)

DICK. (*Stirring sleepily.*) And—and I'm glad I met you, Mister Julius Caesar—and you too, Mister Saint Valentine! (*Girls pause, fingers on lips.*) And I promise—I promise—

JOAN. (*Whispering.*) He's dreaming.

DICK. And I promise you I'll never send another "comic" valentine as long as I live. That I won't. I know now valentines should be beautiful and gay—and KIND. (*Starts. Looks about in confusion.*) Well—Well—I guess—I've been—asleep.

NAN. (*Laughing.*) You certainly were.

JOAN. (*Laughing.*) And dreaming, too.

DICK. (*Doubtfully.*) Well—maybe—but (*Looks about in confusion.*)

NAN. Well, here's the fudge—and do tell us what you dreamed.

JOAN. Yes, yes, tell us.

DICK. (*Rousing and helping himself generously to fudge.*) I—I dreamed—oh, nothing much—only— (*Glances at "comics" in* JOAN'*s hands.*) Here, stick those old things in the wastebasket, will you?—I've sort of changed my mind—I'm not going to send them after all—I'd be always thinking of the lions and old Julius Caesar and good old Saint Valentine.—If you got any pretty ones left (*Helps himself again to fudge as curtain begins to lower.*) I'll send them! Good old Valentine!

(*Girls exchange nods and glances, as*

CURTAIN FALLS

CUPID TAKES A VACATION *

A Play for St. Valentine's Day

By Delle Oglesbee Ross

PERSONS

Saint Valentine, *a very old man*
Dan Cupid, *a child*
Puck, *or* Robin Goodfellow, *also a child*

Girls	*Boys*	
Val	Dan	*Pupils at Meadowbrook School, in their early teens*
Mab	Ted	
Sue	Bob	
Marge	Bill	

Larry Larimer } *movie stars*
Betty Bubbles }

Time: Scene 1: *A week or two before St. Valentine's Day*
　　　Scene 2: *Afternoon of St. Valentine's Day*
　　　Scene 3: *St. Valentine's night*
　　　Present time.

Place: Scene 1: *A lane near the hermit hut of St. Valentine*
　　　Scenes 2 & 3: *Gymnasium of Meadowbrook School*

Notes: *The young people should wear modern afternoon clothes in Scene 1, and evening clothes in Scene 2. The Movie Stars should be very elaborate.* Betty, *especially, must be made up extravagantly.*

St. Valentine *is a very happy looking saint, with a round, rosy face, his beard and long hair shine like silver, and he wears a little crown of red hearts, his monk's robe is white bordered with red hearts, and he carries a long staff tipped with a heart.*

---

* This play may be produced without royalty where no admission is charged. Otherwise a fee of three dollars must be paid to the author, 317 North Marion St., Oak Park, Ill.

He wears silver sandals. CUPID *wears the traditional costume, small wings and his bow and arrows should be gold, silver or bright red.*

PUCK *should wear a bright green, tight-fitting suit; his hair should be red, and stand out in peaks from his head.*

If the stage is large enough more boys and girls could be used at the dance, filling in the picture and making more dancers.

During Scenes 2 and 3, PUCK, CUPID *and* ST. VALENTINE *are always unseen and unheard by the young people.*

SCENE 1

To be played before the curtain. A lane near the hut of ST. VALENTINE. CUPID *is seated on a small mound or rock, his bow and arrows at his feet. He sits with his elbows on his knees, face in his hands, very disconsolate.*

CUPID. (*He yawns.*) Tired out, that's what I am! Worn to a frazzle! There was a time when I shot my arrows—and they *stuck!* Now with all this modern business they just pull 'em out when they get tired—and I have to do the work all over again! (*Sighs deeply.*) Ho—hum! (*Pounds his forehead with his fists.*) Well, I'll have to ask Old Saint Valentine—can't make a move without his permission—'specially this time of the year; he gets so strict around his birthday. (*He starts to get up, then slumps back.*) I'm too tired to move, wonder if he'd be mad if I called him. (*He waits a moment.*) Hi! Saint Valentine. (*Listens.*) Maybe he won't answer. Hi—sir! Hi! Saint Valentine—

(ST. VALENTINE *enters from right.*)

ST. VAL. Were you calling me?

CUPID. Sounds that way, doesn't it?

ST. VAL. Why, Dan Cupid, I didn't know you at first. What's the matter? You seem—well—cross!

CUPID. I am cross—I'm tired.

St. Val. Cross! Tired!

Cupid. Yes, I am—and I called and called and you didn't answer.

St. Val. Sorry, son, you see, I didn't hear you until I turned off the highway to come to my hut.

Cupid. Weren't at home, huh? Well, some folks can gallivant all they like, apparently.

St. Val. I wasn't gallivanting, exactly. I was around to see about the supply of valentines this year.

Cupid. Oh.

St. Val. Almost the 14th, you know. (*He puffs up with pride.*) Birthday, you know.

Cupid. Huh!

St. Val. Great day for lovers, you know.

Cupid. I'm tired of lovers!

St. Val. Wha-a-t!

Cupid. (*Shouts.*) I say I'm tired of lovers!

St. Val. Why Cupid! Why, my dear lad!

Cupid. (*Grumbling.*) Well, I am; drat 'em!

St. Val. I can't bear to hear you talk this way.

Cupid. Used to like 'em. Used to enjoy pairing 'em off, and shooting my arrows at 'em.

St. Val. Well, what's come over you? Don't you still do that?

Cupid. Yes—but they know how to pull them out—these days. They don't stick together. Divorce mills! Broken homes! I don't like it.

St. Val. Well—well—we must do something.

Cupid. I'm tired, I tell you. I need a vacation!

St. Val. A vacation!

Cupid. (*Shouts.*) That's what I need—a vacation!

St. Val. But—but—

Cupid. Look at the thousands of years I have worked—no time off!

St. Val. But—who—

CUPID. (*Grumbling.*) It's a good thing I don't belong to a Union!

ST. VAL. Now, Dan Cupid, you know I don't want anyone weary and unhappy, but who would attend to the sweethearts of the world?

CUPID. Couldn't—

ST. VAL. You wouldn't want all the love affairs to stop short, would you?

CUPID. Now, listen; if I found a substitute, then couldn't I go away for a while?

ST. VAL. But who—?

CUPID. Well—well—

ST. VAL. (*Moving towards left.*) Think fast. I must get home to my hut. A whole new consignment of paper lace came this morning, and I've got to make valentines.

CUPID. (*Suddenly jumping up.*) How about Puck!

ST. VAL. Puck!

CUPID. Sure as anything. He'd like it.

ST. VAL. Can he shoot straight—and can he be trusted?

CUPID. Oh, anything as important as this—make him feel big!

ST. VAL. Where is he?

CUPID. I'll call him. He's somewhere nearby helping Jack Frost trim the fields in silver lace.

ST. VAL. Then call him.

CUPID. Puck—Puck—Robin Goodfellow!

(*A far-off cry, thin and sweet, is heard.*)

ST. VAL. He heard you.

CUPID. He'll come. Who—ee—ee—ee! Puck—Puck— (*The cry is a little nearer.*) Come here—Cupid is calling!

PUCK. (*Still a little nearer.*) I'm coming—coming—coming— (*PUCK comes on, right, as though blown by the wind. He stops by* CUPID.) Here am I—now why did you call me, Dan Cupid?

CUPID. Saint Valentine, you know my old friend Robin Goodfellow—sometimes known as Puck—don't you?

ST. VAL. I've heard of him. Well, my son, will you help us out?

PUCK. Always glad to help. (*He hops around on one foot.*) Hee—Hee! In my own way.

CUPID. Now listen, Puck, you have simply got to be serious.

PUCK. (*Sits down and imitates* CUPID's *position.*) As serious —as serious as the income tax!

CUPID. Well, here it is. You aren't very busy these days, are you?

PUCK. Oh, I haven't been very busy since Midsummer's Night. Hoo! Was that a night! (*He jumps up and dances around, then sits down solemnly.*)

CUPID. I want you to act as my substitute.

PUCK. What!

CUPID. While I take a vacation.

PUCK. Oh, I'd love that!

ST. VAL. (*Wagging his finger.*) But no tricks, mind you.

CUPID. No, and don't fool around those Meadowbrook School kids. They are graduating this month, and must have their minds on their lessons. One couple, I'm about ready to shoot— but not yet.

PUCK. Oh jiminy! (*He leaps up and grabs the arrows and bow.*) Shall I start now?

CUPID. Shall he, St. Valentine? May I go right away?

ST. VAL. Well, I suppose so—but see that you are back by Valentine Day, Dan Cupid. And, Robin or Puck or whatever your name is—*be careful!* I *must* get home. Good-bye, good-bye.

(*He goes off left;* CUPID *takes a small valise from behind the mound, and follows* PUCK, *who has already danced out aiming an arrow.*)

CUPID. Now, let's see—where shall I go—any place where there are no lovers!

CURTAIN

SCENE 2

The gym at Meadowbrook School. Boys and girls are preparing for the Valentine party. Gym equipment is pushed back. At a table, left center front, MAB and SUE are cutting out paper hearts. Near them TED and BOB are stringing them. There are some extra chairs scattered around; there are entrances right and left.

BOB. (*Holding up string of hearts.*) Pretty swell, eh what!

SUE. Swell, all right, but my hands are about ready to quit.

MAB. Patience, my child, we only need a few more.

TED. Where's Dan with that ladder?

SUE. He'll be along; probably had to get the key from the janitor.

BOB. Thought Val was coming to help.

MAB. Yes, and Marge and Bill.

SUE. Marge and Bill went to get the candy hearts.

MAB. But Val?

SUE. Don't know—thought she came with Dan.

BOB. The inseparables!

SUE. They always do everything together, don't they?

(*Laughter is heard.*)

MAB. Here come Marge and Bill.

BOB. They are almost as wacky as Val and Dan.

MAB. Oh, I don't know! Bill asked me for a date the other day.

TED. He did, did he! The big fish!

BOB. Hey! Hey!

SUE. Are you going, Mab?

MAB. Maybe. No one has the key to my lock and chain!

TED. Sez you!

MAB. Sez I, Mr. Smarty.

SUE. Well, dates are out for me. I've got to put on the old spectacles, and get busy with my A B C's.

BOB. Woe is me! Not even the basket ball game?

SUE. Not even the basket ball game. My fond parents have stamped hard with their Number 10's.

TED. Why all the heavy discipline?

SUE. Bad marks last time, old son. Must make the goal this time.

(MARGE *and* BILL *carrying their skates and a large candy box breeze in.*)

MARGE. Hi, everyone!

BILL. Hi-di-ho!

SUE. Hi, Marge. Hi, Bill.

MAB. Did you get the candy?

BOB. Why the skates?

TED. Aren't you going to help us?

BILL. Sure—for a very short time.

MARGE. Then we're going to skate. Ice is fine!

MAB. Let's see the hearts.

BILL. Where's Val?

SUE. Hasn't come yet.

(BILL *places the box on the table, all crowd around while* MARGE *opens the box.* SUE *takes up a candy heart.*)

SUE. Hear this one! "Do you love me?"

(*All laugh.*)

BOB. Regular old fashioned ones, aren't they?

TED. (*Reading another.*) "Kisses won't tell"—Gee!

(*All are laughing and grabbing at hearts when* DAN *enters, left, dragging a ladder; he leaves the door slightly ajar.*)

BOB. Well, you took long enough.

SUE. Maybe he had to *make* a ladder!

MAB. Maybe he doesn't like to cut hearts.

TED. Or string them!

DAN. What you picking on me for?

BILL. You should worry!

MARGE. Don't they like you, Big Boy?

(PUCK *pushes the door open and looks in.*)

DAN. Where's Val?

SUE. Maybe she has found another affinity.

(PUCK *comes into the room.*)

MAB. Maybe you are just too—too—slow!

DAN. Hey! What's the matter around here?

BILL. You don't seem very popular—

TED. Here, give me that ladder—

SUE. You and Bob get busy—

BOB. Sure, we've got to get something done before tonight—

(BOB *and* TED *take the ladder and begin to hang up the strings of hearts.* PUCK *runs across the room and leans against the opposite wall. He winks at the audience, points at* DAN *and shakes his head.* DAN *looks rather sulky and crestfallen. The girls huddle in a group, paying no attention to him.*)

TED. Hey—look! We'll have to get a hammer and some nails.

(TED *and* BOB *go out left.*)

DAN. Looks like I'm the forgotten man!

PUCK. This will never do! Now for some fun! We'll stir up these bits of fluff—

(*He dances gaily while he takes a bunch of arrows, each with a large tag marked* DAN. *He fits them one by one to the bow and shoots them into the group of girls. They do not see them, but give little squeals as though stung by an insect.* DAN *has seated himself on a chair, and acts puzzled and hurt. He doesn't look at the girls.*)

MAB. Ouch!

SUE. Something stung me! Oh, how my heart flutters!

MARGE. There wouldn't be mosquitoes in February, would there?

MAB. No—but— Why, Dan, *darling!* How lonesome you look.

(Puck *hops up and down in glee—*)

MARGE. Have some hearts, Handsome. (*She goes over to him with the box.*)

SUE. Here, let *me* give you some. (*She runs over, picks out a heart and puts it in* DAN'S *mouth.*) This says "Love me, my pet"!

DAN. (*So astonished he is almost speechless.*) Mush!

(*The girls arrange themselves in adoring attitudes around* DAN. PUCK *runs out, right.*)

MAB. Oh, Dan, you are the *grandest* football player!

SUE. And how you can swim!

MARGE. And dance!

MAB. You're not going to bring Val tonight, are you?

MARGE. (*To the girls.*) He's taking *me*. I can shake Bill.

DAN. For cat's sake! What *is* all this?

SUE. Oh, Dan, I just adore your tango.

DAN. What's come over you girls?

MAB. Oh, Dan, I think you have the cutest chin!

DAN. Here, I'll go find the fellows. Oh, here's Val—

(VAL *enters carrying a pile of valentines.*)

VAL. Here are the favors for tonight. Hi, Dan!

DAN. (*Rather blankly.*) Hi, Val.

VAL. Don't you want to see them?

MARGE. Put them on the table over there. Oh, Dan—

SUE. Come on, Dan, let's look at them.

MAB. Dan, dear, do you like fudge? Because I can—

VAL. What in the world—

DAN. Sure I like fudge—but—

(*He jumps to his feet, and goes to the table.* PUCK *dances in, right, looking rather worried.*)

PUCK. This *is* Meadowbrook School, the one Cupid warned me about! My Goodness!

(*Enter* BOB *and* TED, *left, with hammer and nails.*)

BOB. Come on, Dan, get busy!

MARGE. Oh, don't bother Dan.

VAL. Well—and why not?

SUE. Dan wants to talk to me.

TED. Come on, shake a shoe.

MAB. Dan and I are going over to my house.

VAL. (*Looking shocked and disgusted.*) Well—of course he can if he wants to.

MARGE. (*Pulling* DAN's *arm.*) Come on, Big Boy, let's practice our steps.

DAN. (*Confused, but still rather liking the attention.*) Just a minute—

SUE. (*Also pulling at him.*) Oh, Dan, let's go where we can talk.

DAN. But—I—wait—

MAB. (*Taking his hand.*) This way—you know, Dan, fudge?

PUCK. My soul and body! This won't do—what'll Cupid say! This must stop. I'll get Saint Valentine. (*He runs out, appearing almost at once with the* SAINT.)

BOB. What ails you women?

VAL. Well, I think you are nuts! I'm going home.

(*Holding her head very high, she goes out, right.* DAN *looks at her, then settles back with the girls.*)

TED. (*Throws down the hammer.*) Of all the ga-ga performances!

BOB. Let's go!

(*They stamp out muttering. The girls are still pulling at* DAN.)

MAB. Coming with me, Danny?

MARGE. Dan, old dear—

SUE. Do you like music, Dan? (*She starts to sing "You can't stop me from dreaming."*)

DAN. (*To* BOB *and* TED.) Don't go—wait for me— (*He goes out, the girls still talking and dragging at him.*)

ST. VAL. Well, you *have* done it!

PUCK. Cupid will never trust me again; but they *are* funny!

Ha—ha—ha! Ho—ho—ho!

(PUCK *and the* SAINT *roar with laughter*.)

ST. VAL. I suppose we must straighten it out—

PUCK. Oh, do you think you can?

ST. VAL. (*Claps his hands*.) I know! Just the thing—at least I think it'll work!

PUCK. What?

ST. VAL. That handsome movie star, Larry Larimer; he's in town. I'll just send him to the dance tonight.

PUCK. No one can resist *him!* Don't need any arrows.

ST. VAL. Come—I'll send you. You can whisper in his ear.

PUCK. But—I thought he was in love with Betty Bubbles—

ST. VAL. Oh, just publicity, I think.

(*They go out, right, still conspiring*.)

CURTAIN

SCENE 3

The gym that night. The gym is decorated with strings of hearts and other characteristic valentine emblems. On the table there is a large valentine box. As the curtain rises the music is playing a tango, and DAN *enters, left, followed by* SUE, MAB *and* MARGE. VAL *stands with* BILL *by the table, right.*

VAL. I simply can't understand it.

DAN. (*Girls all chattering and pulling at him*.) Whoa there! Whoa there! One at a time, my pretties.

SUE. But, Dan—darling—

MAB. You asked *me* for the first dance.

MARGE. After all, Dan—

ALL THREE. { Oh, Dan—
Now please, Dan—
You remember, Dan—

DAN. I can't dance with all of you at once, can I? Here, I'll count out—

> Eeny, Meeny, Miny, Mo—
> Out you go—
> O-u-t—out!

(*He points at* SUE. TED *and* BOB *run in and* BOB *catches hold of* MAB's *hands.* TED *takes* MARGE *and they dance the tango.*)

BILL. Well, Val, we're not quitters. Come on—le's dance!

(*They join the dancers, and they all finish the figure.*)

VAL. Time for the Valentine Box.

BILL. Come one—come all!

(*They all rush over to the table. The girls leave* BOB *and* TED *and cling to* DAN.)

BOB. Looks like they are standing us up again.

TED. I'm getting sick of it. Heck!

(*They stand together at the edge of the group.*)

MAB. Val, you be the postmistress.

SUE. Your name is Valentine, so it's up to you!

MARGE. Oh, hurry, it's going to be so exciting!

BOB. Simply ducky!

(VAL *pulls out a large envelope.*)

VAL. Dan, one for you.

DAN. Thanks, Val.

VAL. Here, Mab, catch.

MAB. Oh, Dan, how sweet!

TED. (*To* BOB.) Huh, I sent that!

VAL. Dan! Here's another—and another—

BOB. Robert Taylor himself—I don't think!

VAL. Sue—Marge—one for me. Here, Dan—and another— and another.

MARGE. Why Danny's just getting oodles of valentines!

BOB. Come on, Ted, I'm getting out of here.

BILL. So am I.

(*They leave. Left, no one notices but* VAL; *she looks at* DAN, *who is examining the valentines with the girls.* VAL *starts to follow the other boys, then lifts her head proudly and stays where she is.*)

SUE. Let's dance again.

MAB. My turn now.

MARGE. No—mine.

VAL. Too bad Dan isn't triplets.

MARGE. Oh, isn't he wonderful!

MAB. My hero!

SUE. And to think I never knew him before.

VAL. And to think I thought I did!

DAN. Can't you see I'm blushing? (*To himself.*) But Gee! I like it!

(PUCK *and* ST. VALENTINE *enter, right, and cross to left.* ST. VALENTINE *stands by the door.* PUCK *runs around looking at the girls and* DAN, *who laugh and chatter during* ST. VAL's *and* PUCK's *conversation.*)

ST. VAL. I don't like to see my own namesake so disheartened. Poor Val.

PUCK. I whispered to that movie star, what-ever-his-name-is. Just the breath of a whisper that the drama department of this school is pretty important.

ST. VAL. And I put the idea in the Dean's head to invite him to the dance.

PUCK. We'll see, then.

(TED, BOB, *and* BILL *enter, left, with the extremely handsome and well-dressed* LARRY LARIMER.)

TED. Girls—

(*They all turn toward him.*)

BOB. Surprise!

BILL. You'll like this!

TED. Mr. Logan, in the Drama Section, asked us to bring Mr. Larimer to the dance. He happened to be at the school tonight.

Bob. This, my dear young ladies, is Mr. Larry Larimer, of the Super Marvel Films.

Bill. (*To* Ted.) That'll knock 'em cold!

Larry. Charmed, I'm sure.

Sue. Larry Larimer!

Mab. The movie star!

Marge. Oh, isn't he divine!

Val. (*Looks at* Dan, *as the girls surge toward* Larry, *leaving* Dan *with his hands full of valentines.*) I can't believe it!

Sue. Oh, Mr. Larimer, I've always *longed* to meet you.

Mab. I think you are simply marvelous—just marvelous!

Marge. Those eyes! Those shoulders!

Dan. Weren't we going to dance?

Mab. Some other time.

Sue. Don't bother now.

Marge. (*To* Larry.) Oh, you were so wonderful in "Faces Up."

Sue. Your love scenes were so—so—

Val. Convincing?

Larry. (*Rather bored.*) Thank you very much.

Marge. Oh, I must have your autograph. Oh, where is something?

Mab. Our valentines—let's have him autograph them.

Bob. Well, talk about crust!

Ted. Our valentines!

Bill. That we spent our good money—

Dan. Are there any more in the box?

Girls. {Don't bother, Dan.
These will do.
Give me a pencil, Dan.

(*They push the valentines in* Larry's *face. He grits his teeth, but does his duty.*)

Larry. I've writer's cramp now.

St. Val. (*To* Puck.) I told you this would do it.

PUCK. I still wish Dan Cupid would come.

(*The door, right, bursts open and* CUPID *runs in pulling* BETTY BUBBLES *in with him, though it has the appearance that* BETTY *is doing all the rushing.*)

BETTY. Larry! They told me you would be in here.

LARRY. Thought I had walked out on you, eh?

BETTY. Oh, I didn't know what to think. Publicity tells us to stick together—then not to stick together.

SUE. Well—and who may this be?

BILL. Why, that must be—sure it is—Betty Bubbles!

TED. Golly!

CUPID. (*Grabbing his bows and arrows from* PUCK.) Of course, I might have known you would muddle things!

ST. VAL. Don't scold him, Cupid.

PUCK. I didn't mean any harm.

CUPID. Always have to make donkeys of lovers, don't you? Huh! Now you watch me! (*He sends an arrow marked* BETTY *to* LARRY.)

LARRY. Oh, Betty, my sweet, let us do what we want to do.

BETTY. And not pay any attention to Publicity?

(ST. VALENTINE *puts his hands out and beckons to them, they go toward him, walking very slowly, absorbed in each other.*)

SUE. Mr. Larimer—

MAB. Our autographs—

MARGE. Oh, Bill, he won't pay any attention to me.

BILL. What do you care?

SUE. Maybe he isn't real.

BOB. Only on a reel of film.

MAB. He's getting old, too.

TED. Well, on with the dance.

CUPID. I really meant to wait a while for this—but I guess I'll have to.

(*He sends an arrow marked* VAL *to* DAN, *who drops his*

valentines. Puck *claps his hands and leaps upon the table.*)

Dan. Why doesn't the music begin?

Val. The music?

Dan. Well, don't they have music for dances? Come on—
   (*He takes her hands, the music plays softly, the others begin to dance.* Dan *looks at* Val *as though he had never seen her before.*)

Val. Here I am—remember me?

Dan. Gosh, Val—you're beautiful!

CURTAIN

ONLY A VALENTINE! *

Playlet

Written for This Volume

By Elbridge S. Lyon

CHARACTERS

Miss Parker, *a teacher with a blue dress and ideas of her own*

Mr. Newcome, *devoid of ideas but an honorable member of the Board of Education*

Several small children of whom only John, Ben, Mary, Will, Dorothy *and* Emma *have speaking parts.*

Time: *Nine A. M. St. Valentine's Day.*

Place: *Small class room in a school.*

Properties: *Blackboard, white and colored chalk, eraser, ruler, books, teacher's desk that child can hide under, drawer that can be opened, benches or chairs or desks for the children. Only one door for entrances and exits.*

---

* For permission to use, consult author, Chatham, New Jersey.

Curtain rises with two boys drawing a crude picture of their teacher on blackboard.

JOHN. I call that a perfect likeness.

BEN. Of what, a Chinee?

JOHN. Could you do any better?

BEN. Sure. Watch me. (*He draws a child and marks it "Teachers Pet."*)

JOHN. Who's that, Mary Higgins?

BEN. Don't it look like her?

JOHN. I thought it was Mrs. Roosevelt. (*He is giving the teacher's picture a blue dress.*) Miss Parker always wears a blue dress.

(MARY *looks in door observing but unobserved then disappears.*)

BEN. Let's get out of here before we are caught.

JOHN. Just a minute. (*He draws, m–y V–a–l–i–n–t–i–n.*)

BEN. E!

JOHN. E. Valintine, is that right?

BEN. Sure, I hope, I hope. Come on, beat it. (*They rush out.*)

(*Enter* MISS PARKER *in blue dress. She looks at blackboard, starts to erase it but changes mind, a bell buzzes off, she sits at desk but gets up hurriedly and erases the part of picture which is the girl and the words teacher's pet, leaving the teacher intact. She takes seat as several children come in taking seats amidst snickers and sly looks at board.*)

MARY. I know who did it.

MISS PARKER. Never mind.

MARY. It was—

MISS PARKER. Hush. Who knows what day today is?

3 CHILDREN. Friday.

2 CHILDREN. The fourteenth.   }(*More or less together.*)

4 CHILDREN. St. Valentine's Day.

MISS PARKER. Just a minute, I didn't ask what day it is. I

asked who knows what day it is?

SEVERAL. I do, I do. (*Many hands go up.*)

MISS PARKER. Well, Will, you may tell us.

WILL. St. Swithin's Day. (*Laughter.*) I mean St. Valentine's Day.

MISS PARKER. All right, now who can spell Valentine?

(*Several hands go up.*)

DOROTHY. Let me.

EMMA. No, me.

MISS PARKER. Just a minute. John, I see you have blue chalk on your fingers, you should have held up the other hand.

JOHN. Yes 'am, I didn't mean any harm. (*Wipes hands on back of pants.*)

MISS PARKER. Of course not, but I think we will talk about it after school.

JOHN. Yes 'am.

MISS PARKER. Ben, how do you spell Valentine. Don't look at the board.

BEN. Valentine. V—Val—i—n—t—i—n——E.

MISS PARKER. I see. I thought probably it was you.

BEN. It was me what?

MISS PARKER. Helped John with his art effort.

JOHN. How did you know?

MISS PARKER. Teachers sometimes know more than scholars even if members of the Board don't always think so.

BEN. But how did you know that John had any help and how did you know it was me?

MISS PARKER. I, not "me." Valentine, you see, is spelled v-a-l-e-n-t-i-n-e not i-n-t-i-n-e. There were two drawings on the blackboard of such divergent schools of thought that I judged there were two artists. As soon as John confessed his part I looked around and saw you looking guiltily at your hands and when you misspelled the word but made it the same as on the board I assumed for the moment that you were the other villain. You both convicted yourselves.

JOHN. Gee. And *we* belong to the Secret sleuth society.

BEN. I didn't mean any harm.

MISS PARKER. I am not so sure about that, but we will talk it over after school.

BEN. Aw, I've got a date.

MISS PARKER. You have a date with me first.

BEN. Yes, Mam.

MISS PARKER. And now we will settle down to our regular class work, though I do not think our time has been altogether wasted. Emma, you may recite first.

EMMA. (*Reciting after making a deep bow. She starts slowly and quietly and works up to a dramatic climax.*)

PEACE AT HOME

The town is fast asleep; in every house,
From grown-up grandpa to the tiniest mouse,
The drowsy minutes tick away and say
Good night to all, children rest from your play
And parents from your labors.
Sweet dreams attend you and your sleeping neighbors.

What is that light that flickers in the sky
Like warning beacon or a fiery eye?
What is that strangling odor and whence came
Those little tongues of redly leaping flame?

Why do you sleep beside your silly clocks?
Up, up, hurry and burst your stupid locks.
There is no time to lose; the flames creep higher!
God help each one of you, the town's A-FIRE!!
(*Real fire-alarm bell in room rings loud.*)
MARY. The bell—the fire bell.

WILL. It's real!

DOROTHY. Fire!

EMMA. Help!

(*They rush pell-mell for door jamming in door and struggle roughly through.*)

MISS PARKER. Wait—remember your discipline. Line up!

(*But all but two have disappeared.*)

JOHN. Come on, come on, let's go.

MISS PARKER. All right, one two, one two— (*They march out with what little dignity is possible.*)

(*Enter MARY surreptitiously. She takes fancy lacy white envelope from inside her blouse and puts it in teacher's desk. Goes to blackboard and draws, quite well, a man on his knees to the picture of the teacher already there. He has glasses and a bald head. She finishes it off with a red tie and drops red chalk on floor as she hears a noise and hurriedly hides behind teacher's desk. MISS PARKER enters and is amazed at new drawing. She sits in one of the pupils' chairs almost overcome. Seeing red chalk, she picks it up and after carefully looking out into hall goes to board and adds a red nose to picture of man. She backs away as a man enters rapidly. He is the exact image of the man in the Valentine on the board.*)

MR. NEWCOME. Well, well, what is this??

MISS PARKER. It appears to be a Valentine. That is what to-day is, you know.

MR. NEWCOME. Say, that isn't by any chance meant to be me, is it?

MISS PARKER. I am afraid it is, and me, too. I can tell by the blue dress.

MR. NEWCOME. I'd like to get my hands on the boy that did that. Me on my knees!

MISS PARKER. Unaccustomed to such a position?

MR. NEWCOME. In front of women—yes.

MISS PARKER. Meaning me in particular? You once came

pretty near it as I remember before you were elevated to the honor of being a member of the Board of Education and found out how inefficient I am.

MR. NEWCOME. I never did. You were always moon-struck on Robinson. I believe that is why you applied for a job in this school, so as to be near him.

MISS PARKER. Well, if I did, it never did me much good, did it? He scarcely knows I am in the same building.

MR. NEWCOME. I don't think you are inefficient, exactly; but you have no discipline. Look at this blackboard. No other teacher would allow it for a minute. Look at the way your children ran out of your room when the fire drill sounded.

MISS PARKER. There is a reason for that, a very strange one. You would not believe it. I scarcely do and as for this fine cartoon, I consider it a compliment. I will probably have no other Valentine at all. But where are the children? The drill must be over by now.

MR. NEWCOME. They are in the auditorium hearing a lecture on fire prevention. I arranged it all.

MISS PARKER. Then why aren't you there and what, may I ask, are you doing in my room? Oh, you are perfectly welcome. I hope you came to see me.

MR. NEWCOME. Well, to tell the truth, I saw a little girl duck out of the drill line and run upstairs. I followed her and thought she turned in here. Why, by the way, aren't you in the fire practice which I arranged? You see I am on the safety-first committee appointed by the mayor.

MISS PARKER. I see. I know I should have been in line but I couldn't face them after my kids scrammed.

MR. NEWCOME. Say, what sort of talk is that for a teacher?

MISS PARKER. I'm not trying to teach you anything. Nobody could do that.

MR. NEWCOME. Thanks, I did have a pretty good education. Where did you go when the bell rang?

MISS PARKER. I went into the next class room till the procession was over. I didn't like to be in the wrong position. To tell the truth, I do not like these fire drills. This is a 100% fireproof building. The bell goes off like a war-cry when you least expect it. It disturbs classes for hours. I am sure it sets up complexes in some children for a life-time.

MR. NEWCOME. You should be discharged. You are radical. No wonder you have no discipline when you yield to no authority yourself and obey no rules. I pity the man that marries you. It will have to be one who does not care for schedules or precedent.

MISS PARKER. Well, that lets Mr. Robinson out.

(*As they are talking she goes behind her own desk and sits down and as her feet come in contact with the little girl hidden there she starts up but resumes calm.*)

MR. NEWCOME. As I was saying, discipline is organized self-control.

MISS PARKER. Oh, and you think I lack self-control, is that it?

MR. NEWCOME. Exactly. I am afraid that I will have to recommend to the Board that your tenure of office be shortened. As a duty, mind you, only as my official duty.

MISS PARKER. That will be sweet of you.

MR. NEWCOME. I am responsible to the tax payers.

MISS PARKER. You think my duty is to live by rules rather than make human beings out of the children?

MR. NEWCOME. You are not paid to think for yourself but to obey the plans mapped out by the board and other vested authorities.

MISS PARKER. That would mean taking orders from Dan Robinson, wouldn't it?

MR. NEWCOME. How that young squirt ever got to be Principal is more than I can see.

MISS PARKER. That was before the town woke up to your qualifications for managing the school system.

Mr. Newcome. Oh, I am only one member, but I take my duties seriously. Where is the eraser? I will rub out this evidence of your lack of control of these little innocent children.

Miss Parker. How kind! Here it is.

(*She hands him eraser and he notices chalk on her fingers.*)

Mr. Newcome. My gracious, there is red chalk on your hand. I believe you drew these pictures your own self.

Miss Parker. Caught in my own trap. Well?

Mr. Newcome. You drew me—proposing—to you?

Miss Parker. Well?

Mr. Newcome. (*Coyly.*) Well I can only guess what is the wish behind the act. I hardly know what to say. I always hoped you would change toward me some day but I—I—

Miss Parker. Go on—you know all the rules.

Mr. Newcome. I—I— How DO you feel about me?

Miss Parker. (*Taking eraser from his hand, she rubs his picture entirely out.*) There, that is the way I feel.

Mr. Newcome. Well, that is plain enough at all events. I wish you a good morning. (*Stalks out.*)

Miss Parker. (*At door.*) Don't forget to look in each room for that run-a-way girl you thought you saw.

(Mary's *head comes up from behind the desk.*)

Mary. Gee, Miss Parker, you're a peach. All the kids like you.

Miss Parker. You won't when I get through with you.

Mary. (*Dubiously.*) What are you going to do to me?

Miss Parker. Spank you within an inch of your life. (*Picks up ruler.*)

Mary. It's against the rules.

Miss Parker. Making him think I drew silly pictures on the blackboard. Come here to me.

Mary. (*Frightened.*) Honest, Miss Parker, it IS against the law to strike a pupil with a ruler.

Miss Parker. Maybe so; but I doubt if it specifies using a

blackboard eraser. If we have to live so by rules, let's make it complete.

MARY. I'll tell Mr. Robinson.

MISS PARKER. You'll tell him what, that you ran away from the fire drill?

MARY. I'll tell him you love him!

MISS PARKER. You'll tell him what! (MISS PARKER *has been following* MARY *around desks trying to catch hold of her. She now does so and bending her over her lap belabors her with the eraser amidst a cloud of chalk dust.*) Now what are you going to tell him?

MARY. Ouch! Oh, don't. He loves you, too.

MISS PARKER. (*Sitting* MARY *up on bench by her side.*) Look at me, Mary. What are you saying?

MARY. Mr. Robinson loves you.

MISS PARKER. This isn't funny.

MARY. It's true.

MISS PARKER. What makes you think that; how do you know?

MARY. He sent you a Valentine and I read it.

MISS PARKER. Where is it?

MARY. He gave it to me to put in your desk when no one was looking. I came up early, but John and Ben were in here, so I didn't have a chance then. As soon as they went out you came in. When I was in the fire-line Mr. Robinson asked me if I had done it and I said no and he was mad and told me to run and do it right then, rules or no rules. So I didn't leave the line without permission and that old geezer who was in here trying to catch me and you whipping me—boo—hoo—(*But* MISS PARKER *is behind her desk reading the Valentine and as she clasps it to her breast with a beatific expression—*MARY *adds.*) Nobody loves Me! Boo-hoo!

CURTAIN

GREAT-GRANDMOTHER'S VALENTINE

By Katherine Edelman

I ran across it in the attic chest:
  A faded Valentine of long ago,
A little lace-edged card that bore the words,
  "My dear, I love you so!"
A wisp of ribbon that had once been blue
  Held its small pages firmly in their place,
And faded buds of lavender and pink
  Circled a lovely face. . . .
And while with tender touch I held it there
  A dear, quaint lady from an age long gone,
Tip-toed across the room in ruffled gown,
  Singing "Love's Old Sweet Song."
    Pausing a moment, with her hand in mine,
    To softly say, "He's still my Valentine!"

A VALENTINE

[*Sent to a friend who had complained that I was glad enough to
see him when he came, but didn't seem to miss him if he stayed
away.*]

By Lewis Carroll

And cannot pleasures, while they last,
Be actual unless, when past,

231

They leave us shuddering and aghast,
 With anguish smarting?
And cannot friends be firm and fast,
 And yet bear parting?

And must I then, at Friendship's call,
Calmly resign the little all
(Trifling, I grant, it is and small)
 I have of gladness,
And lend my being to the thrall
 Of gloom and sadness?

And think you that I should be dumb,
And full *dolorum omnium,*
Excepting when *you* choose to come
 And share my dinner?
At other times be sour and glum
 And daily thinner?

Must he then only live to weep,
Who'd prove his friendship true and deep
By day a lonely shadow creep,
 At night-time languish,
Oft raising in his broken sleep
 The moan of anguish?

The lover, if for certain days
His fair one be denied his gaze,
Sinks not in grief and wild amaze,
 But, wiser wooer,
He spends the time in writing lays,
 And posts them to her.

And if the verse flow free and fast,
Till even the poet is aghast,

A touching Valentine at last
   The post shall carry,
When thirteen days are gone and past
   Of February.

Farewell, dear friend, and when we meet,
In desert waste or crowded street,
Perhaps before this week shall fleet,
   Perhaps tomorrow,
I trust to find *your* heart the seat
   Of wasting sorrow.

A MAN WHO WOULD WOO A FAIR MAID

By W. S. Gilbert

A man who would woo a fair maid,
Should 'prentice himself to the trade;
   And study all day,
   In methodical way,
How to flatter, cajole, and persuade.
He should 'prentice himself at fourteen,
And practise from morning to e'en;
   And when he's of age,
   If he will, I'll engage,
He may capture the heart of a queen!
     It is purely a matter of skill,
     Which all may attain if they will:
     But every Jack
     He must study the knack
     If he wants to make sure of his Jill!

If he's made the best use of his time,
His twig he'll so carefully lime

That every bird
Will come down at his word,
Whatever its plumage and clime.
He must learn that the thrill of a touch
May mean little, or nothing, or much;
It's an instrument rare,
To be handled with care,
And ought to be treated as such.
It is purely a matter of skill,
Which all may attain if they will:
But every Jack,
He must study the knack
If he wants to make sure of his Jill!

Then a glance may be timid or free;
It will vary in mighty degree,
From an impudent stare
To a look of despair
That no maid without pity can see.
And a glance of despair is no guide—
It may have its ridiculous side;
It may draw you a tear
Or a box on the ear;
You can never be sure till you've tried.
It is purely a matter of skill,
Which all may attain if they will:
But every Jack
He must study the knack
If he wants to make sure of his Jill!

THE NIGHT HAS A THOUSAND EYES

By Francis William Bourdillon

The night has a thousand eyes,
    And the day but one;
Yet the light of the bright world dies
    With the dying sun.

The mind has a thousand eyes,
    And the heart but one;
Yet the light of a whole life dies
    When love is done.

A VALENTINE

By Laura E. Richards

Oh, little loveliest lady mine!
What shall I send for your valentine?
Summer and flowers are far away,
Gloomy old Winter is king today,
Buds will not blow, and sun will not shine;
What shall I do for a valentine?

Prithee, Saint Valentine, tell me here,
Why do you come at this time o' year?
Plenty of days when lilies are white,
Plenty of days when sunbeams are bright;
But now, when everything's dark and drear,
Why do you come, Saint Valentine dear?

I've searched the gardens all through and through,
For a bud to tell of my love so true;

But buds are asleep, and blossoms are dead,
And the snow beats down on my poor little head;
So, little loveliest lady mine,
Here is my heart for your valentine.

SAINT VALENTINE'S DAY

By Coventry Patmore

Well dost thou, Love, thy solemn Feast to hold
In vestal February;
Not rather choosing out some rosy day
From the rich coronet of the coming May,
When all things meet to marry!
    O quick, prævernal Power
That signall'st punctual through the sleepy mould
The Snowdrop's time to flower,
Fair as the rash oath of virginity
Which is first-love's first cry;
O, Baby spring,
That flutter'st sudden 'neath the breast of Earth
A month before the birth;
Whence is the peaceful poignancy,
The joy contrite,
Sadder than sorrow, sweeter than delight,
That burthens now the breath of everything,
Though each one sighs as if to each alone
The cherish'd pang were known?
At dusk of dawn, on his dark spray apart,
With it the Blackbird breaks the young Day's heart;
In evening's hush
About it talks the heavenly-minded Thrush;
The hill with like remorse

Smiles to the Sun's smile in his westering course;
The fisher's drooping skiff
In yonder sheltering bay;
The choughs that call about the shining cliff;
The children, noisy in the setting ray;
Own the sweet season, each thing as it may;
Thoughts of strange kindness and forgotten peace
In me increase;
And tears arise
Within my happy, happy Mistress' eyes,
And, lo, her lips, averted from my kiss,
Ask from Love's bounty, ah, much more than bliss!
   Is't the sequester'd and exceeding sweet
Of dear Desire electing his defeat?
Is't the waked Earth now to yon purpling cope
Uttering first-love's first cry,
Vainly renouncing, with a seraph's sigh,
Love's natural hope?
Fair-meaning Earth, foredoom'd to perjury!
Behold, all amorous May,
With roses heap'd upon her laughing brows,
Avoids thee of thy vows!
Were it for thee, with her warm bosom near,
To abide the sharpness of the Seraph's sphere?
Forget thy foolish words;
Go to her summons gay,
Thy heart with dead, wing'd Innocencies fill'd,
Ev'n as a nest with birds
After the old ones by the hawk are kill'd.
   Well dost thou, Love, to celebrate
The noon of thy soft ecstasy,
Or e'er it be too late,
Or e'er the Snowdrop die!

AN HONEST VALENTINE

Returned from the Dead-Letter Office

BY DINAH M. MULOCK

Thank ye for your kindness,
　Lady fair and wise,
Though Love's famed for blindness,
　Lovers—hem! for lies.
Courtship's mighty pretty,
　Wedlock a sweet sight;—
Should I (from the City,
　A plain man, Miss—) write,
Ere we spouse-and-wive it,
　Just one honest line,
Could you e'er forgive it,
　Pretty Valentine?

Honeymoon quite over,
　If I less should scan
You with eye of lover
　Than of mortal man?
Seeing my fair charmer
　Curl hair spire on spire,
All in paper armour,
　By the parlour fire;
Gown that wants a stitch in
　Hid by apron fine,
Scolding in her kitchen,—
　O, fie, Valentine!

Should I come home surly,
　Vex'd with fortune's frown,
Find a hurly-burly,

House turn'd upside down,
Servants all a-snarl, or
  Cleaning step or stair:
Breakfast still in parlour,
  Dinner—anywhere:
Shall I to cold bacon
  Meekly fall and dine?
No—or I'm mistaken
  Much, my Valentine.

What if we should quarrel?
  —Bless you, all folks do:—
Will you take the war ill,
  Yet half like it too?
When I storm and jangle,
  Obstinate, absurd,
Will you sit and wrangle
  Just for the last word?—
Or, while poor Love, crying,
  Upon tiptoe stands,
Ready plumed for flying—
  Will you smile, shake hands,
And the truth beholding,
  With a kiss divine
Stop my rough mouth's scolding?—
  Bless you, Valentine!

If, should times grow harder,
  We have lack of pelf,
Little in the larder,
  Less upon the shelf;
Will you, never tearful,
  Make your old gowns do,
Mend my stockings, cheerful,

And pay visits few?
Crave nor gift nor donor,
   Old days ne'er regret,
Ask no friends save Honour,
   Dread no foe but Debt;
Meet ill-fortune steady,
   Hand to win with mine,
Like a gallant lady—
   Will you, Valentine?

Then whatever weather
   Come—or shine, or shade,
We'll set out together,
   Ne'er a whit afraid.
Age is not alarming—
   I shall find, I ween,
You at sixty charming
   As at sweet sixteen:
Let's pray, nothing loath, dear,
   That our funeral may
Make one date serve both, dear,
   Like our marriage day.
Then, come joy or sorrow,
   Thou art mine—I thine.
And we'll wed tomorrow,
   Dearest Valentine.

VALENTINE IN FORM OF BALLADE

BY ANDREW LANG

The soft wind from the south land sped,
   He set his strength to blow,
O'er forests where Adonis bled

And lily flowers a-row.
He crossed the straits like streams that flow
   The ocean dark as wine
To my true love to whisper low
   To be your Valentine.

The spring-time raised her drowsy head,
   Besprent with drifted snow,
"I'll send an April Day," she said,
   "To lands of wintry woe."
He came; wan winter's overthrow
   With showers that sing and shine
Pied daisies round your path to strow,
   To be your Valentine.

Where sands of Egypt swart and red
   'Neath suns Egyptian glow,
In places of the princely dead
   By the Nile's overflow,
The swallow preened her wings to go,
   And for the North did pine,
And fain would brave the frost, her foe,
   To be your Valentine.

Envoy

Spring, Swallow, South Wind, even so
   Their various voice combine,
But that they crave on me bestow
   To be your Valentine.

A VALENTINE STORY

"ST. VALENTINE'S DAY OUT"

A Story

By Mabel M. Moran

St. Peter swung open the gates and watched young St. Valentine step off into space—it being February 14th and Val's day off.

"Don't be late returning to the feast," Peter called to the fast moving shade and chuckled at the brisk gesture he received in reply from the lad.

"Nice boy that," he mumbled, turning the great key in the lock.

"Well, what are you girls doing here?" he inquired of the three female saints who were hanging over his shoulders.

St. Joan, ready to speak up on all occasions, answered promptly: "We would like to ask a few questions—she" (pointing to the littlest saint) "never heard of St. Valentine and is curious about him."

"Humph," St. Peter tried to sound harsh, and failed, "saints and sinners, you are all alike where a good-looking boy is concerned; what ails you that you never heard of St. Valentine?"

The littlest saint, dropping a pretty courtesy said:

"In the convent where I was living my earthly life, sir, we never spoke of young men."

Peter made a noise remarkably like a snort and changed it into a cough:

"Suppose we sit down and I will try to remember something

about the case," said he—collecting a bunch of fluffy clouds and sinking into them gratefully, and easing his feet after long hours at the gate.

"Please, sir, do not let us keep you from your duties," St. Ursula urged him anxiously.

"Never you mind about my duties, I'll attend to them myself," replied the beloved old saint testily, as he beckoned to a passing seraph: "Go watch the gate, son," said he, "and if I am wanted you say I'm in conference."

St. Joan sat down on a jasper boulder and the others joined her.

"According to his credentials," said Peter thoughtfully, "St. Valentine is a splendid young man, showing throughout his short life a great devotion to the church. That was somewhere towards the end of the second century—in a place called Italy, I think, but I'll make sure about it by asking St. Francis of Assisi who is coming toward us."

St. Francis hastened his steps as he heard his name called. The littlest saint watched him eagerly, as she had heard all about him in the convent, and was not surprised to see him surrounded by a fluttering mass of heavenly birds.

"Sit down for a moment, St. Francis," urged Peter hospitably. "We are discussing St. Valentine. Did he not come from your country?"

"Ah yes," answered the other—"he came from Rome where he befriended the martyrs in the persecution of Claudius II and was, in consequence, arrested, beaten with clubs, and finally beheaded."

Francis spoke with great cheerfulness. Martyrdom held no horrors for him.

"There used to be a fine gateway in ancient Rome called after him; but the old gate of St. Valentine is now named the Porta del Popolo."

"Ouch!" interrupted St. Peter suddenly, waving his hands

about his head, "I wish you would call off your birds, Francis, they have pulled out a lot of my whiskers! You should train them better!"

"Oh, I AM sorry!" Francis rose in concern. "Come come, little brothers," said he to the birds, "we must be on our way; you will recall, dear Peter, that today the birds begin to pair, and, no doubt they wanted some of your beautiful silvery beard to line their nests; you cannot blame their excellent taste, I trust."

Peter watched St. Francis as he bowed his farewells with all the grace of his early Troubadour days, and passed on amid his twittering and chirping followers.

"Francis is always helpful," said the older man, "he has mentioned a number of items that had quite escaped me. When Valentine was awaiting his execution he was denied all means of communicating with his family or his friends and he had little to occupy his long, sad imprisonment save to cut small pieces of parchment into fancy shapes upon which he wrote a few messages of love with the hope that the jailor's daughter would smuggle them out after his death. Possibly the young female was a little enamored of Valentine, since she arranged to do his bidding, and quite a few of the lacy bits of vellum reached their destination, each signed 'Your Valentine.' "

The three saintly maidens sighed in unison as St. Peter continued.

"Many years passed, as of course they must, before one may be canonized; but at last when Valentine's name appeared on the list of Saints, people recalled the story of those messages and it became the style for young sweethearts to use the anniversary of Valentine's death to send love messages and sign them 'Valentine.'

"St. Valentine has taken a number of trips back to the old Earth since those days; each year on February 14th he goes on his pilgrimage and often he brings back a souvenir of his visit—

the so-called 'valentines' of the period.

"Once it was a composition by a man named Chaucer who wrote a poem with a stanza about February 14. It was called 'The Parliament of Foules,' saying:

" 'For this was on seynt Valentynes' day
Whan every foul cometh ther to choose his mate.'

"This was no doubt what St. Francis referred to when he said his birds 'were pairing.' "

"Please sir, are the 'Valentines' pretty?" asked the littlest saint.

"Some are, and again no," answered Peter. "The earliest ones from England were made entirely by hand; ladies used to do a deal of flower painting in those times. Valentine showed me a very pretty one done on a sheet of embossed paper—it was a nice likeness of a rose very well painted and under it a sentimental verse in fine lettering. On another visit—along in the sixteen-sixties—Val discovered a man named Pepys who kept a well-known diary which, being a curious youth, Val glanced into and found an item which interested him—something about Pepys' wife receiving a valentine from a man named 'Will Mercer' which was 'Writ upon a blue paper in gold letters; done by himself and very pretty.' "

St. Peter paused for a moment to try and untangle his girdle which he had been tying in knots as he talked. St. Joan took the snarled rope out of his hands and straightened it competently.

"Thank you, Joan," said Peter rather dreamily. "Strange how long a habit lasts! It still comforts me to handle a rope as I used to in the old days on Galilee with my good fishing boat running before the breeze!"

"When will St. Valentine come back?" interrupted the littlest saint shyly.

"In good time for his feast," Peter told her. "We hold feast days for a certain few of the saints who enjoy them; most of us are not interested; but Valentine likes them—if he is not too upset over mortals' doings down below."

"You cannot help being upset when you see how foolish mortals are when you visit the earth!" St. Joan spoke forcefully; "I once came across a statue of myself down there and it looked like a thin child riding on a toy horse! Surely all the world knows I was of peasant blood and strongly muscled."

St. Ursula was about to voice her views, when again the littlest saint spoke:

"Please sir, what could upset St. Valentine?"

"The comics," snapped St. Peter violently. "If Val finds another comic he is apt to forget he is a saint. I remember the first and only time he brought one in here to show me! He was pale with anger. 'How dare they use my name to such as this!' he cried, and was so upset that I called to one of those imps of Satan who always hang around the gate and gave the thing to him, telling him to hand it to his master, and the last I saw of him, the little devil was laughing uproariously—it was just his style!"

The maidens shuddered.

"A thing that pleased St. Valentine greatly," continued Peter, "was when that part of the Earth that is called America began to take note of his feast day. It seems that a Miss Howland— a college girl at Mt. Holyoke 'invented' the first valentine in America in 1849. It was almost a copy of the lace-paper sort from England, but she originated the idea of having a ready-made verse printed on it. Since Miss Howland had a brother who was a 'traveling salesman,' he worked up so much popularity for this valentine that before long his sister became the owner of a valentine factory that brought in a hundred thousand dollars a year. And that, my good children, is the way they do things in the U. S. A."

St. Peter may have expected the three maidens to express astonishment over his financial statement but they only looked vague, and he sighed as he continued: "Some mortals are now making collections of valentines—hunting for the silhouette sorts which are hard to find, and the ones with mirrors which are equally scarce, and carry the legend:

" 'Beloved, in the mirror see
All that is beautiful to me.' "

St. Peter was about to add that there was often a sketch of a church on them to show that the lover's intentions were honorable—but changed his mind as a gay whistle sounded at the gate.

"The boy has returned," he shouted, springing to his feet.

There was no need to question the success of St. Valentine's "day off," as his face was wreathed in smiles; nor was there a question of the prettiness of the souvenir he carried, with its dainty lace and gay flowers and crimson hearts spitted on golden arrows.

"This," said Valentine holding it aloft, "is what the world calls SWELL!"

St. Peter smiled as he saw the littlest saint reach out her hand!

ESSAYS

ST. VALENTINE'S DAY

February Fourteenth

By Clara J. Denton

This is the day, February 14, when we mean to be kind to everybody. We want to give, not only loving thoughts, but words as well, to our dearest friends, and we love to go to the stores and buy pretty little tokens to send to them.

It is true that we see in the windows hideous pictures, unlike any people that have ever been seen on earth, and we hear them called "Valentines," but they have no right to the name.

The day was set apart for merrymaking and kind feeling, and not to give pain and annoyance. If people want to make these hideous pictures, and other people are foolish and unkind enough to buy and send them out, I suppose it is not possible to prevent them from doing so; but they have no right to call the ugly things, "Valentines," for that is an insult to the good and holy saint after whom the day was named.

It is true that the good Valentine did not set going this custom of sending valentines, but I am sure he would not object to having messages of love and kindness named after him. Let us keep the holy man in our minds, and so refuse to call by his name the frightful objects displayed in some of the windows at this time.

Very little is known of St. Valentine except that he was a bishop and lived in Rome less than three hundred years after the dear Lord Jesus was on earth.

In those early days, when Christianity had not been in the world very long, the Romans used to put to death the people who owned that they were Christians. These people were called martyrs, and St. Valentine was one of these early martyrs.

In ancient days the Romans held a great feast every February, called "Lupercalia," which was in honor of a god whose name was Lupercus. When Rome was first founded it was surrounded by an immense wilderness in which were great hordes of wolves. So the Romans thought they must have a god to watch over and protect the shepherds with their flocks, so they called this god Lupercus, from the Latin word, *lupus,* a wolf. As they kept special feast days for other gods, they must have one for Lupercus since so much depended on his protection. When the country about the city became cleared up, and there was no longer danger from the wolves, they still kept up the feast day in honor of Lupercus.

One of the amusements on this great day was the placing of young women's names in a box to be drawn out by the young men. Each young man accepted the girl whose name he drew, as his lady love.

The Christian priests, wishing the people to forget about their heathen gods, yet not liking to do away with all their sports, kept the feast, but called it St. Valentine's Day, because the good bishop's birthday occurred about that time, and they also wished to remind the people of his holy life. Not satisfied with this, they went even further, and changed the nature of the festival by putting the names of saints and martyrs into the boxes to be drawn out. The name that each one drew was called his or her "valentine," and the holy life of that person was to be imitated throughout the year.

But as time went on the custom gradually changed again, and the names put into the boxes were those of living people instead of dead saints, and these became the "valentines." From this custom grew quite naturally the practice of sending out messages of kind remembrance.

It was at one time the custom in England for people to call out, "Good-morning, 'tis St. Valentine's Day," and the one who succeeded in saying this first expected a present from the one to whom it was said, so this made things pretty lively on St. Valentine's Day.

Nowadays people have learned to make these little tokens both cheap and pretty, and when you see one that can be bought for a few cents you would hardly think that it went through five or six hands before it became the dainty gift which you buy for your friend.

BY QUILL PEN OR WIRE, IT'S STILL
A VALENTINE

By Frederick Gruin

Long ago, in the days of the goose quill, there began the custom of composing valentines for Feb. 14, a custom now carried on by the super-color press and the telegraph key. Between the scratch of feather pens and the roar of printing machines much has happened to the valentine. Once the fancy of a select few, it now belongs to the masses. First an exercise with ink and paper, then with various stuffs from straw to satin, it has been also a vehicle for gush and guffaws, the while it has borne the best of sentiment.

Yet, compare bygone valentines with those of today. Note the persistence of certain symbols: the valentine cannot escape hearts and flowers and cupids. Above all, in changing phrase and print, read the same old, ever fresh refrain— "I am thine, please be mine." Essentially, what difference between these verses, separated by a century and a quarter?—

A Magic Spell will bind me fast
And make me love you to the last.

Let Cupid then your Heart incline
To take me for your Valentine—

and—

CUPID'S WINGS ARE NOT SO FAST;
I'D RATHER SEND A WIRE.
THEN I'M SURE MY VALENTINE WILL
SET YOUR HEART ON FIRE.

From its hand-made origin, more than 200 years ago, to its machine-made present the valentine has evolved through different phases, each reflecting something of the contemporary taste and manners. What gallant sent and what damsel received the first valentine card is no more known than what St. Valentine (there were at least five of them) gave his name to St. Valentine's Day. The early Christians seem to have adapted for Feb. 14 the pagan festival of the Lupercalia, in which young men drew lots from helmets to find sweethearts for the coming year. The sainted sweethearts' day took firm hold on folkways, out of which emerged the valentine recognizable as the ancestor of today's.

Those first missives were true labors of love, the products of patient and nimble fingers wielding pen and knife. A venerable few of them are still preserved. One of the oldest, dated 1710, is in the collection of Frank House Baer of Cape May, N.J. It is a small card of German origin; its faded India ink conjures up the vision of a bewigged youth, his sword, feathered hat and velvet coat laid aside, composing perhaps by candlelight in a tavern. His dagger cuts leaves and tulips in the parchment, his goose quill draws flaming hearts and turtle doves. "Liebes Voegelein"—"dear little bird"—he apostrophizes in verse, "greet my beloved a thousand times."

The valentine long remained a luxury reserved for those with a flair for rhyme and design. Nor did everyone have the patience of the colonial American girls who cut scallops and hearts in

wheel-shaped pieces of paper, then penned sweet sentiments in
fine script from end to end of their handiwork. Or the skill and
time of the New England tar who passed spare hours on long
voyages either inking or block-printing on linen a pattern of
flowers, cupids, nymphs and verses like:

> *As sure as Grapes grows on the vine,*
> *I drew thee for my Valentine.*

Valentines for the masses had to wait upon the invention of
lithography, that late eighteenth, early nineteenth century child
of the Industrial Revolution. Once designs could be easily repro-
duced, stationers' shops did a rushing business on Feb. 14.

A refined elegance pervaded the best of those first litho-
graphed love tokens. Along with the traditional flowers and
doves they displayed demure maids, with church spires (wed-
ding hints) in the distance. Blushing, gentle-faced creatures they
are, in full skirts and bonnets, often clinging to frock-coated
beaus, or shyly pining for someone absent, thus:

> *Sever'd from thee, in memory I trace*
> *Thy form, the well-known features of thy face. . . .*
> *On recollection, you'll perhaps divine*
> *The name of her who sends this Valentine.*

Another lot of contemporaries—the sweepers, servants and
generally less heroic folk—preferred to copy on gilt-edged paper
verses from pamphlets known as "Polite Valentine Writers." In
such writers could be found proper sentiments for "all trades
and professions" from bricklayer to staymaker. The pungent
fishmonger thus expressed his emotion:

> *You are the girl I take delight in,*
> *Much more than haddock, smelts or whiting.*

Beneath the polite veneer flourished an amazingly different
type of valentine, the "comic," sharp in caricature and unkind
in humor. It lampooned "disagreeable old maids," the skinny,

the fat, the conceited, the smug and the dandified, mincing no words. The demure maid could also send this verse:

> *Dear Sir, you're so foppish,*
> *And scented so fine;*
> *I'll not have a man monkey*
> *For my Valentine.*

After a period of comparative simplicity the more genteel valentine went into the lush and long Victorian era. Machines were developed to emboss and trim paper in lace patterns. From flat cards the taste ran to folders, and people accustomed to over-stuffed parlors liked dried petals, leaves, straw, humming bird feathers, silk, satin, plush, velvet, spun glass, celluloid, shells, seaweed and perfumes on their valentine messages.

In the Seventies and Eighties lace valentines and silk fringes had a heyday. On the delicate embossed paper filigree of these cards appear the eternal cherubs, with roses and swans framing young men and maids. Often the lace is gilded. Usually its fragile whiteness is set off by bits of colored paper, representing forget-me-nots, lilies of the valley, violets, butterflies and birds. Through the lace can be seen lavender or yellow inner pages inscribed with such devotion as:

> *I may wander over land and sea,*
> *Pass many days away from thee,*
> *Yet my heart can never rove*
> *From thee, my own, my only love.*

When the little British Queen had finished her long reign fashions changed. Around 1910 leading American publishers, beset by competition of stilted romantic foreign cards and by cheap and vulgar comics, introduced a plain style which embodied native ideas of friendliness, sentiment and humor. Caustic cartoons were ruled out. "Thee and thou" gave way to Yankee terms, as in the card displaying a heart-shaped piece of sandpaper and this plaint:

Gee, but I like you, oh so much
I fain would hold your hand,
And win your promise to be mine,
But I haven't got the sand!

Curiously enough, in the post-war years of jazz, short skirts, bobbed hair and cynical disillusionment came a revival of ornamental effects. A modified revival, of course, with studied effort to avoid slush, like the card showing a starry-eyed little woman carrying a bouquet, wearing a scalloped yellow skirt, standing on a pink heart and saying: "Valentine greetings to a married man from the lady who married him!" Or the picture of a Negro girl, flashing a diamond ring and warning:

Ashes to Ashes, Dust to Dust,
If you won't be ma Valentine, I'se gonna bust,
Bust right out in an awful wail—
Look out, honey, I'se a Wild Female!

And so down to 1939, wherein St. Valentine's Day calls for 80,000,000 cards that run the gamut of tastes from the flippant to the saccharine; they are sent by all members of the family from babe to grandparent. Add 200,000 or so valentine telegrams, at 25 cents each, with words by Western Union, wired anywhere in the United States. Throw in a good number of valentines sung for customers over the telephone by the telegraph company's dulcet-voiced operators.

Still on greeting cards and telegrams appear the familiar symbols: hearts and cupids, ribbons, lace and scented sachets, loving couples and tender rhymes. There lingers the post-war trick of coating sentiment with banter. Ardent swains at Dartmouth, for instance, like a card showing a war-painted Indian (the college emblem) with tomahawk poised over a pretty squaw's head and threatening: "Be my Valentine or I'll scalp you!"

PARTIES, GAMES, AND OTHER ACTIVITIES

A HAPPILY-EVER-AFTER PARTY

By Hazel Carter Maxon

Oh, Valentine's is the very best day
For romance and fun and laughter,
So come along and we'll show you the way
To live HAPPILY-EVER-AFTER.

This invitation is written on a red cardboard heart and two white pages, to represent a story-book, and bearing the words HAPPILY-EVER-AFTER pasted near the bottom. You can make it into a poster-form if you prefer that form to an individual invitation. It bids your guests to a February party which is mostly a Valentine affair but includes a romantic pantomine to honor Lincoln's and Washington's birthdays.

DECORATIONS: Make a wall-border of red paper hearts which dangle from gold string hung in loops. Make crepe-paper hearts, cut double, to fit over the lights and let gold-cardboard arrows shower down from the hearts by attaching them to gold strings. At the door, where the guests enter the room, nail to the wall a Cupid's Mail Box made of a box with a slit and covered with silver paper. This is to be used in the first game.

DOROTHY DIX CONTEST: Give the girls note-paper and envelopes and ask each of them to write a love problem and mail it to Dorothy Dix by dropping it in the Cupid Mail Box. A "postman" then collects the letters and delivers one to each man who must write the solution. For the best letter and answer award a prize.

PATRIOTIC SENTENCES: Divide the group into two teams and line up each team at opposite sides of the room. Place blackboard and chalk, or a large sheet of paper and crayon, as a goal for each team. When a leader fires a toy cap pistol the first player in each line must run to his goal and write LINCOLN as the start of the patriotic sentence for his team. He then runs back and hands the chalk, or crayon, to the next player in line on his team who quickly runs to the board and makes up a second word to add to the sentence. The fun of the game is not knowing what your neighbor is going to write, so have no sentences planned.

The object of the game is to see which side can complete the best sentence in the quickest time. It is more difficult and exciting than it sounds because, besides speed, it requires that players add words which will give the sentence sense. For example, it is a good idea for the second player to add a verb to get the sentence off to a good start. A good sentence written by ten players might read: "Lincoln liked to swap stories with his friends and neighbors." (You might play on with a sentence beginning with WASHINGTON.)

CUPID'S DICE FORTUNES: Take square white boxes and spot them dice-fashion with red hearts. Let each one roll the dice to see which of these fortunes he rolls:

> *One* will take a tropical trip
> *Two* find romance aboard a ship
> *Three* in marriage will make a slip
> *Four* will inherit money galore
> *Five* will go single evermore
> *Six* will choose mates—two, three, four!

SECRET LOVE LETTERS: Give each person a sheet of paper and a bottle of "ink" which is merely lemon juice. Ask supper partners to write love letters to each other. They exchange letters and by holding the letter over a lighted candle (individual tiny candles are stuck in heart-shaped cup cakes at each plate) the writing magically appears!

BASKET TOSS: Divide your group into two teams and ask each team to sit in a semi-circle on the floor, so that all are equally distant from a market basket in the center. Decorate the handle of the basket with a red, white and blue bow if you wish to make it festive. Give one team a deck of playing cards with blue backs and the other team a deck with red backs. The cards are then dealt so that each player receives six cards.

One player from each team tries to throw his card into the basket, then the next player has a turn and so on. When each player has tossed his card, the cards in the basket are taken out, counted and the team score is posted on a sheet of paper on the wall.

The second round, each player must toss two cards at a time and the third time around each player tosses three cards at a time. Then the final scores are added to see which team has tossed the greatest number of cards into the basket.

MARRIED COUPLES' CHARADES is good fun. Ask each married couple present to re-enact their own engagement. Give a prize for the funniest.

SUPPER TABLE DECORATIONS: Red paper hearts on lace paper doilies, with a centerpiece of roses. The table is lighted by red candles.

SUPPER MENU: Chicken Canapé (toast hearts spread with minced chicken seasoned with curry powder and melted butter and decorated with narrow strips of pimiento); . . . Cheese Salad (molded heart-shape); . . . Bavarian Pineapple Cream with red cherry; . . . Heart Shaped Red and White iced Cakes; . . . and Coffee.

FAMOUS ROMANCES: To match partners for the first dance, give each girl a heart with the name of a famous woman, and give each man a heart with that of a famous man on it. Choose such well-known partners as Napoleon and Josephine, Romeo and Juliet, Franchot Tone and Joan Crawford, Jack and Jill, and Antony and Cleopatra. Ask each hero to find his heroine.

SWEETHEART DANCE: Each man writes a two-line verse asking for a dance. These are collected and tied in a large red tissue-paper bag which hangs from the ceiling. Each person is given a toy bow-and-arrow (which can be taken home for favors). All line up on one side of the room to shoot at the bag. When someone hits the bag and the verses scatter to the floor, the girls rush out and each grabs a verse-invitation. A girl reads her verse aloud and the author steps up to claim her for the dance.

A VALENTINE PARTY

BY THEDA PEARSON HEDDEN

A highly effective valentine party was enjoyed by my rural school of all grades. Each child made a headband of white paper, and when he won a contest, he pasted on his headband a small red heart. While the upper grades were composing telegrams, using a letter in "valentines" for beginning each word, the younger children were outlining on paper a large heart; then, with a small heart for a pattern, each tried to see who could draw the most small hearts within the large one.

Next, all played valentine archery, using graduated hearts drawn on the blackboard for a target and bits of plastic clay for missiles. In another contest, prizes of hearts were given to those making the best animals or men, using hearts for bodies, legs, and heads. Valentines which I had prepared for the children were suspended from a string across the room, just a little higher than the children's heads. Each pupil in turn was blindfolded and given a pair of blunt scissors, with which he cut down a valentine. The party ended with the distribution of valentines from the class valentine box.

VALENTINE GAMES

By Alice Hoffman

Cupid Says Ditto.—Someone is chosen to be Cupid to start the game. All the other players sit or stand about him. He makes a statement, such as "My heart is stabbed by love's dart," and follows it with a ridiculous pantomime action. All the others must imitate his gestures without laughing or smiling. The first to laugh or smile must exchange places with Cupid.

Heartstrings.—Two captains choose sides. The two sides should be equal in number. Each captain is given a shoestring. A large number of heart cut-outs, with holes punched through them, have previously been hidden about the room. When the signal to begin is given, all the players except the captains go in search of hearts. As soon as a player finds a heart he runs to the captain of his side and hands it to him. The captain puts it on his string. The hearts must be taken to the captains one at a time. The game goes merrily on for a set period or until all of the hidden hearts have been found. The side having the most hearts on its heartstring is the winner.

HOMEMADE VALENTINES

By Clifford Cook

My pupils were delighted to receive valentines which I had made as follows. From red construction paper I cut for each valentine two medium-sized hearts. In the center of one heart I cut a small, heart-shaped opening. With a sewing machine threaded with red thread I stitched the two hearts together, running the seam around the edge. Through the opening I filled the valentine with candy motto hearts, sealed the opening with a tiny heart cut from white paper, and then wrote an appropriate message on each valentine.

USING OLD VALENTINES

By Frances Schuetze

Old valentines provided a variety of material for our primary projects. Some of the figures were ready for immediate use; others had to be cut out and have cardboard props fastened to the backs. Figures of children in old-fashioned costumes were used on the sand table to depict the scene of "When Grandmother Was a Wee Girl"; Dutch figures made our study of Holland realistic; and similar uses were found for other characters.

The lace, hearts, verses, and other usable parts were utilized in art class for the making of new valentines. Some of the larger pictures were made into puzzles for seat work. Since most of the pupils had saved the valentines that they received the previous year, we had an adequate supply for all projects in which we cared to use them.

A VALENTINE BOX

By Corinne Kidd

Secure from the grocer a corrugated box in the size desired. Be sure to get one with four overlapping flaps. Two of these sides, partly closed to the desired angle, will form the sloping roof. With a sharp knife or scissors shape the end pieces so that they will meet the sloping roof evenly. It is wise to use the first end piece (triangle piece with the top cut off) as a pattern for cutting the other end piece. You now have the roof with an opening for letters between the sloping roof pieces. Use passepartout tape to bind the edges.

Cover the four walls of the box with white crepe paper. This may be tacked in place with pins or thumbtacks. Use red crepe paper to cover the sloping roof, letting the lower edge hang over the walls and the upper edge slip down into the opening. These ends should be pasted down securely inside the box.

A flat piece of cardboard with a chimney made of cardboard and glued to it is used as a cover for the opening. The cardboard and the chimney are also covered with crepe paper, and the chimney should be marked with white chalk to represent bricks. The children lift the chimney and cardboard to put in their valentines. Heart-shaped doors and windows complete the house.

Celebrations for
St. Patrick's Day

PLAYS

THE POWER THAT WAS PATRICK *

By Mary Stewart Sheldon

Time: 400 a.d.

Five Acts—4 scenes

Act 1—*In Scotland, outside* Patrick's father's *castle. His father was a Roman noble and the scenery and costumes should suggest this. There is a massive door in the wall of the castle; vines grow over it; small trees and bushes are on either side.*

Act 2—*In Ireland, bare hill-side, rough bush at right, sheep painted upon canvas placed in front of back-drop to left.*

Ten years pass.

Act 3—*Same hill-side, evening.*

Act 4—*Druids' Circle. This is merely part of mountain with high stone pillar in center back, ornamented with gold and silver, and on either side of it, forming a semi-circle, smaller, squat stones. These must all be on painted canvas so they can topple, or "crumble."*

Act 5—*Seashore. Large rock and bushes to left, small rocks at right, sea-scene painted on back-drop.*

The chief incidents in this play are taken from traditional history and some of the phrases used by the Bard *and by* Patrick *are true quotations.*

---

* Where no admission is charged, this play may be produced free. Otherwise, written permission must be secured by sending a fee of $5.00 to Mrs. Raymond Sheldon, Chestnut Ridge Road, Mt. Kisco, N.Y.

CHARACTERS

Printed in the order in which they appear on stage.

PATRICK, *predominating quality a kind of joyousness even in danger or surrounded by hardships. He is about twelve years old in first act, fifteen in second, twenty-five in third and fourth, and ninety in last.*

CEDRIC, PATRICK'S *boy friend in Scotland*

PATRICK'S FATHER, *a Noble*

CEDRIC'S FATHER, *a farmer*

5 IRISH PIRATES

COLIN, *Patrick's friend in Ireland, much poorer than Cedric and more wistful.*

COLIN'S TWO SISTERS *and* YOUNGER BROTHER

ANGEL

THREE SMALL CHILDREN

CHIEFTAIN DICHEI

THREE GUARDS *in armor*

MILCHU IN DALARIA, *Druid Priest and Patrick's master*

4 DRUID PRIESTS

IRISH KING

KING'S BARD (*He also appears before curtain before third act; this is his first appearance on stage.*)

Three or more IRISH CHIEFTAINS

PAGES

MAIDENS

MINSTREL

ANIMALS: Two rabbits, deer, birds, wolf, SNAKES.

　(*These are all important. They may be painted on flat cardboard and managed with wires from above, if possible, otherwise from the sides. The Snakes must be manipulated from sides. Bird notes may be imitated by a whistle containing water.*)

ACT 1—SCOTLAND

Enter PATRICK *and* CEDRIC. *Both boys are dressed in tunics which fall from shoulders to knees which are bare.* PATRICK *has a white tunic, a crimson belt with a golden dagger thrust through it, golden sandals, a band of gold or crimson around his forehead and around his neck, hung by a crimson cord, he carries a small silver whistle.* CEDRIC'S *tunic is of unbleached muslin, his belt of brown leather, a brown band around his forehead, brown sandals. The boys are talking eagerly and with extreme friendliness.*

PATRICK. Are you sure it was a white fox, Cedric? Perhaps it only looked like that in the moonlight.

CEDRIC. No, I am positive. It glistened like silver, but its eyes were red and cruel. As I watched, hidden behind the bushes, I saw it pounce upon the fattest duck in the poultry yard and carry it off squawking, with its blood dripping upon the stones.

PATRICK. Oh dear! That was the mother-duck, the best one we have. Her twelve eggs were almost ready to hatch—and now they are cold. Cedric, (*impressively*) I must find that fox and make friends with him. Then he will obey me and leave the poultry alone.

CEDRIC. Take care he doesn't spring at you first! Oh, I know, Patrick, there hasn't been an animal around here yet who wouldn't follow you! Even the wild ones come when you whistle. I don't see nor hear a single one now, but there may be some hiding. Blow your whistle and see.

(PATRICK *puts his whistle to his lips and blows, softly at first, but gradually it becomes loud and clear. From the bushes two rabbits hop out to him; birds appear and sing on the vines upon the castle wall; and a deer's head with antlers looks out from between the branches of a tree.*)

CEDRIC. What fun! I wish I could do that! Wasn't it grand in school today when the teacher was asking questions none of us could answer and you blew your whistle ever so softly? Two big turtles walked right up the aisle. Three frogs hopped onto the teacher's desk, and a bat circled around his head. He forgot to ask us any more questions, didn't he!

(*Both boys laugh and the animals, frightened, disappear.*)

CEDRIC. Now let me try and blow your whistle. I don't see why I can't call the animals too.

(PATRICK *takes the cord with whistle off over his head and hands it to* CEDRIC *who whistles awkwardly several times. Nothing happens. He hands it back to* PATRICK, *who blows once and again the animals appear.*)

PATRICK. I know what I'll do. My mother expects me for supper right off, but I'll be a little late and go now to the woods by the poultry yard. It's just the time to find that fox. Goodbye, Cedric, I'll see you tomorrow.

(*He runs off at left and the rabbits hop after him. The other animals disappear.*)

CEDRIC. (*Calling.*) Goodnight, Patrick! I hope the old fox doesn't bite your nose off!

(CEDRIC *turns and goes off to right. The birds are still chirping in the vines, they cease only when the fathers enter. They are dressed very much like the boys except that their tunics are long and the* NOBLE'S *costume is as great a contrast to the* FARMER'S *in richness of color and material as* PATRICK'S *was to* CEDRIC'S. *Both wear short beards. The* FARMER *may carry a rake. They are much disturbed.*)

FARMER. Ah my lord, this is bad news. Pirates' ships you say near our coast? Did they weigh anchor or did they seem to be sailing on toward the south of Scotland?

NOBLE. Alas, they were weighing anchor. I could see their fierce faces as they stood upon the deck. They were pointing toward this castle. I fear they plan to attack us here. There is no time to lose. Go, call my tenants, your neighbors. Tell them to bring their weapons—bows and arrows, daggers and spears— and stand ready to defend this spot tonight. Be sure your boy, Cedric, stays at home. No young person must venture out until these wild Irish have sailed away. Patrick is sure to be within the castle now, for it is past supper time and he never forgets that.

FARMER. Nor Cedric either. I could swear that both boys are eating their porridge this minute. I will hasten and call the tenants together.

NOBLE. Do so, and I will see that my servants are armed and on guard. This is bad, bad! No good comes to us from Irish shores.

(*He opens great door and closes it after him. Exit* FARMER, *right. Stage grows darker. Forms of* PIRATES *steal in from left. They have red and green handkerchiefs knotted in caps on their heads and around necks, black painted moustaches, long knives. They are very fierce and terrifying.*)

1ST PIRATE. (*In stage whisper.*) This is the spot. The King's Bard foretold we would find great riches here. "Treasure to make all Ireland shine with glory," he promised.

2ND PIRATE. Shall we steal into the castle and carry off the chests of gold we are sure to find there?

3RD PIRATE. No, no, it would take many a weary hour to find a Scotchman's hiding place for his treasure. We would lose our lives before the hunt was over. We'd better just take what first we can lay our hands on swiftly.

1ST PIRATE. That's what the Bard said: what we met first would be the treasure we're seeking. Shhh—someone is coming!

(*They crouch down silently.* PATRICK *enters from left.*)

PATRICK. (*Speaking to himself.*) The fox wasn't there at all. I must go again before dawn.

(*He goes to the door to open it and the* PIRATES *stand up.*)

1ST PIRATE. A goodly lad, he would bring a fine price in the slave-market.

3RD PIRATE. Yes, yes, he may be the very treasure we seek.

ALL. Fine! Let's take him! Quick!

(*They spring upon* PATRICK *who draws his dagger. They tear it from him, bind a cloth over his mouth, tie his hands behind him and drag, or carry, him off stage.*)

CURTAIN

ACT 2

Scene—Bare hill-side with a few scrubby bushes at right.

PATRICK *is alone. He is dressed literally in rags, barelegged, with bits of rags tied on to form sandals. One arm is bound with rough bloody bandage. His hair is disheveled, his face pale and dark lines are painted under his eyes. He carries a shepherd's crook. He is evidently half-starved but looks cheerful in spite of it and still carries his whistle on the crimson cord around his neck. He blows a few notes upon it softly and the head of a wolf appears over the bushes to the right.* PATRICK *walks over to it and pats its head as he speaks.*

PATRICK. It was trouble you brought me last night, Brother Wolf, but sure you didn't mean no harm. Whist—I am speaking the Irish tongue to you, the Gallic I have learned these years from my friend Colin. (*A hulloo from a boy's voice sounds off stage—presumably from down the valley.*) There he is now, and it's food he'll be bringing me I swear—good lad. My Master, the Druid Priest, would like to starve me into bowing before his hateful old stones, only Colin keeps me alive now.

(*He forms a trumpet with his two hands and hulloos through them. Then he turns to the wolf again.*)

PATRICK. It's quiet you must be now, Brother Wolf, and don't, don't let me hear one whimper of a growl out of you while Colin is here. Good beastie!

(*The wolf apparently crouches down behind the bushes and a boy appears at left. He wears blue peasant's smock and short breeches, all shabby, but whole. He carries a jug of milk in one hand and a crust of bread in the other.*)

COLIN. I couldn't come sooner. The cow had strayed over the moor and after I found her I had to milk her. Are you famished, lad?

PATRICK. Bless you, Colin! (*He takes jug and crust.*) Food first, talk afterward.

(*While he drains the jug and bites ravenously into the crust, COLIN is gazing at PATRICK'S arm in horror.*)

COLIN. What have they done to you, Patrick? Has your wicked old master who prays to stocks and stones given your blood as an offering to one of his gods? I know he threatened to if you lost another sheep,—but they are all here and the wolf has gone. (*The wolf's head appears again over the bush.*) May the saints defend us, here he is again!

(*He starts to run, but PATRICK stops him, laughing.*)

PATRICK. No, no, my friend, you don't understand. The wolf is my friend too, my brother. He didn't know that a week ago when he carried off a lamb. He knows it now. But it was on account of him that I got these wounds. You see my master is a timid soul in spite of his grand title of Chief Druid Priest and his name of Milchu in Dalaria. He drove along the road last night in his golden chariot as I was taking the flock home. As luck would have it, Brother Wolf was walking beside me. Milchu swore that I must be a friend of Evil Spirits to have a wolf for a companion. He commanded me to kill the animal, otherwise he would have me tortured. I refused—well, you see what happened.

(*Children are heard crying, "Patrick! Colin!" in agonized voices.*)

COLIN. My sisters' voices, something must be wrong! (*He calls.*) Hulloo! Here we are, on the hill-side!

(*Two GIRLS and a little boy enter. They are dressed as Irish peasants. The* Girls *have gay handkerchiefs over their heads tied under their chins, short striped skirts, bodices laced over white chemises. Little boy wears short breeches and smock. All have bare legs and sandals. They rush in, all talking at once, wringing their hands and crying.*)

1st Girl. Patrick, Patrick, Milchu is calling the Druids from near and far to come to his Circle tonight as the moon rises! He says there will be a sacrifice before the stones of a boy who walks with wolves— Ah Patrick, he means—*you!*

(*All, including* Colin, *cluster around* Patrick, *clinging to him, sobbing.*)

2nd Girl. We'll never see you again. Nothing can save you now. There are soldiers on all the roads, the people are pouring in to see—alas! alas!

(Patrick *stands very straight and quiet, looking over their heads.*)

Patrick. Milchu in Dalaria swore that if I would worship his great, cold stone he would let me live—

All. Oh do, do, Patrick! Worship the stone, it can't hurt you, and we will keep you with us! Please! Please!

Colin. Why should you not, laddie? We don't understand.

Patrick. (*Speaking slowly and quietly.*) Listen and try to understand. The wolf was wild and fierce. When he heard my whistle and my voice he became quiet and my friend. He will not harm the sheep again. While I lived on these mountains under the sun and stars, or under the rain and snow, I knew Some One was always with me, Some One so strong that he gave me courage and I prayed to him. Your mother told me his name, he is— Lord God Almighty, Maker of heaven and earth. I pray to him many times a day and often in the night. He gives me power to conquer evil with goodness, to tame the wild wolf, to make him my brother. He is strong enough to shatter the power of Milchu in Dalaria—I do not know how. So I must trust him. He will never forsake me. Even if this night I am slain before the Druid's altar, he will be with me. Go now, my dearest friends. If you are found with me harm will come to you also. Milchu has tortures you know not of.

(*He touches his bloody arm, and with bowed heads the children leave, sobbing as they go. It grows dark and* PATRICK *kneels, burying his head in his hands. Suddenly, in a bright light, an* ANGEL *stands before him. He lifts his face and gazes at her.*)

ANGEL. Patrick, the Lord is with you. Fear neither the soldiers who watch for you at night, nor the fierce Druids who seek you by day. Take the path down the other side of the mountain and walk onward to the sea. From there you will sail homeward to Scotland. He has given His angels charge over you, to watch you in all your ways.

CURTAIN

Act 3

The KING'S BARD—*an old man with long, white beard, dressed in flowing robes and carrying a harp, steps in front of the curtain and relates the following.*

BARD. Ten years have passed. Patrick found a ship sailing for Scotland and reached home safely. Then he traveled in France and Italy, learning all he could about the Christian church. He was made a Bishop, and offered gold and jewels by those whose lives were transformed by his teaching. But he refused riches, and, dressed as a simple monk, he traveled, preaching and singing beautiful songs as he went. But he kept having a dream of Irish children calling to him, "Oh holy youth, come back and walk with us once more!" Although warned that the power of the Druids had spread over Ireland and that his life would be taken at once if he returned, he sailed there and walked to the hill-side where he had tended the sheep ten years ago. His friends have married, they and their children are on the hill-side.

CURTAIN

Scene—Same hill-side, powdered with snow. COLIN *is there, also his two sisters who are now grown up and married, and their children—three or four of them. The women are dressed in the same manner as in the second act, but their skirts are longer, their hair pinned back, and, as it is cold, they wear shawls and scarves.* COLIN *has a moustache to show his age. The children are in gaily colored cottons and wear bits of shawls over their heads.*

ONE CHILD. Oh, we are so cold! Why can't we have a fire in our cabin and cook some hot porridge, Mother?

1ST MOTHER. Listen, poor wee ones, and I will tell you again why we must shiver. On the top of yonder mountain a high bonfire is laid. Look, you can see that black pile from here. That is near the Druids' Circle where the King, the nobles and the Druids are meeting tonight. The people, for hundreds of miles around, have been forbidden to light a fire for a day and night until his great fire shines out as a signal. Run now and gather up sticks so that we may light a little fire here at dawn and warm ourselves.

(*The children run and pick up sticks, laying a fire.*)

COLIN. (*To his sisters.*) Yes, we will have our fire at dawn, but that will not keep us from shivering with terror. When the great fire is lighted that will be a signal for—you know!

2ND MOTHER. Hush, Colin, don't speak so loud. The children are terrified already.

1ST MOTHER. No, they are so busy picking up sticks they cannot hear. Tell us, Colin, is it just a horrible fear? When the King's fire is lighted and the Druids show their power, what will happen?

COLIN. (*Speaking slowly.*) You remember Patrick, our good friend whom the Druid priest, Milchu, tried to murder?

BOTH MOTHERS. Of course, of course. Go on!

COLIN. Well, Milchu in Dalaria is the Chief Druid Priest in all Ireland now. Each year he has grown more cruel. He is in charge of this great meeting. Nobles and chieftains have come from all over Ireland to worship his gods and see the proof of their power that he has promised. To please his gods he has announced that he will first throw into the fire all strangers who have dared travel these paths during the last weeks. His spies are watching for any chance traveler. No wonder the hill paths have been deserted. But see—there is a man climbing the hill now, coming here, and he looks familiar. He is—can it be?—Ah joy!

(*He rushes out and comes back with* PATRICK, *his arm around his shoulders.* PATRICK *is dressed in a coarse brown robe with a hood at back, a rope for his girdle. Otherwise he is almost unchanged. In spite of the years he still looks young and gay and the dark lines have gone from under his eyes.*)

MOTHERS. Rushing to him—Patrick, is it really yourself? After all these years—where, oh where have you been?

(*The children drop their sticks and circle around him wonderingly. One touches his robe and he takes its hand and holds it.*)

PATRICK. Dear, dear friends. Always when I traveled in strange lands I had dreams of these children crying to me to come back here and help them, to tell them about the God I found on these mountains.

COLIN. And surely they need you, Patrick. Such horrors the Druid priests have brought to us.—Oh!—in the joy of seeing you I had forgotten— Your life is not safe here for one moment! You must hide, dear friend, for the King's guards are out now searching for all travelers, to burn them in the great fire which the Druids will kindle at dawn on yonder hill-top. That is why we shiver here—with cold and with terror. Hide quickly!

PATRICK. Hide, did you say? Ah no, old friend, I am here to help, not to hide. But the children are cold, let us first light the little fire they have laid and warm us all.

1ST MOTHER. You don't understand. It has been commanded that no fire shall be lighted until the Druids' fire on yonder hill shines out at dawn.

PATRICK. (*Scornfully.*) Druids' Fire! To bring horror and blood-shed! I came back to Ireland to bring joy and peace, and this little fire shall be the sign of the great glory which will one day shine over the land.

(*They draw back, bewildered, while* PATRICK *lights the fire. This can be done safely and effectively with "cold fire." The children laugh and run to it warming their hands, while the older ones gaze in wonder which turns to terror as they see the King's guards coming up the hill. They enter at left, led by* CHIEFTAIN DICHEI. *He is very fierce, dressed in armor, his visor open, a drawn dagger in his hand.*)

CHIEFTAIN DICHEI. What does this mean? A fire lighted before the signal? Ah, I see—a traveler is responsible for this. He is needed to burn in the great fire yonder! Also I will take a child or two as a warning to you all to obey the King. (*He beckons to his men.*) Here you, catch those!

(*The children run screaming to hide behind* PATRICK.)

DICHEI. (*Advancing upon* PATRICK *with drawn dagger.*) Come immediately, and give us those children, or this dagger shall be in your heart!

(PATRICK *stands quietly, holding the hands of the children.* DICHEI *steps nearer, his dagger upraised over* PATRICK's *heart—then his arm is frozen stiff. He cannot move it.*)

DICHEI. (*Bewildered.*) What does this mean? I cannot move my arm, *it is frozen!* And this man—I took him to be a common traveler who would burn in the Druids' fire. I see him now shining with glory! (*He falls to his knees before* PATRICK.) *Who* are you? *Who* sent you here? I will follow you to the ends of the world.

PATRICK. (*Raising him.*) You have seen the glory which I too found on these mountains. Others shall see it also before the dawn breaks or the Druids' fire is lighted. Come, my new friend, let us go together to the King. I would meet with him and his nobles and the Druid priests. We must show them all that the glory of God Almighty is stronger than their evil spirits.

(PATRICK *and* DICHEI *go out together, followed by the guards shaking their heads. The group gazes after them with shining eyes.*)

CURTAIN

ACT 4

Druids' Circle: As described in beginning this is composed of one great stone in center and others at each side in semi-circles.

At extreme right and left two DRUIDS *are standing. They are dressed in long white robes, have white hair and beards and wear circlets of green around their foreheads and heads. They carry white wands. When the curtain rises the scene is still rather dark and mysterious. This feeling can be enhanced by weird music off stage played softly.*

Enter MILCHU IN DALARIA. *He is dressed as the other priests, but must be made more imposing. He is taller, older, fiercer. His voice is deep. The other priests step forward and bow before him.*

MILCHU. The dawn will soon break, are the victims in readiness?

1ST DRUID. They are bound, and at your signal for the fire to be lighted they will be thrown upon the flames.

2ND DRUID. Would it not give the gods pleasure if we should

first offer some victims *here,* before the prisoners are burnt to ashes?

MILCHU. A sharp knife, cut throats and blood upon the stones! Yes, that would be best. I might forget then the loss of the slave Patrick who was to have been a victim here ten years ago. His face laughs at me in my dreams. (*Aside.*) He brings terror to my soul, I know not why.

(*From without there is the sound of drums. Enter* KING, *purple cloak over his armor, crown upon his head, brown beard. With him is his* CHIEF BARD, *guards and nobles, as many as there is room for. They all bow before* MILCHU *and he and the* KING *stand together, talking, in the center of stage. The others speak with* DRUIDS *at sides.* BARD *stands at front, right side, watching.*)

KING. A fire was lighted yonder upon that hill, defying our command. I sent Chieftain Dichei to drag the villain here. He shall be our first victim to die.

BARD. (*Speaking toward audience.*) That little fire which shone like a mere spark, shall blaze forever in this land, unless this very night it be extinguished.

(*Enter* DICHEI *and* PATRICK.)

KING. (*Angrily.*) What does this mean? Is this the culprit who lighted the fire yonder? Why is he not bound?

MILCHU. (*Aside.*) A miracle! That is the slave Patrick of whom I have dreamed with terror. His hour has come. His blood shall flow and I shall be content.

(*The stage grows lighter and* PATRICK *steps to center, facing* KING.)

PATRICK. There was no need to bind me. I wish to come. Upon the hill around us I see thousands gathered, Irish folk waiting for your fire here to be lighted. Around us are your nobles, chieftains, Druids—prepared, when the flames rise, to shed blood and spread terror over this land. There is One stronger than all of you, stronger than these piles of stone you worship, One whose power can quench your flames and shed the light of joy upon this land.

DRUIDS. (*Starting forward.*) A test! A test! Try to prove your words before your blood streams upon our stones.

PATRICK. Call your demons of death and darkness, let them strive with light and life.

MILCHU. A challenge! Call the demons, let them come with blackness,—then lift the clouds so all may see our victims writhe in agony. (DRUIDS *give awful calls, they fall flat upon the ground before the stones, shrieking.*) Powers of darkness, demons of terror, fill the sky with your clouds! Prove to the watching throngs of Ireland that you are—*gods!*

(*There is a rumble of thunder, and the stage grows dark. Wails of terror are heard from the people off stage.*)

KING. (*Falls kneeling upon the stage with his head on the ground, as do all the others except* PATRICK.) Enough, enough! We tremble, we are choked! We suffocate! Call the demons off, great priests! Milchu in Dalaria, bring us light!

MILCHU AND PRIESTS. (*Chanting, beseeching.*) Oh gods of stocks and stones, demons of force and fury, let light shine out! The people die of terror!

(*There is more thunder and the stage grows absolutely dark. Wails and cries of terror are heard.* KING *and* NOBLES *and* PRIESTS *moan and sob.*)

ALL. Light! Light! We are strangled, we cannot breathe, we perish! Help! Help!

(*There is more thunder. Then—a glimmer of light shines upon* PATRICK *who is standing in the center of the stage. He lifts his face heavenward and the light increases until, when he finishes his prayer, he stands in a stream of glory.*)

PATRICK. Lord God of Light, scatter these clouds of evil. Let thy goodness and strength and peace shine into these poor hearts.

(*All is quiet and the* KING *and others, still kneeling, lift their faces and look toward* PATRICK. *Birds are heard singing, the stage grows golden with light, like full sunshine. All rise and gaze dazed at* PATRICK.)

BARD. (*Speaking toward audience.*) This is the treasure I foretold, the one who would bring golden glory to Ireland.

(*The stones totter, shake, and fall with a crash to the ground. The four* DRUIDS *give a loud shriek of terror, and rush from stage.*)

MILCHU. The slave that I tortured—victorious! Never can I face him. I shall burn my home and throw myself into the flames!

(*He rushes out. The* KING, NOBLES *and* CHIEFS *kneel around* PATRICK *who stands quietly looking out to left, to the mountains. Voices are heard from there singing. The volume increases until it is a triumphant chorus, singing*

Holy! Holy! Holy! Lord God Almighty,
Early in the morning our song shall rise to Thee.
Holy! Holy! Holy! merciful and mighty,
God in three Persons, Blessed Trinity.

Holy! Holy! Holy! Though the darkness hide Thee,
Though the eye of sinful man Thy glory may not see;
Only Thou art holy, there is none beside Thee,
Perfect in power, in love and purity.)

CURTAIN

ACT 5

Scene—On seashore, represented by painting of sea on backdrop. There is a large rock at left upon which PATRICK *is seated. Behind it and beyond it are small trees and bushes. On the other side of stage are small rocks.* PATRICK *is now ninety years old. His hair beneath his head-dress is white. He is dressed in full Bishop's regalia, as gorgeous as possible, brocade robe, high-pointed golden headdress, a mitre, etc.*

PATRICK. (*Talking to himself.*) Nearly seventy years have I spent in this green isle. The power of the Druids has been broken, and my labor is nearly ended. How sweet and peaceful it is here. (*As he pauses and looks around him, birds twitter.*) But my life has not been all peaceful. Twelve times was I taken prisoner by the Druids, twelve times was I loaded with chains and thrown into a dungeon,—and twelve times the angel of the Lord delivered me. Soon shall I see him again, in all his glory, calling me to my eternal home.

(*From off stage there is the sound of voices calling* "Where is the Holy Father?" "We must find him!" "Father Patrick!")

PATRICK. Here, here I am, my children!

(*Enter maidens and pages, two nobles, the* KING, *with a white beard this time; a young* MINSTREL *with a much ornamented harp. They all bow before* PATRICK, *and some of the young people kneel beside his rock.*)

PATRICK. What can I do for you? You seem disturbed.

KING. Holy Father, we are wretched! You have brought us many blessings. The Druids with their frightful sacrifices have gone, services to God Almighty are held in every village and town in Ireland, but Oh Father, the curse which has come to us now is driving us from our homes!

PATRICK. Curse? I do not understand. (*They all try to explain and there is a chorus of* "Holy Father, the snakes!" "They are everywhere!" "Ouch, I thought that was one now but it is only a twig," "We live in terror!" "Help us!")

KING. Hush, all of you. Let the minstrel explain so that Father Patrick can hear.

(MINSTREL *steps forward.*)

MINSTREL. You see, Father, where you live here by the seashore you don't see the slimy creatures. But inland the snakes are ruining the land and terrifying the people. When I put my cloak around me this morning a green snake slid from it down my leg.

Another was in my shoe. My harp-strings often have small snakes coiled around them. The children walk on top of the hedges to school, for fear of the snakes sunning themselves in the road. They have grown so bold they sleep in the hens' nests—

ONE MAIDEN. Yes, we thought at first the eggs were hatching out into snakes there were so many there.

A PAGE. They crawl into the cushions on the chairs. My old grandmother sits on the branch of a tree all day, knitting, to escape them—

2ND PAGE. And mine too. The trees seem to bloom with old people who cannot run away, and babies' cradles are hung from the branches.

SMALL BOY. They ate my porridge this morning and curled up in the bowl.

ALL. Oh dear, dear Father, can you help us?

KING. Holy Father, there are stories that when you were a boy you called wild animals to you and tamed them; even the wolves followed you. How did you do it, Father, can you tell us?

PATRICK. Yes, friends, I can tell you.

(*Listeners smile and nod at one another.*)

PATRICK. It was by the power of music, shown through friendship. (*They look wonderingly at one another and one exclaims,* Friendship? Not for snakes!)

PATRICK. (*Smiling.*) Perhaps. Try first the music. (*To the* MINSTREL.) You can play a good tune I know. Let us see whether you cannot charm the creatures.

(MINSTREL *touches his harp and apparently plays upon it a gay Irish tune. He ends and looks around. Nothing happens.*)

PATRICK. No, that did not answer, did it? There is horror of the snakes in your heart and they knew it. Perhaps some of the maidens can do better. Sing, my children, sing some song of Ireland that you love.

(MAIDENS *sing* **Londonderry** *or any sweet Irish song.*

When it is finished they look around fearfully—nothing happens.)

PATRICK. That was a sweet tune, well sung; but all the time you were fearing the snakes. In the faraway of long ago I had a whistle. (*He puts his hand beneath his robe and brings out the whistle on the crimson cord.*) When the animals heard me blow this they knew I was their friend and they answered.

(He blows, softly, then loudly. There is the sound of rustling and dozens, if possible hundreds, of snakes appear. [They can be made out of paper, painted, and drawn in by strings from both sides. They must be large enough to look truly horrible.] All, except PATRICK, shriek and jump upon rocks, holding up their gowns, clinging to one another. The KING'S crown tips to one side, he lifts his robe high disclosing yellow stockings. The snakes pause in front of PATRICK and he stands up.)

PATRICK. (*Speaking to snakes.*) My friends, the land of Ireland is no place for the likes of you, but the sea around will make a convenient spot for your homes. Crawl you now into the sea and become good, happy eels. Crawl, my friends!

(In a mass they all crawl, many lifting their heads from which forked tongues protrude. With a splash they vanish into the sea. [This can be managed by having a low strip of painted water in front of the back-drop. This can be drawn aside when the snakes withdraw to the back and replaced when they are close to the back scene.] When they have vanished the KING, etc., exclaiming "Wonderful!" "Magical!" "A miracle!" "The Holy Father has saved Ireland!" step down from the rocks, and gaze with wonder at PATRICK. He blows his whistle again softly. Deers' heads look out from between the branches; rabbits hop in and stand beside him; birds appear [if possible to arrange they circle around PATRICK'S head]; a white fox comes from behind the big rock to left and stands beside him. The KING kneels before him. Then he rises

and addresses all his followers—pages, maidens, minstrel.)

KING. Behold the power which was Patrick. Let music sound, music which contains our love and the heavenly faith which the Holy Father has brought to Ireland.

(*The* MINSTREL *touches his harp,* ALL *sing.*)

Holy! Holy! Holy! Lord God Almighty,
Early in the morning our song shall rise to Thee;
Holy! Holy! Holy! merciful and mighty,
God in three persons, blessed Trinity.

Holy! Holy! Holy! Lord God Almighty,
All thy works shall praise thy name in earth, and sky, and sea;
Holy! Holy! Holy! merciful and mighty,
God in Three Persons, blessed Trinity.

(MINSTREL *steps to front of stage, at side, facing audience and signals for all to join in singing, with the cast, the last verse.*)

CURTAIN

FOOTPRINTS OF ANGELS *

A Folk Play for St. Patrick's Day

In One Act

BY OLIVE PRICE

CHARACTERS

OLD WOMAN, *Rosaleen's servant*
ROSALEEN, *a young Irish exile*
NORA, *her needle woman*
MICHAEL, *heir to Castle Mourne*

* For permission to produce, consult the author, 101 Delaware Ave., Freeport, L.I., N.Y.

ELLEN, *Rosaleen's friend*
DENNY, *Michael's older brother*
HUGH, *Michael's friend*
SAINT PATRICK

MINSTRELS, GUESTS

TIME: *Centuries ago.*

PLACE: *A cottage in the valley of the Braid in the shadow of Slemish "which rises magnificently from the moors."*

SCENE: *The interior of* ROSALEEN'S *cottage. It is a large bare room with a door, center-rear, that looks out across the moors to Slemish—mystic mountain of St. Patrick. Inside, there is a fire-place, down right, with a shelf upon which are a few silver plates and a hunting horn. Nearby is a bench and a tapestry-frame with an unfinished piece of work. There are also a table with accompanying benches, a heavy oak chest, and a couch strewn with leaves. Down left, is a door to an inner room.*

OLD WOMAN *is discovered at work at the tapestry-frame. From time to time, she looks anxiously toward the door—finally rises and stirs the contents of a kettle hanging over the fire—and at last goes to the door and opens it—murmuring, meanwhile, as she stands peering out into gathering evening.*

OLD WOMAN. Sure, stars of fire hang over Slemish—glittering swordpoints in the dusk—(*As she wraps her shawl more closely about her.*) Rosaleen—Rosaleen—Rosaleen! Come home this night!

NORA. (*Entering from the inner room, a dress of silver cloth over her arm.*) You see nothing of her?

OLD WOMAN. I see only the river and moors and the darkness lowering down upon them.

NORA. (*As the sound of a young girl's laughter is heard.*) That's Rosaleen—sure, and that's Rosaleen!

OLD WOMAN. (*Darkly.*) I think I should rather hear her cry —than laugh like that on the wind.

NORA. Her laughter makes strange music. It is high and clear and exultant. Sure, and Michael must know and be charmed by it.

OLD WOMAN. (*Leaving the doorway.*) Charmed he is, but frightened too. She is like a bird in his hand—but the moment he loosens his fingers—she's off on the wing and he is alone.

NORA. (*Sighing.*) Ah! Strange it is, too, when the heart o' her loves him.

OLD WOMAN. (*Stirring the fire.*) She shouldn't walk on Slemish. That mountain says dark things to her. (*Brooding.*) Dark and rather wonderful. . . .

NORA. It is the mountain of St. Patrick. Sure, and no evil could come of that.

OLD WOMAN. (*As* ROSALEEN *enters.*) Who can tell? Who can tell?

ROSALEEN. Ah! Good-evening it is to you both! (*She is a tall, slender girl who carries herself like a princess. Her hair is as dark as night.*)

OLD WOMAN. God's love! You are late. And this night the night of your nuptial dance.

ROSALEEN. The harp will play in this room as at Tara—the minstrels will sing to its music—and Michael will come from his Castle Mourne—

NORA. Sure, and gay it will be with your dancing here in your silver dress.

ROSALEEN. (*Crossing the room to her.*) It is ready?

NORA. (*Holding it up for her inspection.*) Aye. And how it will gleam in the candle-light!

ROSALEEN. (*Looking at it, stirred.*) It is the color of moonlight on Slemish. . . . Its rustle will be as the wind in the mountain grass when I move. . . . Its lace will lie softly on my throat like his lips lie on mine in his kiss.

OLD WOMAN. (*Laughing.*) Aye. Michael's kiss is a coveted one in this valley!

ROSALEEN. (*With a bit of defiance.*) It is not of Michael I speak.

OLD WOMAN. (*Incredulously.*) Not of Michael, my Rosaleen?

ROSALEEN. (*As the women exchange frightened glances.*) I talked with a man at St. Patrick's Well. He told me of another kiss. A kiss of love and light and legend.

NORA. (*Derisively.*) An old woman's tale as she sits in her dun or herds her geese!

ROSALEEN. No! No! This happened. This really happened and not so far away. (*As she sits at the table plainly enamoured by what she is telling.*) It was in County Monaghan—

OLD WOMAN. (*Lighting candles on the table.*) You should believe no tales that do not come from the High Kings at Tara.

ROSALEEN. I believe this somehow. It happened at a dance like we shall have this night. And the kiss was from a stranger.

OLD WOMAN. (*Sharply.*) Do not tell it! Do not dwell on it at all! It is something weird you've gathered from your wanderings on Slemish!

ROSALEEN. (*As knocking is heard on the door.*) I tell you there is truth in it! (*As she laughs exultantly again and moves toward the door.*) Perhaps the stranger's come!

NORA. (*Frightened.*) Sure, the mountain says dark things to her just as you were telling!

A MALE VOICE. (*From outside.*) The gods save you, Rosaleen!

OLD WOMAN. (*Relieved.*) It's the minstrels come with their music.

NORA. (*Devoutly.*) Praise be to Heaven's name!

ROSALEEN. The gods save you, good friends! Come in! Come in!

(*Three* MINSTRELS *enter, carrying harps or violins. They*

are gnome-like and joyous.)

FIRST MINSTREL. We will set up our harps as at Castle Mourne.

SECOND MINSTREL. And our young lord Michael bids us sing the song of his heart to Fair Rosaleen.

ROSALEEN. (*Gaily.*) Sing, Minstrels all! (*As one of them turns and closes the door.*) No, let the door open! Your voice will ring down the soft spring wind and who can tell what stranger may be listening!

OLD WOMAN. This song is not for strangers. It is Michael's song this night—from his heart to yours.

ROSALEEN. (*With a strange, inscrutable smile.*) I will listen —and dream—and hope—

THE MINSTRELS. (*Tuning their harps and beginning to sing.*)

"My dark Rosaleen!
My own Rosaleen!
Shall glad your heart—"

ROSALEEN. (*Interrupting.*) No! No! I do not like that song this night!

FIRST MINSTREL. But it is chosen for you by our young lord Michael!

ROSALEEN. (*Softly.*) There's another one, Minstrels, you must sing to please me!

THIRD MINSTREL. (*Deep in admiration of her.*) You have only to name it!

ROSALEEN. "The Golden Shore of Far Away." . . .

OLD WOMAN. Always your mind like your feet are wandering! (*Pleading.*) Stay here this night, my Rosaleen! Stay here!

ROSALEEN. (*Lying back on her couch, already dreaming.*) Sing, Minstrels! Sing!

THE MINSTRELS.

"There grows the Tree whose summer breath
Perfumes with joy the azure air,

And he who feels it fears not Death
  Nor longer heeds the hounds of Care.
Oh, soft the skies of Seskinore,
  And mild is meadowy Mellaray;
But sweet as honey running o'er,
  The Golden Shore of Far Away."

ROSALEEN. (*When the song is ended.*) That is a song that speaks and lets one dream . . . (*Singing softly, her hands folded lazily under her head.*) "The Golden Shore of Far Away" . . .

NORA. There is no more time to dream this hour. You must dress for the dance.

OLD WOMAN. (*As a horn sounds outside.*) Listen! It is Michael's horn! The guests are already here!

ROSALEEN. (*Laughing recklessly.*) Hasten off with me, Nora! (*Rising.*) Hasten!

OLD WOMAN. Play, Minstrels! Play! Let your harp-strings swell with the gay lilt of music while I make in this room brightness and light!

(*The* MINSTRELS *do as she commands. Meanwhile, she lights many candles and the room becomes festive and ablaze as the* GUESTS *enter. There are* MICHAEL [*young and tall and good to look at*], *and* HUGH *and* DENNY. *Among the colleens are* ELLEN *and* BRIGID.)

MICHAEL. (*Merrily.*) The gods save you, Old Woman!

OLD WOMAN. (*Curtsying.*) And you this night! And you!

MICHAEL. Where is my beautiful Rosaleen? (*Tenderly, as the others laugh at his ardor.*) My own beautiful, beautiful Rosaleen!

OLD WOMAN. She dresses this hour for the dance.

MICHAEL. (*Frowning.*) What? Late this time as every time?

OLD WOMAN. She was walking abroad on Slemish with only the dusk to warn her of the lateness of the hour. (*Apologetically.*) She bids you make merry until she appears.

HUGH. (*As the* MINSTRELS *drift into an old refrain.*) Dance, colleens, dance! Let Michael sulk if he will!

(*Couples form merrily and the scene becomes one of motion and light. Candle-light gleams on the silken gowns of the dancing colleens and glitters upon the young men's swords. Only* MICHAEL *stands alone and watching as* OLD WOMAN *brings forth a flask of wine.*)

DENNY. (*Jesting, as he passes* MICHAEL.) The night is long, young Michael! Even now we are dancing before the rising of the moon!

MICHAEL. (*As the music grows softer and* ROSALEEN *appears on the threshold of the inner room.*) My Rosaleen!

ROSALEEN. (*Lovely and gay in her silver dress.*) Michael! God shield you! Ah, boy of my heart! (*Taking his hand as she turns to the others.*) And this evening be good to you all!

MICHAEL. (*Staring at her.*) You are too beautiful tonight!

ROSALEEN. (*Laughing.*) Hear! Hear! There is madness on his lips like the madness of the rushing of the river!

DENNY. (*Jesting again.*) When he looks in your eyes he is pierced with the light of a thousand new stars!

ELLEN. (*Softly.*) Such love was meant for starlight and the cool green of the grass. It is there we should be dancing!

HUGH. (*Taking her arm.*) Out, Minstrels! Into the night!

(*Playing merrily, the* MINSTRELS *file out into the darkness. The dancers and* OLD WOMAN *follow; only* MICHAEL *and* ROSALEEN *are left in the room.*)

MICHAEL. (*Shyly.*) Aye. What Ellen says is true. This night is one for the stars to bless us.

ROSALEEN. (*Laughing and scolding.*) Ah, Michael! Michael! Always so sober!

MICHAEL. What else should one be as one nears one's betrothal? The responsibilities of love are grave as well as gay.

ROSALEEN. And I so love laughter!

MICHAEL. But there is laughter, too, within the walls of Castle

Mourne! Harps play there as here tonight and there is all the color of the halls at Tara.

ROSALEEN. (*Musing.*) And I shall be the Lady of it all!

MICHAEL. (*Eagerly.*) You like to play with that thought?

ROSALEEN. (*Looking away.*) No . . .

MICHAEL. I do not understand you! You, a princess, born to splendor, exiled here on lonely Slemish—

ROSALEEN. (*Protesting.*) Slemish is never lonely. If it is, I've learned to love the wildness of its crags and the darkness of its forests. (*Looking at him with sudden awe.*) Strangely, Michael, they can speak! Its hills are where Saint Patrick stood, a captive, waiting for a ship—

MICHAEL. You think too much of saints because you've been so much alone. At Castle Mourne, my Rosaleen, you'll come back to the world which gave you being! (*Dreamily.*) A princess in a castle-keep—

ROSALEEN. (*Covering her face with her hands.*) Sometimes I fear I am not meant for that.

MICHAEL. Your dreams are dark this night. Come, lay them aside, until the brightness of the morning!

VOICES. (*As the music continues outside.*) Rosaleen! Rosaleen! Michael!

MICHAEL. Come! They are our guests! We, too, must dance!

ROSALEEN. Go quickly! I will follow! Sure!

(*He stands looking down at her, concerned for a moment, then does as she bids him. She is completely alone in the room. . . . Suddenly, as if by a gust of wind, the candle-flames are extinguished and all is blue darkness. As she stands, not afraid, but wondering, a bright golden light falls across the threshold of the inner room and reveals a tall young man who stands there watching her gravely. He is gracious of presence and handsome. He is the young* SAINT PATRICK.)

SAINT PATRICK. Rosaleen . . .

ROSALEEN. You . . . The—the stranger!

SAINT PATRICK. Is it not as it was told you in the tale? "The stranger will come to the last one left in the room . . ."

ROSALEEN. And I am the last.

SAINT PATRICK. You are the last . . . (*Coming toward her.*) And I have come to feel that it is by your own choosing.

ROSALEEN. What is your name?

SAINT PATRICK. (*Gently.*) Some say it is Death. Others, Saint Patrick.

ROSALEEN. Death could not have such laughing eyes! He could not be so young and ardent! I shall call you Saint Patrick!

SAINT PATRICK. I have walked with you often on Slemish . . .

ROSALEEN. I have heard you speak to me from the rocks . . . I have seen you stand, young as you are now, looking out to sea. You were a captive here, as I am. You were lonely, too, for one to speak your language.

SAINT PATRICK. I had my white sheep to herd on the hills—stars to worship above the waste-land—and always my dream of Heaven.

ROSALEEN. (*Softly.*) Always your dream of Heaven . . .

SAINT PATRICK. And you, I know, must have that too. Today I saw you kneel and kiss the footprints of the angels.

ROSALEEN. I found it all so beautiful! The little church on top of Skerry—the bird's song in the roses—and the stone that marks the place where the angel's footprint lay clear and shining in the dust.

SAINT PATRICK. You are not of this world, Rosaleen. Not of Michael's castle.

ROSALEEN. I do not know . . . I do not know . . . (*Pondering a bit wildly.*) From his arms I fly to Slemish to be alone with all its wonder—then again I'm faint with joy at the thought of being near him.

SAINT PATRICK. If I should bend and kiss your forehead—

ROSALEEN. (*Backing away from him, frightened.*) Then, if the tale be true, you could forever claim me!

SAINT PATRICK. (*Repeating as in litany.*) I could forever claim you . . .

ROSALEEN. (*Bewildered, confused.*) This world is sweet—but sweeter still is Heaven—

SAINT PATRICK. Sweeter still is Heaven . . .

ROSALEEN. The bells ring here but there they ring with music—

SAINT PATRICK. There they ring with music . . .

ROSALEEN. And love is here—young and dear and ardent—but there it shines most heavenly bright—

SAINT PATRICK. There it shines most heavenly bright . . . (*Coming closer to her as* MICHAEL *is heard calling her name outside.*) Most heavenly bright!

MICHAEL. (*Appearing in the door-way.*) Rosaleen!

ROSALEEN. (*Looking helplessly from one to the other.*) Michael! My Michael!

SAINT PATRICK. You are young and lovely as the morning star I loved so long ago on Slemish. Rosaleen! Rosaleen! I give you your choice. My kiss—forever mine—or his—

MICHAEL. (*Facing him, angered.*) You are the Spectre who appears at dances and gives to one the fatal kiss!

ROSALEEN. He is the stranger I have known on Slemish a thousand, thousand years!

SAINT PATRICK. (*Gently.*) You have made your choice?

MICHAEL. (*Crying out, struggling with him futilely.*) No! No! NO!

ROSALEEN. (*Approaching him, radiant.*) Kiss me, Saint Patrick . . .

SAINT PATRICK. Some are not meant for this world. All their dreams are of another. Here in a valley of little stars you reach for those above Slemish. . . . (*As he walks back to the threshold of the inner room and stands again in the blaze of golden light, she follows him as one under a spell.*) The winds and the rain and I make answer . . . (*He bends and kisses her on the*

forehead.) Go, Rosaleen—dark Rosaleen—in the footprints of
the angels. . . .

(*She falls lightly against him—the golden light blazes even
more splendidly for a moment—then all is darkness complete.
. . . There is a frustrated cry from* MICHAEL *as*

THE CURTAIN FALLS

THE DUMMY *

A Play

BY ELBRIDGE S. LYON

CHARACTERS

JOHN
TERRY
ST. PATRICK
RUTH
HELEN
AMY
ROSE
TOM
BILL

TIME: *The present.*

SCENE: *The loft of a barn.* RUTH, HELEN, AMY, ROSE, BILL
and TOM *are seated in two rows, on boxes.*

RUTH. Why doesn't he come?

HELEN. What are we here for anyway?

RUTH. John is going to rehearse his act before going to the city
to try and make a big name for himself.

HELEN. What kind of an act is it?

* For permission to produce, consult the author, Chatham, N.J.

BILL. He's a entril-i-kist.

TOM. A what?

AMY. He means a ventriloquist.

HELEN. What in the world is that?

ROSE. It's where a man talks without letting his lips move, and a dummy moves its lips, and you think the dummy is talking.

RUTH. Well, where is John? Why doesn't he come?

BILL. He's putting on his stage clothes.

AMY. If his father finds out he is wearing his tuxedo around in this barn, he'll get it.

HELEN. Why does he have to practice in a dress suit?

BILL. He calls it atmosphere.

TOM. I should think there was enough atmosphere up here over these stables for anybody.

RUTH. Do you think Major Bowes will like his act?

AMY. You betcha. It's better than Charlie McCarthy any day. You can see this dummy. Who ever saw Charlie McCarthy?

BILL. I have—lots of times.

AMY. Not really. Only in pictures, and you've never heard him except on the radio.

BILL. Well, that's better than this dummy in the trunk over there, which we've never seen nor heard anywhere.

AMY. I have. His name is Terry and he's great. He may be a dummy, but he's awful smart. At least, John makes him seem smart.

TOM. Why in the world doesn't he come?

BILL. Hi—John. Where are you?

(*They stamp and clap and get into a rhythm of stamping. Bang, bang,—bang, bang, bang, etc. Enter* JOHN, *who is a large older boy. He has on a tuxedo or better yet, a full dress suit.*)

JOHN. (*Bowing to his audience of six.*) Ladies and Gentlemen, hello, kids; sorry to keep you waiting. Ladies and Gentlemen, I will now demonstrate for your edification.

TOM. What does that mean?

BILL. Shut up.

JOHN. Ladies and Gentlemen—

TOM. You said that.

RUTH. Give him a chance, can't you!

JOHN. I will now demonstrate that great science known as ventriloquism.

HELEN. Whatever that is.

ROSE. It's what Edgar Bergen does.

JOHN. Hello, Terry, over there in the trunk. How are you?

TERRY. (*Muffled voice from trunk.*) O.K., boss.

JOHN. Want to come out and see your audience?

TERRY. Any blondes out there?

JOHN. Now, never mind that.

(*Goes to trunk and lifts lid. Takes dummy by coat collar and drags him out.* TERRY *is a very small live-boy with an Irish false face with staring eyes. The lower jaw is to be hinged so that it moves when he talks. He has an empty sleeve with a glove pinned to it. There is also a glove on the other sleeve with a fist in it, leaving the fingers empty. Dummy is completely relaxed and falls naturally into whatever position* JOHN *lets him go.* JOHN *leaves him in a heap on floor and goes back to trunk to close the lid. Comes back and drags dummy to special chair. He sits, props dummy up on his lap placing one hand behind. Dummy moves his head from side to side and back and forth stiffly, as good dummies do when propelled by hand of the master.*)

JOHN. Well, here we are, all set.

TERRY. Maybe you're all set, but look at what I drew to set on.

JOHN. Maybe you'd like to sit in the chair and hold me on your lap.

TERRY. I'd rather sit in that third chair over there. (*Indicating where* ROSE *is sitting.*)

JOHN. Aren't you rather forward? You haven't even been

introduced yet.

TERRY. Well, get on with it.

JOHN. Ladies and Gentlemen, this is Terry O'Rourke fresh from Dublin.

TERRY. You're pretty fresh your own self.

JOHN. I'm not from Dublin.

TERRY. They wouldn't have you over there.

JOHN. Well, they ran you out pretty young.

TERRY. G'wan, I ran myself out, but I'd not 'a' done it, had I known I'd have to associate with you.

JOHN. Tell me, why did you come to America?

TERRY. Looking for St. Patrick.

JOHN. But he was in old Ireland.

TERRY. I couldn't find him there.

JOHN. But he's dead.

TERRY. That's what you think.

JOHN. You're the queerest dummy I ever had!

BILL. It's the only one you ever had.

JOHN. Don't interrupt me. I've got to learn to think.

TERRY. I'll say you do.

JOHN. Yes, and for you, too.

TERRY. Don't call me a blockhead!

AMY. He is a wooden head and a wooden body too.

RUTH. Hush up.

HELEN. He is not all wood. He's mostly sawdust. Isn't he, John?

JOHN. Yes, but sawdust is wood.

HELEN. Maybe it was wood once, but it's sawdust now.

ROSE. I suppose hash isn't meat.

HELEN. Well, it isn't a leg of lamb.

JOHN. Come now, enough of that. How did you lose your arm?

TERRY. Elephant hunting.

JOHN. Hunting elephants? You never hunted elephants.

TERRY. Well anyway, you know very well you dropped the

trunk on it.

AMY. Go on, John. What comes next?

RUTH. Make Terry sing.

JOHN. All right. Come on, Terry. Will you sing for us?

TERRY. Huh? What did you say?

JOHN. Stop staring at that little girl. We want you to sing for us.

TERRY. Who's us? Where's the microphone?

JOHN. We have to practice first. Some day we will be acting for the great unseen audience.

TERRY. You mean we won't see who we are talking to?

JOHN. Yes, that is right.

TERRY. And they won't see you?

JOHN. Correct.

TERRY. What a break for the audience.

JOHN. Come on. Sing.

TERRY. I'll sing for her on the end there. She's Irish.

JOHN. That's right, and her name is Rose. What are you going to sing?

TERRY. You tell me. It's you who does it all anyway.

JOHN. Who, me?

TERRY. Sure. I'm only sawdust.

JOHN. Well, why not "My Wild Irish Rose"?

TERRY. Whoopee! (*Clears throat. Sings "My Wild Irish Rose." Audience of six applauds loudly.*)

JOHN. That was very nice.

TERRY. Thank-you. Thank-you. (*To* JOHN.) Now, you sing. Oh, that's right, you were singing, weren't you?

JOHN. Me? I can't sing. You know that.

TERRY. You can't do much without me, can you?

JOHN. I guess you are right. Now, what can I do for you to show my appreciation?

TERRY. You can give me a new face.

John. All right. I will get some paints. What do you want to be—a Chinaman or a little darky or what?

Terry. None of them. Once Irish, always Irish. I'm not for changing my nationality, but I want soft skin like the rest of you. I want to really live.

John. Well, I am afraid I can't do that.

Terry. St. Patrick could if he was here. (*Cries out.*) St. Patrick, where are you? Come and help me.

(*Enter through panel in rear wall a patriarchal personage with flowing robes.*)

St. Patrick. Well, well, Terry. Here I am. What is the matter?

Terry. St. Patrick, is it really you?

St. Patrick. Of course, I always help my children when they call to me.

Terry. But I am not a real child.

St. Patrick. Oh yes you are. You had faith that I could make you alive, and I have. Get up.

(Terry *stands and walks a few steps.*)

Terry. I can stand alone!

St. Patrick. Not alone, yet. I am holding you.

Terry. But you are not touching me.

St. Patrick. What is the matter with your arm?

Terry. It's all right, only it came off.

John. (*Goes to trunk and gets a false arm. Holds it out to* St. Patrick.) Here it is, sir.

(All *gather around* Terry *screening him from view, as* St. Patrick *takes false arm and helps* Terry *put his real arm into his coat sleeve. They remove both gloves, and false face. They all step aside.*)

St. Patrick. There you are.

(Terry *feels his face and examines his hands.*)

Terry. I'm real! I'm real!

ST. PATRICK. Of course you are, and you always were, only these dummies here didn't know it.

TERRY. Whoopee.

(*Prances over to* ROSE. *Bows. She bows, and together they dance an Irish jig.*)

CURTAIN

A DAY OF MEMORIES

By Katherine Edelman

St. Patrick's day brings memories—I see the old home place—
The friendly row of hawthorn trees—my mother's sainted face—
My father picking shamrocks in the field before the door—
And my bitter tears are falling for the days that are no more.

St. Patrick's day brings memories of a crooked little lane,
Where bluebells peeped through grasses all wet with dew and
    rain;
Of a singing stream that wandered through meadows sweet and
    green—
And my lonesome heart is crying for the miles that lie between.

I am longing for the happy things I lightly left behind—
The linnet singing in the hedge—the friends so true and kind—
The peace of little sheltered field—the peat fire's ruddy glow—
For all the dear remembered things I used to love and know.

MARCH SEVENTEENTH

By Julia Boynton Green

Saint Patrick, he deserves his Day,
I wouldn't clip his crown a fraction;
To rid a land of serpents—say!
That surely was a noble action.

But listen—I've a worthy plan
To put before a heedless nation;
There's one hard-worked deserving clan
That has no Day for celebration.

They drudge and sweat and slave and toil,
Our fine undaunted dose-concoctors;
They saw a leg or lance a boil—
Up with your drink, lads! TO THE DOCTORS!

Give them the palm, the golden hats;
At top of Heaven's own legions list 'em;
Their job is bigger, far, than Pat's,
They chase bugs from the human system.

They delve with messy microscopes
For years to mix a useful serum.
For every ill they've proper dopes.
A mighty decent bunch. Let's cheer 'em!

Dear Sister, if you limp or wheeze
They hand a crutch or cough-drop, yes'm.
They rush to reach, these kind M.D.s
The glad hand to the Stork, God bless 'em.

Saint Patrick, he deserves his Day;
So do policemen, preachers, proctors.
But look—here goes my best bouquet—
"Our latest-model Saints—THE DOCTORS!"

THE FIGHTING RACE

By Joseph I. C. Clarke

"Read out the names!" and Burke sat back,
     And Kelly drooped his head,
While Shea—they call him Scholar Jack—
     Went down the list of the dead.
Officers, seamen, gunners, marines,
     The crews of the gig and yawl,
The bearded man and the lad in his teens,
     Carpenters, coal passers—all.
Then, knocking the ashes from out his pipe,
     Said Burke in an offhand way:
"We're all in that dead man's list, by Cripe!
     Kelly and Burke and Shea."
"Well here's to the *Maine*, and I'm sorry for Spain,"
     Said Kelly and Burke and Shea.

"Wherever there's Kellys there's trouble," said Burke.
     "Wherever fighting's the game,
Or a spice of danger in grown man's work,"
     Said Kelly, "you'll find my name."
"And do we fall short," said Burke, getting mad,
     "When it's touch and go for life?"
Said Shea: "It's thirty odd years, bedad,
     Since I charged to drum and fife
Up Marye's Heights, and my old canteen
     Stopped a rebel ball on its way.
There were blossoms of blood on our sprigs of green—
     Kelly and Burke and Shea—
And the dead didn't brag." "Well, here's to the flag!"
     Said Kelly and Burke and Shea.

"I wish 'twas in Ireland, for there's the place,"
　Said Burke, "that we'd die by right,
In the cradle of our soldier race,
　After one good stand-up fight.
My grandfather fell on Vinegar Hill,
　And fighting was not his trade;
But his rusty pike's in the cabin still,
　With Hessian blood on the blade."
"Aye, aye," said Kelly, "the pikes were great
　When the word was 'Clear the way!'
We were thick on the roll in ninety-eight—
　Kelly and Burke and Shea."
"Well, here's to the pike and the sword and the like!"
　Said Kelly and Burke and Shea.

And Shea, the scholar, with rising joy,
　Said: "We were at Ramillies;
We left our bones at Fontenoy
　And up in the Pyrenees;
Before Dunkirk, on Landen's plain,
　Cremona, Lille, and Ghent;
We're all over Austria, France, and Spain,
　Wherever they pitched a tent.
We've died for England from Waterloo
　To Egypt and Dargai;
And still there's enough for a corps or crew,
　Kelly and Burke and Shea."
"Well, here's to good honest fighting blood!"
　Said Kelly and Burke and Shea.

"Oh, the fighting races don't die out,
　If they seldom die in bed,
For love is first in their hearts, no doubt,"
　Said Burke; then Kelly said:

"When Michael, the Irish Archangel, stands,
  The angel with the sword,
And the battle-dead from a hundred lands
  Are ranged in one big horde,
Our line, that for Gabriel's trumpet waits,
  Will stretch three deep that day,
From Jehoshaphat to the Golden Gates—
  Kelly and Burke and Shea."
"Well, here's thank God for the race and the sod!"
  Said Kelly and Burke and Shea.

DAWN ON THE IRISH COAST

BY JOHN LOCKE

Th' ANAM THO' DIAH! but there it is,
  The dawn on the hills of Ireland!
God's angels lifting the night's black veil
  From the fair, sweet face of my sire-land!
O Ireland, isn't it grand you look,
  Like a bride in her rich adornin'?
And with all the pent-up love of my heart
  I bid you the top o' the mornin'.

Ho—ho! upon Cliona's shelving strand,
  The surges are grandly beating,
And Kerry is pushing her headlands out
  To give us the kindly greeting;
Into the shore the sea-birds fly
  On pinions that know no drooping;
And out from the cliffs, with welcome charged,
  A million waves come trooping.

O, kindly, generous Irish land,
  So leal and fair and loving,

No wonder the wandering Celt should think
 And dream of you in his roving!
The alien home may have gems and gold,
 Shadows may never have gloomed it,
But the heart will sigh for the absent land,
 Where the love-light first illumed it.

And doesn't old Cove look charming there,
 Watching the wild waves' motion,
Leaning her back against the hills,
 And the tips of her toes in the ocean?
I wonder I don't hear Shandon's bells!
 Ah, maybe their chiming's over,
For it's many a year since I began
 The life of a Western rover.

This one short hour pays lavishly back
 For many a year of mourning;
I'd almost venture another flight,
 There's so much joy in returning—
Watching out for the hallowed shore,
 All other attractions scornin';
O Ireland, don't you hear me shout?
 I bid you the top o' the mornin'.

For thirty summers, asthore machree,
 Those hills I now feast my eyes on
Ne'er met my vision, save when they rose
 Over Memory's dim horizon.
Even so, 'twas grand and fair they seemed
 In the landscape spread before me;
But dreams are dreams, and my eyes would ope
 To see Texas' skies still o'er me.

Oh! often upon the Texan plains,
   When the day and the chase were over,
My thoughts would fly o'er the weary wave,
   And around this coast-line hover;
And the prayer would rise that, some future day,
   All danger and doubtings scornin',
I'd help to win my native land
   The light of young Liberty's mornin'.

Now fuller and truer the shore-line shows—
   Was ever a scene so splendid?
I feel the breath of the Munster breeze;
   Thank God that my exile's ended.
Old scenes, old songs, old friends again,
   The vale and cot I was born in!
O Ireland, up from my heart of hearts
   I bid you the top o' the mornin'!

ST. PATRICK WAS A GENTLEMAN

BY HENRY BENNETT

Oh, St. Patrick was a gentleman,
   Who came of decent people;
He built a church in Dublin town,
   And on it put a steeple.
His father was a Gallagher;
   His mother was a Brady;
His aunt was an O'Shaughnessy;
   His uncle an O'Grady.
     So, success attend St. Patrick's fist,
       For he's a Saint so clever;
     Oh, he gave the snakes and toads a twist,
       And bothered them forever!

The Wicklow hills are very high,
    And so's the Hill of Howth, sir;
But there's a hill, much bigger still,
    Much higher nor them both, sir.
'Twas on the top of this high hill
    St. Patrick preached his sarmint
That drove the frogs into the bogs,
    And banished all the varmint.

There's not a mile in Ireland's isle
    Where dirty varmin musters,
But there he put his dear fore-foot,
    And murdered them in clusters.
The toads went pop, the frogs went hop,
    Slap-dash into the water;
And the snakes committed suicide
    To save themselves from slaughter.

Nine hundred thousand reptiles blue
    He charmed with sweet discourses,
And dined on them at Killaloe
    In soups and second courses.
Where blind worms crawling in the grass
    Disgusted all the nation,
He gave them a rise, which opened their eyes
    To a sense of their situation.

Oh, was I but so fortunate
    As to be back in Munster,
'Tis I'd be bound that from that ground
    I nevermore would once stir.
For there St. Patrick planted turf,
    And plenty of the praties,
With pigs galore. ma gra, ma 'store,

And cabbages—and ladies!
　　Then my blessing on St. Patrick's fist,
　　　For he's the darling Saint, O!
　　Oh, he gave the snakes and toads a twist;
　　　He's a beauty without paint, O!

ON ST. PATRICK'S DAY

By Katherine Edelman

A thousand miles of prairie and two thousand miles of sea
Are stretching out their weary wastes—their barriers to me—
But their unrelenting reaches are defeated—swept aside—
As the magic wings of memory conquer land and rising tide.

For it's Ballybree I'm seeing—I am walking as of old
Where the buttercups and cowslips flaunt robes of yellow gold;
Where the softest rays of sunshine and the slanting silver rain
Fall down like benediction on a crooked little lane.

I have left the world of hurry—every foolish, futile thing—
For the dewy, ferny meadows where the lark and linnet sing;
I have cast aside the knowledge and the wisdom of the years
For the innocence of childhood and its lack of frets and fears.

Far away from walls and canyons—from the city's wear and
　　grind—
I have let the things of glamour fill my heart and soul and mind;
Even mystic veils are lifted, as I plainly hear and see
The home of my forefathers—in beloved Ballybree.

A BIT OF GREEN

By Grace L. Schauffler

Your neighbor may come
From the Emerald Isle—
Let's all wear a bit of green!
He's homesick perhaps
For his old domicile—
Let's all wear a bit of green!
Saint Patrick it was
Who started the style—
Let's all wear a bit of green!
For the Irish a cheer,
For the shamrock a smile—
Let's all wear a bit of green!

CUSHLA-MA-CHREE *

By John Philpot Curran

Dear Erin, how sweetly thy green bosom rises,
    An emerald set in the ring of the sea,
Each blade of thy meadows my faithful heart prizes,
    Thou Queen of the West, the world's *cushla-ma-chree.*
Thy gates open wide to the poor and the stranger,
    There smiles hospitality, hearty and free;
Thy friendship is seen in the moment of danger,
    And the wanderer is welcomed with *cushla-ma-chree.*

Thy sons they are brave, but, the battle once over,
    In brotherly peace with their foes they agree,
And the roseate cheeks of thy daughters discover

* *Cushla-ma-chree,* pulse of my heart.

The soul-speaking flush that says *cushla-ma-chree.*
Then flourish forever, my dear native Erin,
 While sadly I wander an exile from thee,
And firm as thy mountains, no injury fearing,
 May Heaven defend its own *cushla-ma-chree.*

CORRYMEELA

BY MOIRA O'NEILL

Over here in England I'm helpin' wi' the hay,
 An' I wisht I was in Ireland the livelong day;
Weary on the English hay, an' sorra take the wheat!
 Och! Corrymeela an' the blue sky over it.

There' a deep dumb river flowin' by beyont the heavy trees,
 This livin' air is moithered wi' the bummin' o' the bees;
I wisht I'd hear the Claddagh burn go runnin' through the heat
 Past Corrymeela, wi' the blue sky over it.

The people that's in England is richer nor the Jews,
 There' not the smallest young gossoon but thravels in his
  shoes!
I'd give the pipe between me teeth to see a barefut child,
 Och! Corrymeela an' the low south wind.

Here's hands so full o' money an' hearts so full o' care,
 By the luck o' love! I'd still go light for all I did go bare.
"God save ye, *colleen dhas,*" I said: the girl she thought me
  wild.
 Far Corrymeela, an' the low south wind.

D'ye mind me now, the song at night is mortial hard to raise,
 The girls are heavy goin' here, the boys are ill to plase;

When one'st I'm out this workin' hive, 'tis I'll be back again—
Ay, Corrymeela, in the same soft rain.

The puff o' smoke from one ould roof before an English town!
For a *shaugh* wid Andy Feelan here I'd give a silver crown,
For a curl o' hair like Mollie's ye'll ask the like in vain,
Sweet Corrymeela, an' the same soft rain.

THE LANE TO BALLYBREE

By Katherine Edelman

There's a little lane a-winding, a crooked little lane,
A dewy, woodbine-scented lane, that leads to Ballybree;
Where the hawthorn boughs are laden with their wealth of starry
bloom,
And sweetly singing little birds are heard on bush and tree.

There's a little lane a-winding, a little, winding lane,
Where the furze is all in blossom like a wave of yellow gold.
And every turning in the brake you hear the leaves a-stirrin',
'Tis the little fairy people—oh, they're very brave and bold.

There's a little lane a-winding, a crooked little lane,
And there's someone at the end of it who's wishing hard for
me;
There are soft winds gently blowing—a peat fire brightly
glowing—
Oh! I'm aching to be wandering the lane to Ballybree.

ST. PATRICK

BY WILLIAM MAGINN

A fig for St. Denis of France,
    He's a trumpery fellow to brag on;
A fig for St. George and his lance,
    Which spitted a heathenish dragon;
And the saints of the Welshman or Scot
    Are a couple of pitiful pipers,
Both of whom may just travel to pot,
    Compared to the patron of swipers,
        St. Patrick of Ireland, my dear.

He came to the Emerald Isle
    On a lump of a paving-stone mounted;
The steamboat he beat to a mile,
    Which mighty good sailing was counted.
Says he, "The salt water I think
    Has made me most bloodily thirsty,
So bring me a flagon of drink
    To keep down the mulligrubs, burst ye,
        Of drink that is fit for a saint."

       *   *   *   *   *

You've heard, I suppose, long ago,
    How the snakes in a manner most antic
He marched to the County Mayo,
    And tumbled them into the Atlantic.
Hence not to use water for drink
    The people of Ireland determine;
With mighty good reason, I think,
    Since St. Patrick has filled it with vermin,
        And vipers, and other such stuff.

THE WEARIN' O' THE GREEN

OLD BALLAD

O Paddy dear! an' did ye hear the news that's goin' round?
The shamrock is by law forbid to grow on Irish ground!
No more St. Patrick's day we'll keep, his color can't be seen,
For there's a cruel law agin the wearin' o' the green!
I met wid Napper Tandy, and he took me by the hand,
And he said, "How's poor Ould Ireland, and how does she
    stand?"
She's the most disthressful country that iver yet was seen,
For they're hangin' men and women there for wearin' o' the
    green.

An' if the color we must wear is England's cruel red,
Let it remind us of the blood that Ireland has shed;
Then pull the shamrock from your hat, and throw it on the sod,—
And never fear, 'twill take root there, tho' under foot 'tis trod!
When law can stop the blades of grass from growin' as they grow,
And when the leaves in summer-time their color dare not show,
Then I will change the color, too, I wear in my caubeen,
But till that day, plaze God, I'll stick to wearin' o' the green.

IRISH MOTHER

BY KATHERINE EDELMAN

There's a little mother waiting in a cabin by the sea,
Oh, the aching and the longing that's in her heart for me.
Sure, I'd give a thousand years away to feel her arms once more
And to hear her whisper brokenly, "You're welcome back,
    asthore."

There's a little mother waiting and her eyes are dim with tears
With the weariness of watching through all the lonely years;
And I'd give the very heart of me to feel her kiss once more
And our hands a-clasping tightly as we entered at the door.

There's a little mother waiting where the peat fires brightly
    glow,
Where the air is sweet and mellow as the soft winds gently blow;
And I'd give up all the wealth there is in money or in land
To be sitting by an Irish hearth a-holding of her hand.

THE BIRTH OF ST. PATRICK

By Samuel Lover

On the eighth day of March it was, some people say,
That Saint Pathrick at midnight he first saw the day;
While others declare 'twas the ninth he was born,
And 'twas all a mistake, between midnight and morn;
For mistakes will occur in a hurry and shock,
And some blamed the babby—and some blamed the clock—
Till with all their cross-questions sure no one could know
If the child was too fast, or the clock was too slow.

Now the first faction-fight in ould Ireland, they say,
Was all on account of St. Pathrick's birthday;
Some fought for the eighth—for the ninth more would die,
And who wouldn't see right, sure they blacken'd his eye!
At last, both the factions so positive grew,
That each kept a birthday, so Pat then had two,
Till Father Mulcahy, who show'd them their sins,
Said, "No one could have two birthdays, but a twins."

Says he, "Boys, don't be fightin' for eight or for nine,
Don't be always dividin'—but sometimes combine;

Combine eight with nine, and seventeen is the mark,
So let that be his birthday,"—"Amen," says the clerk.
"If he wasn't a twins, sure our hist'ry will show
That, at least, he's worth any two saints that we know!"
Then they all got blind dhrunk—which complated their bliss,
And we keep up the practice from that day to this.

THE SHAMROCK

By Maurice De Guerin

When April rains make flowers bloom
    And Johnny-jump-ups come to light,
And clouds of color and perfume
    Float from the orchards pink and white,
I see my shamrock in the rain,
    An emerald spray with raindrops set,
Like jewels on Spring's coronet,
    So fair, and yet it breathes of pain.

The shamrock on an older shore
    Sprang from a rich and sacred soil
Where saint and hero lived of yore,
    And where their sons in sorrow toil;
And here, transplanted, it to me
    Seems weeping for the soil it left:
The diamonds that all others see
    Are tears drawn from its heart bereft.

When April rain makes flowers grow
    And sparkles on their tiny buds
That in June nights will over-blow
    And fill the world with scented floods,
The lonely shamrock in our land—

So fine among the clover leaves—
For the old spring times often grieves,—
I feel its tears upon my hand.

THE BREASTPLATE OF ST. PATRICK

(Part of an old Gaelic poem)

I arise today
Through a mighty strength, the invocation of the Trinity,
Through a belief in the Threeness,
Through confession of the Oneness
Of the Creator of creation.

     *   *   *   *   *

I arise today
Through the strength of the love of cherubim,
In obedience of angels,
In service of archangels,
In the hope of resurrection to meet with reward,
In prayers of patriarchs,
In predictions of prophets,
In preachings of apostles,
In faith of confessors,
In innocence of virgins,
In deeds of righteous men.

I arise today
Through the strength of heaven;
Light of the sun,
Radiance of the moon,
Splendor of fire,
Speed of lightning,
Swiftness of the wind,
Depth of the sea,

Stability of the earth,
Firmness of the rock.

I arise today
Through God's strength to pilot me;
God's might to uphold me,
God's wisdom to guide me,
God's eye to look before me,
God's ear to hear me,
God's word to speak for me,
God's hand to guard me,
God's way to lie before me,
God's shield to protect me,
God's hosts to save me,
From snares of the devil,
From temptations of vices,
From everyone who desires me ill,
Afar or near,
Alone or in a multitude.

Christ with me, Christ before me, Christ behind me,
Christ in me, Christ beneath me, Christ above me,
Christ on my right, Christ on my left,
Christ when I lie down, Christ when I sit down,
Christ when I arise,
Christ in the heart of every man who thinks of me,
Christ in the mouth of every man who speaks of me,
Christ in the eye that sees me,
Christ in the ear that hears me.
I arise today
Through a mighty strength, the invocation of the Trinity,
Through a belief in the Threeness,
Through a confession of the Oneness
Of the Creator of creation.

THE IRISH TE DEUM

Thanks be to God for the light and the darkness;
Thanks be to God for the hail and the snow;
Thanks be to God for showers and sunshine;
Thanks be to God for all things that grow;
Thanks be to God for lightning and tempest;
Thanks be to God for weal and for woe;
Thanks be to God for His own great goodness;
Thanks be to God that what is, is so;
Thanks be to God when the harvest is plenty;
Thanks be to God when the barn is low;
Thanks be to God when our pockets are empty;
Thanks be to God when again they o'erflow.
Thanks be to God that the mass-bell and steeple
Are heard and are seen throughout Erin's green isle;
Thanks be to God that the priest and the people
Are ever united in danger and trial.
Thanks be to God that the brave sons of Erin
Have the faith of their fathers as lively as aye;
Thanks be to God that Erin's fair daughters
Press close after Mary on heaven's highway.

ESSAYS

THE CELEBRATION OF ST. PATRICK'S DAY

FROM HONE'S EVERYDAY BOOK

It is impossible to say when the 17th of March in each year began to be set apart as St. Patrick's Day and observed as a popular holiday of Ireland. But whatever may have started it there can be little doubt that the day is a national holiday in Ireland and is observed with much enthusiasm, and that it renews and intensifies the patriotism of the people. In most of the large cities of America it is celebrated by the Irish national societies and other citizens of Irish birth or blood by a parade through the streets.

In Ireland itself the celebration is less formal but more universal. The shamrock is worn everywhere in commemoration of the fact that when St. Patrick was preaching the doctrine of the Trinity he made use of this plant bearing three leaves upon one stem as a symbol of the great mystery. In every household "Master and Mistress" are expected to "drown the shamrock" in generous drafts of whiskey and then send the bottle to the kitchen for the servants. In Dublin the higher classes conclude the festivities of the day by attending a great ball at St. Patrick's Hall, Dublin Castle.

None can be admitted who have not been presented and attended the viceroy's drawing room; and of course everyone must appear in court dress or full uniform. In the smaller hamlets the local inn used to be a place of universal resort for young men. A "Patrick's Pot" of beer or whiskey and a small allowance of oaten bread and fish to each one was benevolently contributed by the host. All additional orders had to be paid for. Where the village or hamlet had no inn the largest cabin was sought out, and poles extended horizontally from one end of the apartment to the other; on these poles doors purposely unhinged and brought from the surrounding cabins, were placed so that a table of considerable dimensions was formed, round which all seated themselves, each one providing his own oaten bread and fish. At the conclusion of the repast they sat for the remainder of the evening over a "Patrick's Pot" and finally separated quietly.

On Patrick's Day while the bells of churches and chapels are tuned to joyous notes the piper and harper play up "St. Patrick's Day in the Morning," old women with plenteous supplies of trifoil are heard in every direction, crying, "Buy my shamrocks, green shamrocks," and children have "Patrick's crosses" pinned on their sleeves. These are small prints of various kinds; some of them merely represent a cross, others are representations of St. Patrick trampling the reptiles under his feet.

THE TWO IRISH BULLS

Curious expedients were sometimes resorted to, according to monastic chroniclers, to determine the ownership of saints' relics and the locality for the shrine, when a contention arose between rival churches for such an honor. After the death of St. Patrick there was a keen contest between the churches of Saul and Armagh. Two bulls were yoked to the cart which bore his body and left to go whither they would. They stopped at a spot where now stands the church of Dunpatrick and there we are told he was buried. In 1186 Combrensis says his body was found in that place with the bodies of St. Columba and St. Bridget and that when they were translated from so terrible a position the following couplet was written:

In Down's fair church one hallowed tomb contains
Bridgit, Columb, and Patrick's blest Remains.

J. CHARLES WELLS.

A ST. PATRICK CIRCUS PARTY

By Hazel Carter Maxon

Step right this way—ladies and gents,
A St. Patrick Circus! Cost—non-cents.
Peanuts and popcorn and pink lemonade,
Side-shows and side-splitting circus parade.
Stupendous! Colossal! Terrific!—It's great,
So come—and come early
And stay—and stay late.

Here's a party appropriate for St. Patrick's month—or any other time. Print the above verse on top hats cut out of green cardboard to resemble the ringmaster's hat.

Decorations. To lend circus atmosphere paint red tent-like stripes on white canvas or cardboard and arch it, canopy-fashion, over the door where the guests come in. Sprinkle some sawdust on the floor, at least in the entrance. Tie a bunch of bright balloons over the top of each window, and fasten on the walls some six-sheets, as circus posters are called. For these use vivid green or red paper and letter in yellow the usual ballyhoo of superlatives: SEE THE GREATEST BIGGEST AND ALSO LARGEST SHOW ON EARTH! WITNESS THE MOST SPECTACULAR DARING AND AMAZING FEATS! GAZE ON FEROCIOUS ANIMALS FROM JUNGLES OF INDIA!

Side Shows come first at the circus. Divide the group into fours, each four to go into a huddle and present a side-show. One

327

of each four will be Barker for his show and should be given a cane, a megaphone and a sheet to screen his performance. To hang the sheets, fasten a clothes line at each end of the room, a distance from the wall. Thus sheets can be stretched from the clothes line to the wall to form little separate booths. Fill a small wagon (or Junior's baby-carriage) with costume accessories which can be rolled along to supply make-up—such accessories as false faces, crepe-paper beard for the bearded lady, snakes for the snake-charmer, dunce caps for clowns, etc. These will help to suggest acts. While the three persons of each four are rehearsing their acts, the barkers will be busy with charcoal, drawing sketches to advertise the acts, and thinking up their stirring ballyhoo speeches. When all are ready the whole assembly passes along in front of the booths for the shows. As they come to the various booths four at a time drop out to go "back stage" and put on their act. A prize is awarded for the most hilarious performance. Be sure the prize is appropriate for four people—bags of peanuts, or pop-corn balls.

It's in the Hat! Place hat on the floor and at a distance of five foot lengths place a chair. Each person has a turn at sitting in the chair with a deck of playing-cards in his left hand. His right elbow on his knee, he deals the cards one at a time from the deck into the hat. He can't push the cards, but must flick them from the wrist as though dealing across a table. If a card falls on the brim of the hat it doesn't count, unless another card later knocks it in. The person who gets most cards out of the deck into the hat wins.

Walk the Tight Rope: Place a string on the floor. Put empty bottles or mason jars at intervals of two feet. The first bottle should be placed so that the performer's foot touches it. Ask him to walk the tight-rope with his eyes open to rehearse the act for a blindfold test later. He must be careful not to knock over any bottle. After he has thus rehearsed, blindfold him and then remove all bottles except the one touching his foot. His unnecessary antics to avoid the bottles will afford fun for all.

Bring 'Em Back Alive! is an amusing Jungle Hunt using animal crackers for ferocious animals. Each person is given a paper bag and told to "bag your game." The ringmaster fires a toy pop-gun and they're off! The hunter who can find the most hidden animals wins a trophy—the toy pop-gun.

A Gay Circus Table for Eats can be made to resemble a tent by fastening green and white, or red and white paper streamers from the chandelier to each cover-place at the table. Use green and white checked gingham cloth, paper plates (or tin ones such as real circus people use), paper glasses, etc. For centerpiece have a huge Merry-Go-Round Cake—someone's best white cake baked in a circular tube cake-pan.—Ice it in white and stick green-iced animal crackers on it. From stick in the center, run a green ribbon to each cracker.

If the crowd is large, make it a buffet supper with Tuna Fish à la Newburg (or creamed on toast). Stuffed Olives, Merry-Go-Round Cake, Clown Ice Cream, and Coffee or Hot Chocolate. . . . For a smaller crowd you might serve Spiced Baked Ham, Erin Potato Salad, Pickles, Shamrock Rolls, Merry-Go-Round Cake, Clown Ice Cream and Coffee.

Recipes: *Tuna Fish à la Newburg:* 2 tablespoons butter, 2 tablespoons flour, ½ teaspoon salt, little pepper, ¾ cup evaporated milk or cream, ¾ cup water, 2 egg yolks, 2 cups white tuna fish, 1 teaspoon chopped parsley and one-half tablespoon Worcestershire sauce. Make a white sauce of the butter, flour, seasonings, milk and water. Add slightly beaten egg yolks and cook 3 minutes. Add flaked tuna fish and parsley. Heat thoroughly and add Worcestershire sauce just before serving in patty shells or on toast.

Erin Potato Salad: 2 cups diced cooked potatoes, one-fourth cup vinegar, 1 small diced onion, 2 slices bacon, one-half cup sugar, 1 teaspoon salt. Cut bacon in squares. Fry. Brown onions in fat. Add vinegar, salt, sugar and potatoes. Heat thoroughly and serve with a parsley garnish.

Clown Ice Cream: Place a slice of fresh or canned pineapple on each serving plate, top with a ball of vanilla ice cream. Sprinkle with coconut hair. It has red candy features, and an ice cream cone hat.

CONFETTI DANCE is a good finale. Before the dance begins give each man several small paper bags filled with confetti and tell them to "bag" instead of tag partners. The bagger blows up a bag and bursts it on the back of the man whose partner he wishes to capture.

CIRCUS FORTUNES are fun to take home. A long narrow box, painted to resemble a circus wagon, is placed on the table near the door. As the guests take leave each grabs an animal cracker. A tag on its neck tells some such fortune as:

(On the elephant) ...This "trunk" denotes travel to far foreign lands,

We'll greet your return with blaring brass bands.

(Camel) ....You'll inherit some treasures from countries afar

For this camel denotes you've a bright lucky star.

(Dog) ....A dog is a faithful friend, 'tis true,

But you have friends who are faithful, too.

(Lion) ....A social "lion" will court you soon

Under a mellow tropical moon.

(Pig) ....Paddy's pig vows you'll be stuck,

Stuck with good old Irish luck.

A GREEN HAT PARTY

By Hazel Carter Maxon

Invitation: Cut green cardboard in the shape of a shamrock and letter in white ink:

> Oh, do be a-comin'
> To our IRISH FAIR
> And bring in a bundle
> Some green thing to wear.

Decorate the room in green and white. In one corner, you might even have a picturesque little Erin cottage. It's simple to make if you bend gray cardboard to make walls to be somewhat circular in shape and cover the cardboard roof with straw. Make a vine of red roses out of paper to climb on the walls of the cottage.

Names: As the guests arrive, they are given Irish names (such as Norah, Bridget, Maggie, Mollie, Katie, Rosie, and Peggy for the girls, and Pat, Mike, Tim, Terry, Dennis, Jimmy, etc., for the men). The names are printed on little shamrock cards and pinned on conspicuously, and anyone failing to address another by his or her Irish name during the evening must pay a forfeit. The forfeits are later redeemed by telling Irish jokes. . . . All should use Irish brogue in talking during the evening.

Pig-in-the-Poke Costume Grab: Place a large box covered with green paper (you might put a brim on it to make it look like a hat) at the door. As each guest enters, ask him to drop his bundle of "something green to wear" in the box. After all costumes have been deposited and the guests have had time to greet each other, play "Wearing of the Green" while the guests file past the box and each grabs a bundle; and continue the music while the guests costume themselves. Since each guest will have provided something to wear himself, the grab-box exchange should produce some amusing effects. Girls may draw green suspenders or socks while men may come out wearing hair bows and bonnets.

MAD HATTERS: Have green ribbons, strings, and paper and such millinery materials as pie pans, fresh vegetables on a table, and enough chairs, with working space around them, lined up for the women guests. The men are to each choose a model and make a hat for her. Give a prize for the most up-to-the-minute model.

PIPE AND BUBBLE WAR: Give each player a clay pipe and a small green bowl filled with soapy water. Divide the group into two opposing teams and draw a chalk mark across the floor to separate opposing territories. At the crack of a toy pistol everyone starts blowing bubbles. The object of the war is to blow out the opposing team's bubbles while your own team keeps bubbles floating in the air. The side caught with no bubbles afloat is vanquished. If you wish to make the war more orderly, let each team choose a captain who delegates a certain number of his warriors to blow out bubbles on the opposing side, and a certain number who keep bubbles afloat. The captain can use his own strategy in deciding the most effective number to keep in his home territory and the number to send out on the offensive.

HOW-MANY-PIGS CONTEST is a quiet game to follow the lively one. Ask each person to write as many words as he can think of which contain the letters P-I-G somewhere in the word. They need *not* be in succession, but each word in which they do (s*pig*ot, for example) scores five while others (such as "gallo*pi*ng," "*p*orr*i*dge," "*ga*pi*ng") score one point each. Allow ten minutes for this game.

PAT AND MIKE: See which two men can give the best Pat and Mike jokes. You might give three pairs of them and use these jokes to start the thing off:

Pat: "Begorra, that's a funny pair of socks you have on, Mike
—one's white and the other's green."

Mike: "Sure, and I've got another pair like 'em at home."

* * *

Pat: "My house ought to be real warm this winter."

Mike: "Why?"

Pat: "Faith, an' the painter gave it three coats yesterday."

* * *

Mike: "I live on a boat."

Pat: "You do now?"

Mike: "Sure, and my boat makes twenty knots an hour."

Pat: "Think of that now. And who the divil unties them all?"

* * *

And how about an IRISH JIG CONTEST for the women?

* * *

PAT AND MIKE jokes also make a good supper-partner plan.
Print halves of Pat-and-Mike jokes on different slips of paper
and let guests match jokes so that the correct parts of the joke
indicate the two partners for supper. You will find very non-
sensical jokes result when the players search for their right
partners.

A CAFETERIA SUPPER is simple to serve. Cut white doilies
out of plain white paper in shamrock shape. If it is a money-
raising affair place price tags on each dish by printing the price
on small green shamrocks stuck in the food with toothpicks.

AN EMERALD ISLE MENU

Fruit cocktail with green mint cherry

Casserole   Chicken salad with shamrock pepper-rings

Pear and cottage cheese salad on lettuce

Lime Jello with Whipped Cream

Green Mints   Nuts dipped in Green Fondant

Fortunes with Your "Dish o' Tay"! Serve hot tea, too, and ask if someone in the group is entertaining at reading tea-leaves. The fortunes can be such brief couplets as:

You have-a-way-with-you, me lass,
You'll marry a professor from Boston, Mass.

With your handsome face and jaunty air
You'll have your pick of colleens fair.

So help me, a fortune's comin' your way
But don't sit and wait, says your cup-'o-tay.

Pixies down by the wishing-well
Say you'll travel quite a spell.

ST. PATRICK'S DAY GAMES

By Berenice Mueller Ball

A week's program of St. Patrick's Day games may be conducted by the pupils themselves, each being given a certain game to learn and teach, which also means the preparation of, caring for, and putting away of, all materials or equipment used for the game. Permanent teams for the week may be chosen and contest results tabulated in green chalk by the team captains at the end of each play period. The games that follow are also suitable for special parties held on St. Patrick's Day.

Outdoor Games

St. Patrick and the Snakes.—Have two equal teams line up facing each other, with each player having one foot on a line drawn across the center of the playing space. Designate one side as "Snakes," and the other as "St. Patricks." A leader calls either name, hissing the "s" as long as possible. Should he call "Snakes," all on that side run for safety to their goal line, which is behind them, chased by the other side. Any player tagged before reaching his goal must join and help the other side. The game continues until all on one side are caught. Much strategy should be used by the leader.

Orange and Green Relay.—Divide class into two equal teams, the Orange Snakes and the Green Snakes, and line them single file, facing front, behind two start lines. Place five Indian clubs about two feet apart in a straight line in front of the players. At the start signal, the leaders in turn run to the goal line and back, winding in and out between the clubs. Displacing clubs must be righted at once. On returning to his own line, each tags the outstretched hand of the waiting runner.

INDOOR GAMES

Find the Shamrock.—A hider and a St. Patrick are chosen. The latter leaves the room while a shamrock is hidden. On his return, the group hisses like snakes, softly when he is far away from the shamrock, and louder as he nears it. He becomes the hider on finding the shamrock.

Irish Relay.—Seat children in even rows. Give first in each row colored chalk. At signal, each writes on blackboard the word "shamrock," returns, hands chalk to next in row, who does likewise, and so on. For second round, each draws shamrock beside his word.

Celebrations for Easter

PLAYS AND A PAGEANT

PARABLE IN A PARK *

An Easter Play

BY JEAN MILNE GOWER

TIME: *The present*

PLACE: *Any city*

PERSONS

In order of their appearance

DINNIE O'FLAHERTY, *eight years old*
ANNA BROWN, *seven years old*
NED BROWN, *nine years old*
ALICE MERRIGAL, *eleven years old*
JAMES MERCHANT, *ten years old*
PATRICIA LOFTY, *twelve years old*
RICHMOND LOFTY, III, *twelve years old*
HERMES, *ageless*

SCENE: *Corner of a City Park where two paths converge. There are clumps of shrubbery on either side with a flowering peach tree sheltering a park bench on the right. Through the opening of the main path is a vista of city buildings above the greenery. It is Easter morning. The city churches, concluding their chimes as services are about to begin, ring out the hymn, "He is risen, He is risen; Tell it out with joyful*

* For permission to produce this play, apply to Mrs. J. H. Gower, 56 W. 70th St., New York City.

voice." As allelulias have been heard for some minutes before the curtain rises, it is a surprise to find a small ragged boy busily breaking the Sabbath. DINNIE O'FLAHERTY *is his name.*

DINNIE. (*Shouting as he chases his self-made little wooden plane across the path.*) Hould on, whilst I whittle ye a bit more,—contrayry spalpeen that ye arre! (*Catching it as it is about to land up-side-down, he takes a jack-knife from his pocket and uses it expertly, talking meanwhile.*) Wid yer wings a bit thinner, ye'll do fine. Oi'll try ye out here where the gang can't bust in, thin Oi'll take ye home fer a Easter surprise fer Mike tied up wid a lame leg—bad 'cess to ut. (*Launching the plane again.*) Git goin' an' may the Saints go wid ye!

(*This time the craft goes straight and true across the stage with* DINNIE *whooping along after it. Enter, right,* NED BROWN *and his young sister* ANNA. *They are plainly though neatly dressed and carry Sunday-school books and papers.*)

NED. (*Pausing to watch proceedings.*) Hi, there, Kid! That's some crate. Make it yourself? Let's have a look at it.

DINNIE. (*Handing it over.*) It's me foist try at 'em—though Oi've made gobs of other truck fer me kid brother.

ANNA. (*Pulling at* NED'S *sleeve.*) Let's go home, Neddy. You know Mom don't want us to play comin' home from Sunday-school— 'Specially on Easter an' such.

NED. Jest a minute, Sis. I wanta have a look at this gadget, then we'll go.

(*The three retire to the bench, right center, for a confab. Enter, right,* ALICE MERRIGAL, *a pretty, gaily dressed youngster with a smiley face. She is squired by* JAMES MERCHANT *who carries her Sunday-school books and is obviously her slave.*)

ALICE. (*Glancing at the group.*) Hello, there's that cute, funny little Brown girl who lives 'round the corner from us on

Third Street—her brother too. I wonder what that boy is showing them.

JAMES. (*In a bored voice.*) Some kid gadget, I guess. Come
along, let's find a bench where we can talk by ourselves—

NED. (*Spying the newcomers.*) There's one of our Sunday-
school boys. (*Waving* DINNIE'S *plane.*) Hi, there, Jim! Come
see what this little guy's made. It's swell.

ALICE. Let's look at it, Jim. (*Crosses to bench.*)

JAMES. (*Following glumly.*) Gosh! (*Examines plane per-
functorily.*) Not bad for a kid, but can it fly?

DINNIE. *Kin* ut! Jist kape yer oye peeled an' see if it kin.
(*He launches it up the pathway.*)

ALICE. (*Applauding as they all follow it along the path.*) I'll
say it's a peach! My brother used to make some before he
became an aviator but they weren't a patch on this one.

(*Enter, right,* PATRICIA LOFTY *fashionably correct in the
latest of Spring costumes, with her twin brother,* RICHMOND
LOFTY, III, *a tall frail boy with a languid air. They also
carry Sunday-school books.*)

RICHMOND. What goes on here? (*Observing group witness-
ing the successful landing of* DINNIE'S *plane.*) Lively encore
to Sunday-school.

PATRICIA. Awful mob. Let's hurry home, Rich, rest a while,
then pretty ourselves up a bit and surprise Mummy and Dad
by appearing on the Church Parade after Church. Pity to
waste my new togs on the desert air.

RICHMOND. No Church Parade for me, thank you. I can
think of 'steen things I'd rather do than watch a lot of stuffed
shirts in silk hats strutting along with their wives in spike-
heeled slippers and tiny flower gardens tied on one corner of
their silly heads.

PATRICIA. You're simply impossible, Richmond Lofty! So—
well, plebeian and almost sacrilegious.

RICHMOND. Sacrilegious, eh? Irreligious, maybe. I don't

want to be. What I'd really have liked to do today is to have gone to some quiet little church in the country where— (*Noticing* DINNIE's *crowd returning, he pauses and lifts his hat to* ALICE *whom he has met at Sunday-school.*) Hello, Alice. What's all the excitement?

ALICE. (*Her hand on* DINNIE's *shoulder.*) This boy's made a swell model plane out of a cigar-box. My aviator brother used to make good ones but not so— (*She remembers that she has not greeted* PATRICIA, *so she addresses her.*) Hello. I see you're in our class now—

PATRICIA. (*Haughtily.*) Well, hardly.

RICHMOND. (*To the rescue.*) Pat realises that she's out of your class so far as brothers go—yours being able to make planes and pilot them, and hers being a complete washout in every way—I can't even ride in one without being dizzy.

ALICE. (*Puzzled and nervous.*) But—but I only meant that they'd put us in the same class at Sunday-school—though we've never been introduced—

(*Enter from left,* HERMES. *He is a somewhat mysterious, romantic looking young man wearing a Byronic hat and collar. A sprig of peach blossom adorns his coat and at once one knows there is something atmospheric and universal about him. The tension that has recently been present seems to be relaxing. Even* PATRICIA *and* JIM *look peaceful.*)

HERMES. I hope I'm not intruding but I was sitting just round the corner (*Motioning toward path and shrubbery at at left.*) when I realised that aerial activity was in progress. As I'm much interested in things with wings, I just couldn't resist. (*Crossing to* DINNIE *and inspecting plane.*) Good work, son.

DINNIE. Well, mebby it'll do fer a starter. We've got lotsa other gadgets Oi've whittled outa cigar-boxes an' things. An' you'd oughta see a crutch I made fer Mike, me little brother, an' a shoe-polishin' kit to use whin Oi git the toime.

HERMES. I'd love to see them and the other gadgets. Where do you live so that I can come and have a look at them?

DINNIE. (*Suddenly shy.*) It's 27 Water Front Street, Mister. 'Tain't much of a dump but Oi try to keep it slicked up when Ma's out on a job clanin' an' sich. Me Dad's in a blind institootion, so he's all right.

HERMES. I'm sure he is, and he must be proud to have someone taking his place at home and keeping things going when your mother is out. Hurrah for you!

JAMES. I guess there's not much grass growing under your feet—as my mother says it grows under mine. Don't you ever get tired?

DINNIE. Shure Oi do—whin they make me go to school, bad 'cess to 'em.

NED. That's what it does to me too. I'd like to run away, an' mebbe I will.

ANNA. Why, Neddy Brown, I'm 'shamed of you! You just quit talkin' such foolishness.

HERMES. That's right, little sister. Give him fits. What would we men do without the women-folks to keep us in order? (*He strolls over to the bench where the other three are sitting, RICHMOND between PATRICIA and ALICE who seem now to be quite friendly.*) There's an Irishman who'll bear watching, that young fellow!

RICHMOND. (*Rising and offering his place on the bench to HERMES.*) You mean he'll be a Ford or a new edition of the Wright Brothers?

HERMES. (*Seating himself.*) Great as they and many of our famous discoverers and manufacturers have been, I seem to sense in this child a quality that will endue whatever he accomplishes with an enduring value— I can't quite put it into words—not yet—

ALICE. You mean that this little boy who has whittled an airplane out of a battered old cigar-box would—

HERMES. (*Interrupting, hand over his eyes.*) Wait—wait—there you have it! Wings—cigar-box—unselfish service—the perfect allegory. (*He sighs and opens his eyes.*) I beg your pardons. You must all be thinking I'm absolutely batty. It's partly the lovely day, you happy young people, and above all the compelling vibration over all the earth of the Great Resurrection. There are periods in most lives when one feels caught in a vise—static—unable to move or even to think, then comes some tiny jar—a vibration even—and one is free.

RICHMOND. (*Still standing before them.*) I think—I think I sort of understand.

HERMES. Hardly likely. You're much too young, my boy. But I'm afraid I must be boring you stiff. Perhaps I'd better push off.

PATRICIA. (*Intrigued.*) Oh, please not yet. It's all so different—nobody ever talks to us like this. Are you— I mean I seem to have seen you somewhere—

HERMES. (*Smiling.*) Well, I do get about a bit at times.

RICHMOND. I think it was at one of Mother's shindigs—Yes, it was,—now I remember but I can't recall your name—I'm terrible at names.

HERMES. Mine is "Hermes."

RICHMOND. (*Still uncertain.*) Why, yes, Mr. Hermes.

HERMES. No, just "Hermes" without the "Mr."

ALICE. But wasn't he the mythological god with wings on his heels?

PATRICIA. Yes, the Greek name for the god Mercury. We've just had him in school, wings and all. (*She glances at* HERMES' *heels.*) You seem to have lost yours.

HERMES. Not at all. Mine are ingrowing. I'm full of them at times. Now, for instance.

ALICE. What does it feel like? Sort of tickly?

HERMES. (*Regarding her quizzically.*) With that smiley face of yours I'm sure you know. Don't you agree with me, Richmond?

RICHMOND. (*Slightly embarrassed.*) Well, give me time. I've never thought much about wings but as to smiles—they certainly hit the mark.

PATRICIA. (*Slightly miffed that* ALICE *is getting all the bouquets.*) I think, Rich, that we ought to be going, especially as we're headed for the Church Parade.

RICHMOND. (*Seating himself firmly beside* ALICE.) Well, I'm not going to any Church Parade. It's lovely right here and I want to hear more about these wings and things.

JAMES. (*Approaching with the other children and resenting* ALICE'S *interest in* RICHMOND.) Oh, Gosh, who wants to be a sissy and gab about feathers. Come on, Ned, let's wrestle, have a boxing match or something to steam things up!

ANNA. No, no, Neddy, you mustn't! Mom don't let you play rough on Sundays. Besides, if you fight with Jimmy, his papa won't have you for a bell-hop in his big hotel when you're through school, like he promised he would.

NED. (*Glad to escape combat with his stronger challenger.*) Aw, keep your hair on, Sis! Nobody's gonto fight—not that I'm scared but I twisted my arm yesterday—

ANNA. That's all right then, an' mebbe Mr. Hermes'll tell us a story, mebbe. (*Sidling up to his knee.*) Will you?

HERMES. (*Putting his arm around her.*) If you like. A short one, perhaps.

ANNA. Goody, goody, goody! A Sunday one—all about Easter—

HERMES. (*Lifting* ANNA *to his knee.*) I suspect you've all been hearing in Sunday-school a lot about this wonderful season of the Resurrection so we'll try to think of some everyday happening that might turn sad things into glad things; some selfless or kind action that brings to life happiness in someone—you know what I mean.

ALICE. Something like the parables in the New Testament—they were all little made-up stories to make people think.

PATRICIA. (*Uneasily rising.*) Well, we've really had quite a lot given us this morning to think about, so I guess Rich and I had better be running along, if you don't mind.

RICHMOND. Not just yet, Pat, please. I started this thing by asking information about internal wings and I'd like to stick round till I get it. Right, Mr. Hermes?

HERMES. Right.

PATRICIA. (*Reseating herself reluctantly.*) Oh, well, for a little while, maybe.

HERMES. (*Smiling at her.*) I'll make it snappy. (*To* JAMES, NED *and* DINNIE *on the side-line.*) If you boys want to join this session, just borrow three stumps, stones or something from around the shrubbery for seats—and pray that the cops won't catch you. There were some loose stones over where I was sitting.

DINNIE. Come on, fellers, an' divil take the cops! (*Hands model plane to* HERMES *and starts off left.*)

NED. (*Following.*) I'm a good dodger. Watch me if one shows up.

JAMES. (*Glaring at* ALICE *and* RICHMOND *chatting on the bench, grumbles as he goes.*) I guess folks that live on Park Avenue get the box seats. Some toffs!

(*As construction of the impromptu auditorium progresses, the "box-holders" help with suggestions and comments.*)

ANNA. Neddy's kinda lazy at home but I bet he brings the biggest one to show how strong he is.

PATRICIA. Exercise wouldn't hurt you any, Rich. Why don't you help?

RICHMOND. Having much too pleasant and comfortable a time here, thank you.

ALICE. (*Dreamily.*) It certainly is heavenly—the spring flowers and all.

NED. (*Emerging first from shrubbery at left rolling a large piece of rock.*) Lookit, what a whopper I found! With kinda shiney pimples o' green on it.

PATRICIA. Perhaps you've discovered an emerald mine.

NED. Oh, boy! Then we could buy Mom a new washing machine an' pop a jaloppy.

(JAMES *and* DINNIE *appear with smaller spoils.*)

JAMES. Ned got the only big one.

ANNA. I told you so!—I told you so!

DINNIE. Oi don't moind. Oi'd as lave sit on the ground. Anything does fer me.

HERMES. Not at all. Since your flying machine has brought us together, I think Ned will want you to sit on the emerald throne. How about it, Ned?

NED. (*A bit dashed.*) Oh, sure—sure. I'll sit on his piece of concrete—it's flatter anyway.

HERMES. (*Motioning* DINNIE *to the higher central stone.*) Take the place of honor. By the way, I don't think any of us knows your name.

DINNIE. Me name? Well, me rale name is Dinnis O'Flaherty afther me dad but they call me Dinnie fer short.

HERMES. All right, Dinnie-for-Short, you hold the airplane which maybe will make a good symbol.

ALICE. (*To* RICHMOND *as they settle back.*) I wonder what the Rector would think if he saw us holding this camp-meeting with an airplane for a text.

RICHMOND. He's pretty broad and rather a jolly old codger; but, at that, he might think it a slightly pagan proceeding.

PATRICIA. (*Glancing at the mixed company.*) You couldn't blame him.

HERMES. It wouldn't be the first time I've been accused of

promulgating pagan ideas. I'll try now, however, to be as orthodox as possible. Those who are nervous had better escape now.

ANNA. (*Snuggling up.*) Dunno what those big words mean, but I'm not scared an' I'm gonto stay.

HERMES. Thanks, Anna. It's nice to have friends whom you can trust and who aren't afraid to trust you.

JAMES. (*Enigmatically.*) I used to think that; but I'm learning things lately.

ALICE. Poor Jimmy! You must have eaten something to upset you.

JAMES. Nuts!

HERMES. (*Smiling.*) Now, let's get on with our story. Once, ages ago, some mineral—an emerald, perhaps—awakened from her life-long sleep in the dark earth to find herself trembling with ecstasy. "I have had a wonderful dream," she cried. "I have been flying on beautiful wings through clear, bright air. What may I do to be free?" she asked of the *Great Silence* surrounding her, and gently the *Voice of All Wisdom* revealed to her that she must sacrifice her life as a precious stone and give her substance to the building of some growing thing— grass, grain, shrub or tree.

"Oh, may it be a tree," she sighed, "where birds may shelter between their flights."

ANNA. (*Eagerly.*) Like in her dream! Like in her dream!

HERMES. Exactly. Then *All Wisdom* told her how she, as a tree, might be called upon, after long years of growth, to sacrifice her new substance for the use of man.

JAMES. Some continuous program, if you ask me.

HERMES. That's life, all right. However the essence of her dream lived on through changing seasons as her emerald quality of green strength was being absorbed by the spreading cedar tree which now held her spirit and personality. Some day, she knew, she might be called to man's service by giving up her

strong fine body for the building of beautiful homes, for helping form great ocean vessels, or—dream of dreams—to be a
part of some shimmering airship. "Oh, may I be an airplane
with staunch wings bearing happiness through the sky!"

RICHMOND. (*Aside to* ALICE.) Not only happiness flying
round these days, I'm afraid.

HERMES. When the woodmen came to fell the cedar tree and
her companions, she rejoiced that her vision might be going to
be realised. In every particle of her still coursing sap she knew
there was a trace of her freely-given emerald strength to help
resist possible storm and stress. Even when the final crash
came and the sap congealed, she gloried in the persistence of her
dream which permeated every tiniest twig. But, when her
beautiful tree-body reached the sawmill, she found that, instead of being sawn into long slender segments for the purposes
of which she had dreamed, the wood was being divided into
thin, short lengths. A rough foreman overseeing the work remarked casually, "This-here cedar'd oughter turn out two-
thousand cigar-boxes."

ALICE. What a terrible disappointment—

HERMES. Yes, but Emerald tried to see its possibilities.
"What are cigars?" she wondered. Maybe they were some sort
of precious stone. Perhaps the boxes would be beautifully
joined and carved into jewel-caskets to be treasured by those
who possessed them. But even this dream of a shelter for
jewels—such as she herself had been before she was resurrected
into a tree—was rudely shattered when she found the small
segments of her noble tree-body being transformed by weary
factory workers into endless identical boxes to hold rank-
smelling cylinders of a brown substance called tobacco.

PATRICIA. (*Tensely.*) It's silly of me—but this is getting
tragic—

HERMES. Most of the cigars were sold at smart clubs and
hotels where the "Lords of Creation" did their part in evolution

by returning them to the elements in billows of smoke. Modern incinerators did as much by the boxes so that in process of time—aeons, perhaps—the minute particles of emerald might again have a chance of bringing happiness to someone. One of these empty boxes, however, found itself one morning in a rubbish can outside a disreputable resort near 27 Water Front Street. It faced nothing but a dismal and inglorious fate, still the emerald in its fiber vibrated to the memory of an old dream as the shadow of a cruising pigeon dappled its dusty surface. Then, suddenly, above the rim of the rubbish can a small freckled face appeared, two eager blue eyes grew big and round and a happy voice rang out:

"Glory be! A rale cedar box! Shure now Oi'll be makin' young Mike a illigant airplane that'll bate anny burud a-flyin'!"

DINNIE. (*Amazed.*) Faith, 'twas almost me verry wurruds whin Oi seen the box in the rubbidge foreninst a pair of ould shoes—

HERMES. (*Drawing him closer.*) And you rescued the box and have given it wings and the chance to bring happiness to little Mike.

DINNIE. God love 'im—

ALICE. (*Rising.*) Well. Something's brought something to all of us I guess, eh, Jimmie? (*Takes his arm.*)

JAMES. (*Radiant.*) I'll tell the world! What say we all chip in on a little Easter treat for Dinnie's folks and see Mike get his Easter present?

DINNIE. (*Somewhat uncertainly.*) Well, but there's mebbe too manny uv us. Me dad's home frum the institootion fur Easter an' there's me Granny an' two sisters an'—

HERMES. The more the merrier. Jim's idea sounds grand to me.

ANNA. (*Hopping up and down.*) Me an' Neddie'll give the two nickels Mom gave us for chocolate eggs, won't we, Neddie?

NED. Sure. An' I've got another—the one I didn't put in the

collection.

PATRICIA. (*To* RICHMOND.) I've got a tenner to spend. I think it's going to be the greatest lark ever—

RICHMOND. (*Softly to* PATRICIA.) Lark! Let's make it a couple of turkeys and trimmings. I've not tapped my allowance yet, so the sky's the limit, eh, Pat old girl?

HERMES. (*Joining them.*) Let's get along. We'll plan as we go. (*To* DINNIE.) Skip along to the park entrance, Dinnie-for-Short, and hail a taxi for us.

DINNIE. (*Amazed.*) Taxi! Arre we goin' in a taxi? Shure they'll be bungin' out their oyes whin we come ridin' down Water Front Strate. (*He rushes off right, waving his plane and shouting* "Taxi! Taxi!")

HERMES. (*Half aloud as he pauses while the others follow* DINNIE.) I don't think we really need that taxi—(*Looking up toward the sky.*) There are wings enough around here to float a universe.

CURTAIN

DAWN IN AN UPPER ROOM *

A Play for Easter

BY DELLE OGLESBEE ROSS

PERSONS IN THE PLAY

MARY OF NAZARETH, *the Mother of Jesus*

MARY, THE MOTHER OF MARK, *a woman of position and importance*

MARY MAGDALENE, *a young woman of Magdala, healed, by Jesus, of sin*

---

* This play may be produced without royalty where no admission is charged; otherwise, a fee of $3.00 must be paid to the author, 317 North Marion St., Oak Park, Ill.

SALOME, *Wife of Zebedee, mother of his sons, John and James, sister of Mary of Nazareth*

JOSEPH OF ARIMATHAEA, *a rich man*

MARK, *a youth*

JOHN, *the beloved disciple*

JAMES, *his brother, another disciple*

SIMON PETER, *the disciple who denied Jesus*

ANDREW, *his brother, also a disciple*

THOMAS, *a slow-witted man, who must see to believe, a disciple*

JOANNA, *wife of a steward of Herod, a follower of Jesus*

TWO CHILDREN

TIME: *April, 27 A. D. Late in the night of the Sabbath following the crucifixion of Jesus, the Christ.*

SCENE: *An upper room in the house of* MARY, THE MOTHER OF MARK, *not far from Golgotha, in Jerusalem.*

NOTES: *The characters are dressed in the manner of the Biblical period.* MARY OF NAZARETH, *if possible, should wear a mantle of the rich blue associated with the Madonna, her head is swathed in a veil.* MARY, MOTHER OF MARK, *is soberly, but richly dressed,* JOANNA *is a court lady, and should be attired accordingly,* JOSEPH OF ARIMATHAEA *and* MARK *wear clothes fitting their positions, the others are more poorly clothed.*

The Twenty-third Psalm may be sung using any desired arrangement, or may be recited.

Any Easter Alleluia may be used by the choir at the end of the play.

An upper room in the house of MARY, THE MOTHER OF MARK. *It is late in the night, and the room is dimly lighted with small Syrian lamps on the tables. A door, right front, leads to the roof. At right center is a long table with benches at either side. A chair at the end faces the audience. Center back are two windows with closed shutters. Another table stands between the windows. Upon this are flagons, platters of fruit and bread, a shallow basket with boxes and jars nearby. At right of this table is a low ottoman, and at left, a little advanced to the front, is a large chair or bench. In the corner, left back, are pallets upon which two* CHILDREN *are sleeping. At left, front, a door leads to the stairs and lower part of the house. Both doors are curtained.* JOSEPH OF ARIMATHAEA *stands at the door, left. Upon the chair, left, sits* MARY OF NAZARETH, *bowed in grief.* MARY MAGDALENE *stands beside the window back of her.* SALOME *sits upon the ottoman spinning from a distaff.* MARY, THE MOTHER OF MARK, *sits in the large chair at the head of the table. Her son* MARK *leans against her. On the bench at right of the table are* SIMON PETER, ANDREW *and* THOMAS. *At left are* JOHN *and* JAMES. *They are in various attitudes of grief.* PETER'S *head is bowed upon his arms.*

JOSEPH. Nay, you need not fear—

MARY, MOTHER OF MARK. So far none have molested us—

ANDREW. We have stayed quietly in this house—

SALOME. Today being the Sabbath we could do so without question. We but obeyed the law—

JOSEPH. True—and you have been wise—

SALOME. So it seemeth to us.

JOSEPH. There has been rioting in the city, and Pilate—because he is not satisfied that he gave Jesus over to the High Priest's demands—has given orders to the centurions to be especially diligent.

MARY MAGDALENE. But the tomb?

JOSEPH. 'Tis safe, Mary of Magdala.

MARY MAGDALENE. I have not dared to go since we laid the beloved Master in its darkness—

JOHN. I, myself, saw Joseph place the huge stone before the opening—

JOSEPH. Fear not—'twill be difficult to move—

MARY, MOTHER OF MARK. Then think ye our enemies can not take away the body?

JOSEPH. Nay, Lady—

JAMES. There are guards?

JOSEPH. Yea, that boon I asked of Pilate—and he charged two Roman soldiers to guard it well.

ANDREW. 'Twill serve two purposes—

JAMES. How so, Andrew?

ANDREW. 'Twill prevent our Master's body being removed—

MARY MAGDALENE. And—

ANDREW. They can bear witness that we have made no attempt to do so—

MARY, MARK'S MOTHER. That is true, Andrew—

SALOME. Then nothing has been done since you placed him in the tomb?

JOSEPH. Nothing, Salome.

MARY, MARK'S MOTHER. Think you we have been remiss—

JOSEPH. Nay. What would you? It is unsafe for his followers to be abroad in the city—

MARK. What did you tell me, Simon Peter, that he said about the temple?

SIMON PETER. That though they destroyed this temple—in three days would he build it up again.

JOSEPH. Strange—

JOHN. But think you he meant the temple of stones and clay?

JAMES. Who knows—he spoke in parables—and said many strange things—

THOMAS. Strange things—and confusing—

JOHN. Be not troubled, Thomas. In days to come his meaning will be clear to us—

(THOMAS *looks bewildered, there is a moment's silence.*)

MARY MAGDALENE. I shall wait no longer—

SALOME. What mean you?

MARY MAGDALENE. At the first hint of day I go to the tomb to see that all is well—

MARY, MARK'S MOTHER. I will go with you—

SALOME. And I—

MARY OF NAZARETH. I, also—

MARY MAGDALENE. Nay, you are not strong enough—

MARY, MARK'S MOTHER. Stay you here, Mary, it is not meet that you should go—

MARY MAGDALENE. See—I have spices and rare ointments—

MARY OF NAZARETH. For him?

MARY MAGDALENE. Ay, to anoint him—

SALOME. How will you enter the tomb?

MARK. The great stone—

JOSEPH. Tell the centurions, with my sign, that I have sent you— They will remove the stone.

MARY MAGDALENE. Then very early in the morning we shall go.

JOSEPH. It grows late—

(*There are shouts and the sound of people running. Those in the room gasp—and are very still until the noise passes.*)

SIMON PETER. (*Listening.*) Naught but the watch pursuing some late revellers—

MARY OF NAZARETH. Each time I hear a noise I am affrighted—

JAMES. Be not disturbed—

JOHN. I will protect you—did he not leave you in my care?

MARY OF NAZARETH. Dear nephews, I know in truth ye would do your best—

JOSEPH. All is now quiet, and I must leave you—

MARY, MARK'S MOTHER. I fear to have you go into the street—

MARY MAGDALENE. Need you?

JOSEPH. I must return to Arimathaea—

MARK. Then will I see you to the outer door—

ANDREW. Nay, Mark, I will—

JOSEPH. Stay—

ANDREW. If you must go I will light you down.

JOSEPH. Then, farewell to you, friends, fear not—tomorrow is now the third day—and they have not harmed you—

SALOME. True. Farewell—Joseph—

JOSEPH. God be with you—

ALL. Farewell

JOSEPH. Farewell—

(ANDREW *takes a lamp from a table and goes with* JOSEPH *through the door, left.*)

MARK. I should like to see the city, Mother, since the storm and the earthquake—

SALOME. Joseph said the veil of the temple was riven in twain—

MARY, MARK'S MOTHER. 'Twas a sudden storm and violent—

MARY OF NAZARETH. Violence! Violence! Oh—my son! My son!

SALOME. Nay—Mary—start not thy weeping again—

SIMON PETER. 'Tis I should weep—I who denied my Lord—

MARY MAGDALENE. Peter—you whom he called the rock—

SIMON PETER. I know—I know—

MARY MAGDALENE. But why—

SIMON PETER. (*Getting up to pace the floor.*) 'Twas the evil one—for I had no wish to do this— I would have gladly given my life—

JOHN. You were afraid—Peter—afraid! We were all afraid—

JAMES. In truth Jesus warned us—

JOHN. He told us all that was to come—and yet we could not help him!

JAMES. We all failed him—all!

JOHN. We slept when we should have watched—

THOMAS. And ran away when they came to take him—

JOHN. We loved him and we failed him— Woe—woe—

MARY, MARK'S MOTHER. It helpeth not to go over and over the mistakes ye made—

SALOME. It but addeth to your torment—

JOHN. But he told us—and we should have been alert—

THOMAS. It confuseth me—that he said—"A little while ye do not see me—and a little while ye do see me"—

JOHN. For something was he preparing us—

THOMAS. Then said he, "The way I go ye know not"—

ANDREW. (*Coming in, left.*) But he also said he was sending us a Comforter, "the Spirit of Truth"—

JOHN. And when that is come all will be made plain.

THOMAS. My thoughts are in confusion—I go to the roof— and there alone will see this clearly. (THOMAS *leaves through the door, right.*)

SIMON PETER. And this also he said, "I leave the world and go unto my Father."

JAMES. He charged us to bear witness to all that he has taught us—

JOHN. And to love one another.

MARY OF NAZARETH. Always he spoke of love and forgiveness and peace—

MARY MAGDALENE. How can we forgive Judas Iscariot?

(*Again there is noise in the street, and again the little group is silent with fear. The* CHILDREN *cry out and whimper,* MARY MAGDALENE *hushes them and returns to lean against the window.*)

MARY, MARK'S MOTHER. Didst see aught in the street, Andrew?

ANDREW. Nay, nothing, Mary. Joseph went swiftly, no one disturbed him—

JOHN. You speak of Judas Iscariot, Mary Magdalene, think you not that Jesus forgave him?

SIMON PETER. Ay—he must have—he forgave me!

MARY MAGDALENE. It seemeth too great for me to forgive Judas—

JOHN. No wrong against himself was too great for Jesus, the Christ to forgive—are you more than he?

MARY MAGDALENE. (*Hiding her face and sinking to her knees.*) Who am I to withhold forgiveness?—I—whom he forgave and healed of grievous sins!

JOHN. Ah, Judas—Judas—that misguided man!

JAMES. Think ye his ill-gotten money will be of any value when his heart breaks with remorse?

(*Voices are head, and a loud knocking on the outer door. The* CHILDREN *on the pallets stir and cry out.* MARY MAGDALENE *runs to them.*)

SIMON PETER. What is that? (*He turns to the door left.*)

MARK. Mother—'tis someone at the outer door—

MARY, MARK'S MOTHER. Yea, my son. (*To* SIMON PETER.) Should we answer?

JAMES. Peter—we will go—

JOHN. I go also—

MARY OF NAZARETH. Pray God no harm come to you!

(SIMON PETER, JAMES *and* JOHN *go out the door, left.*)

1ST CHILD. What is it— Oh—what is it?

2ND CHILD. Are the soldiers coming?

MARY MAGDALENE. Hush, thee, hush!

MARY OF NAZARETH. Surely they will not harm babes!

SALOME. Fear not, children of my daughter, no harm will come to ye—

(MARK, *who has come over to the door, left, steps out.*)

MARY, MARK'S MOTHER. My son—my son—Mark—do not leave us!

MARY OF NAZARETH. Come. babes, to me. See, I will wrap you in my mantle. The air is chill before the dawn—

(*The* CHILDREN *crouch on either side of her, and she*

covers them with her mantle.)

MARY MAGDALENE. Once he said— "Suffer little children to come unto me."

(*She covers her face and weeps. Voices are heard on the stair.*)

MARY, MARK'S MOTHER. Sh—they come—

(MARK *runs in.*)

MARK. Mother—Mother—'tis but a woman—a great lady. She is alone—

(JOANNA *enters, followed by* SIMON PETER, JAMES *and* JOHN.)

JOANNA. Greetings—and pardon—Lady—

(MARY, MARK'S MOTHER *rises and goes to her.*)

MARY, MARK'S MOTHER. The Lady, Joanna! What brings you from the palace in the late night?

JOANNA. I heard news—news that I thought ye all must know—

(MARY *leads her to her own chair, then drops down upon the bench by her side. The others who stood at her entrance, and made obeisance to her, resume their places.* MARK *goes to the door, right,* PETER, JAMES *and* JOHN *remain standing by the door, left.*)

MARY, MARK'S MOTHER. Speak then, Lady, what tidings?

JOANNA. I heard the officers of Herod talking—there have been more earthquakes—know ye?

MARK. We feared so, Lady, and the thunder and lightning come again and again—

SALOME. But we have not left this house since the night— since the night— (*She covers her face. There is silence.*)

JOANNA. Think ye I do not know your sorrow?

MARY OF NAZARETH. Oh—woe—woe—

MARK. But thy tidings, Lady—

JOANNA. Yea, yea, my tidings—I must tell you—

SIMON PETER. Speak—Lady—

JOANNA. I overheard the captain of the household guards tell my husband that Judas—

MARY MAGDALENE. Judas Iscariot?

JOANNA. Yea—Judas Iscariot. He hath tried to return the thirty pieces of silver to the chief priest and the elders—

JOHN. His heart repenteth him—

JOANNA. But they would not take the silver—

JAMES. They refused it?

JOANNA. Yea— But hark ye—he went away—

SIMON PETER. Away—

JOANNA. And tonight they found him—hanged!

MARK. Hanged!

(*There are exclamations from them all.*)

JOANNA. He had destroyed himself!

MARY OF NAZARETH. Lo—shall the wicked perish!

(*They are silent from amazement and horror.*)

JOHN. Who has claimed his body?

JOANNA. None.

JOHN. Then what—

JOANNA. The elders have bought a field with the thirty pieces of silver where they may bury the homeless and friendless—it will be called The Field of Blood!

SIMON PETER. The Field of Blood!

JOANNA. And there will the shamed body of Judas Iscariot be buried!

JOHN. Verily the wages of sin are death.

MARY, MARK'S MOTHER. How considerate of you, Lady Joanna, to come to us.

JOANNA. All day, Lady, hath my heart been with you—your sorrow is mine also— I loved the gentle Master and his teachings—

MARY, MARK'S MOTHER. That we know full well—

JOANNA. Thus when I heard this dreadful news, I asked two centurions to bring me here. They also have listened to the words of our Teacher.

MARY OF NAZARETH. (*Musingly.*) Strange—the life of this man—the son of my body—yet the Son of God!

JOANNA. A great Man! Though they crucify him—yet will he never die!

SIMON PETER. In the hearts of those who hear his words will he live forever!

MARY OF NAZARETH. At his birth there was a great star— and shepherds—and wise kings—worshipping—

JOHN. And angels singing—you have told us—

MARY OF NAZARETH. Yea—great and marvelous things at his birth—

SIMON PETER. And great and marvelous things hath he showed us.

MARY OF NAZARETH. (*Talking as though to herself.*) The wise men greeted him—that tiny babe—as a King—though born in a stable—

JOHN. Always he was poor and humble—

SIMON PETER. But always one felt his Kingliness!

MARY OF NAZARETH. Then they crucify him—and the earth trembles—the veil of the temple is rent! Storm and wind as though the elements themselves were angered by this cruel deed—

MARY MAGDALENE. Yet has he said— "I will come again."

JOANNA. And you have faith?

MARY MAGDALENE. (*Her head raised, exalted.*) Yea—I have faith!

(*There is silence.*)

JOANNA. (*Rising.*) It groweth late. Soon will come the dawn, and I must be back before I am missed.

(MARK *steps forward, and with her hand on his arm they go to the door, left.*)

MARY, MARK'S MOTHER. Our deep gratitude, Lady Joanna, for your kindness—

JOANNA. Could I do otherwise, knowing of your grief and fear? Farewell!

ALL. Farewell—

(*She leaves,* MARK *accompanying her.*)

ANDREW. So Judas is no more!

JOHN. So doth evil destroy itself—

JAMES. Then why was our Master also destroyed?

SIMON PETER. Why did he not save himself?

JOHN. He said it was to fulfil the prophecies.

SALOME. He was so good—so gentle—why—

MARY MAGDALENE. Think ye that he really died?

JOHN. It was his wounded body that Joseph of Arimathaea wrapped in linen and—

ANDREW. Yea—and laid within his own newly-hewn tomb in the rocky garden—

JAMES. And he was not living—I saw for myself—

(MARK *returns.*)

MARK. It is nearly dawn. The first gray shows in the eastern sky.

MARY MAGDALENE. We must not delay if we would take the spices to the tomb—

(*She busies herself at the table, center back, placing boxes and jars in the basket.* SALOME *rises and puts down her distaff, she with* MARY MAGDALENE *and* MARY, THE MOTHER OF MARK *wrap themselves in veils and mantles.* MARY MAGDALENE *opens the shutters of one of the little windows. A dim light shows.* SALOME *goes to* MARY OF NAZARETH *and kisses her face.*)

SALOME. Peace, sister, we will soon return.

(MARY MAGDALENE *bows before her,* MARY, MARK'S MOTHER, *takes her hand and presses it.*)

MARY, MARK'S MOTHER. Comfort you, Mary of Nazareth, comfort you thinking of your son. God's gift to men—

SIMON PETER. Shall we go with you?

SALOME. Nay, soon the light cometh—

MARY, MARK'S MOTHER. And few are now abroad—

(*They leave through door, left.*)

MARY OF NAZARETH. The little ones are again asleep—

(*The smaller one has fallen cuddled up to her side, the larger one's head is upon her shoulder.*)

JOHN. I will lift them to their beds.

(*He comes forward and takes the little one in his arms, placing her upon the pallet.*)

MARY OF NAZARETH. How gentle you are, John—

JOHN. (*Helping the other child.*) I was taught by One— meek and tender.

MARY OF NAZARETH. Now help me, John, help me to walk about. I have scarcely moved this night—so fearful was I—

MARK. (*Coming to them.*) I too, Mary of Nazareth, I too will help you—

(*With their help she walks back and forth.* PETER, JAMES *and* ANDREW *are grouped around the table, right.*)

MARY OF NAZARETH. (*Pausing before the open window, which shows a little stronger light.*) How fresh and sweet the dawn wind—

JOHN. Yet the thunder rumbles in the hills—

MARK. And there—another lightning flash—

MARY OF NAZARETH. Methinks 'twill seem long ere they return from the tomb—

JOHN. But it is not far—

MARY OF NAZARETH. They may be delayed—

MARK. You are impatient—

MARY OF NAZARETH. Ay, impatient—that I am—

(SIMON PETER, JAMES *and* ANDREW *have been softly singing a Psalm, their voices grow louder and* JOHN *and* MARK *join in.* MARY *sinks down in her chair, her face lifted as though she saw a vision. Voices of women are heard.*)

THE MEN. (*Singing.*) Yea, though I walk through the Val-
           ley of the Shadow of Death,
           I will fear no evil—
           For Thou art with me—

    (SALOME, *and* MARY, MARK'S MOTHER, *rush in.*)

SALOME. The tomb! The tomb!

SIMON PETER. What say you?

MARY, MARK'S MOTHER. The tomb is empty!

JOHN. (*Angrily.*) The chief priests and the elders—they have
removed him—

JAMES. (*Clenching his fists.*) Stolen his crucified body!

MARY, MARK'S MOTHER. They have taken the Lord out of
the sepulchre, and we know not where they have laid him!

SIMON PETER. Come, we must see this thing—

JOHN. But the stone—the stone?

SALOME. It was rolled away—

SIMON PETER. Haste you, John—

JOHN. Our Lord Jesus—where have they taken him?

    (SIMON PETER *and* JOHN *hurry from the room, left.* MARY
OF NAZARETH *is lying back in her chair.*)

ANDREW. What, then, saw you?

JAMES. Where is Mary of Magdala?

SALOME. She came not with us—

MARY, MARK'S MOTHER. She stood by the tomb, weeping—

ANDREW. But saw ye anything?

SALOME. The empty tomb—

MARY, MARK'S MOTHER. The stone rolled to one side—

SALOME. And on either side of the entrance it seemeth a man
in shining raiment stood—

JAMES. They were the soldiers—

SALOME. Nay, James, the soldiers lay as though dead beside
the sepulchre—

ANDREW. (*Shaking his head.*) I do not understand— Men in

shining garments—

SALOME. (*Timidly.*) It seemeth—perhaps—they were angels—

MARY OF NAZARETH. More marvels! More mysteries!

(PETER *is heard.*)

SIMON PETER. Haste you, John—we must tell them of these wonders.

(*They enter, left.*)

ANDREW. What did ye find?

JOHN. I reached the tomb before Peter, and, stooping, looked within. There was no body—only the linen lying—

JAMES. Didst go in?

JOHN. Nay, I entered not.

SIMON PETER. I did—

ANDREW. And you—what saw you?

SIMON PETER. I also saw the linen clothes lying there—

ANDREW. Nothing more?

SIMON PETER. The napkin, that was about his head, not lying with the linen, but wrapped together in a place by itself.

JOHN. Then went I in also, and found that it was true—he was gone!

MARK. But Salome and my mother saw men in shining garments.

JOHN. Once it seemed so to me—

SIMON PETER. I too—but the light and the shadows mingled —and I know not—

ANDREW. Think ye they were men—or angels?

JOHN. It was not given me to know.

SALOME. This is a time of marvels—but Mary Magdalene— she is not with you?

SIMON PETER. She still wept—kneeling by the tomb.

JOHN. We thought she prayed—so we disturbed her not.

MARK. (*Suddenly.*) What did Jesus say about the third day?

THOMAS. (*Enters from the roof, right.*) What is happening?

You are excited—and Mary Magdalene is running toward the house—

JOHN. They have taken away our Lord!

THOMAS. What sayest—art mad?

SIMON PETER. The tomb is empty—the grave clothes lying nearby—

JOHN. We have been there—

SIMON PETER. And have seen!

(MARY MAGDALENE *bursts into the room, her face is radiant.* MARY OF NAZARETH *rises from her chair, the* CHILDREN *sit up in their beds, then get up and run to the windows.*)

1ST CHILD. The dawn—the dawn!

2ND CHILD. Let the light into the room!

(*She opens the closed window, a pale rosy light streams in.*)

MARY MAGDALENE. He is risen! He is risen!

MARY OF NAZARETH. Risen! Mean you Jesus?

MARY MAGDALENE. Jesus the Christ! He is risen indeed!

THOMAS. You are distraught! What tale is this?

MARY MAGDALENE. Hearken—

SIMON PETER. Haste—tell us—

MARY MAGDALENE. I was weeping by the sepulchre. When you left I arose and bending low looked in—

JOHN. Did you see—?

MARY MAGDALENE. The tomb was empty save for two angels—

SIMON PETER. Angels!

MARY MAGDALENE. In white, one sitting at the head, one at the foot where the body of Jesus had lain—

JAMES. Strange—

MARY OF NAZARETH. Did they speak?

MARY MAGDALENE. Yea. They said, "Woman, why weepest thou?"

SALOME. And you—

MARY MAGDALENE. I said unto them, "Because they have taken away my Lord, and I know not where they have laid him."

JOHN. Then—

MARY MAGDALENE. Then one said, "Ye seek Jesus of Nazareth which was crucified! He is risen!"

MARY OF NAZARETH. Risen!

MARY MAGDALENE. "He is risen—he is not here. Behold the place where they laid him."

1ST CHILD. The light is stronger over the world—

2ND CHILD. 'Twill soon be day!

MARY MAGDALENE. They told me to bring the word to his disciples—and I turned to hasten home.

MARK. And that was all?

MARY MAGDALENE. (*Triumphantly, jubilantly.*) Nay—not all! Not all!

SIMON PETER. What then?

MARY MAGDALENE. There was a man standing—I supposed he was the gardener— He said, "Woman, why weepest thou? Whom seekest thou?"

MARK. Was it the gardener?

MARY MAGDALENE. Hearken ye! I said unto him, "Sir—if thou hast borne him hence, tell me where thou hast laid him, and I will take him away—"

MARY OF NAZARETH. Did he tell you, child?

MARY MAGDALENE. Then he smiled at me and said, "Mary— Mary—"

JOHN. He knew you—

MARY MAGDALENE. Then I looked and saw—it was my Lord, Jesus, and I went to him crying "Rabboni"!

JOHN. Why came he not with you?

MARY OF NAZARETH. Yea—why?

MARY MAGDALENE. He said to me, "Touch me not, for I have not yet ascended to my Father"—

THOMAS. 'Twas his spirit?

MARY MAGDALENE. 'Twas Jesus! Think ye I know not? He further said, "Go to my brethren and say unto them: I ascend unto my Father and your Father—to my God and your God."

SIMON PETER. Thus he meant—when he said "The third day I will arise."

THOMAS. Still will I not believe except I shall see in his hands the print of the nails, and put my finger into the print of his nails, and thrust my hand into his side!

MARY, MARK'S MOTHER. Oh, Thomas—Thomas—thou doubting man!

THOMAS. Still I cannot hold this as truth—

MARY MAGDALENE. (*Firmly.*) It was Jesus! It was the risen Christ!

MARK. Of a verity ye believe this is true?

MARY MAGDALENE. I do believe!

SIMON PETER. And I—

JOHN. So did he tell us it would come about when we ate of the Passover together.

SALOME. His prophecy we must accept—

MARY MAGDALENE. So are the ancient writings justified! With mine eyes saw I the risen Christ!

MARY OF NAZARETH. (*Looking at the windows.*) The night is spent. The blessed day hath come!

(*There is a glow of golden light. A thrilling, tender Voice says,* "Peace be unto you."

The members of the group stand with outstretched hands, or kneel reverently. There is a burst of triumphant music and a choir, as of angels, sings Alleluia!)

CURTAIN

THE NEWS THAT CAME TO NAZARETH *

An Easter Play

By Ivy Bolton

CAST OF CHARACTERS

The Five Angel Watchers
Ruth, *a maid of Nazareth*
David, *her younger brother*
Judith, *her grandmother*
Naomi
Esther
Miriam
Judah, *an old man*
Ephraim
Nathan
Issachar
Jesse, *a lad*
Benjamin, *a lad*
Gideon, *brother of Ruth and David*

Before the curtain rises "Who is this in garments gory?"—or some other hymn of the Passion is sung.

The Scene (*which does not change although there are two short pauses in the play*): *The well and market place of Nazareth. There are hills in the distance. If desired, a village street may be portrayed.*

The time is Good Friday about three o'clock. At the well the five angels *watch with wonder and adoration in their faces.*

The stage is rather dark; outside Keble's "Ave Maria" or "Blest are the pure in heart" is sung.

* For permission to produce, apply to The Woman's Press, 600 Lexington Ave., New York City.

Scene I

FIRST ANGEL. It was here she came, Mary, sweet Maid of Nazareth and here the great Archangel Gabriel spoke his greeting and hailed her Mother of the Lord.

SECOND ANGEL. Behold the handmaid of the Lord, she said. How heaven rejoiced to hear that word!

THIRD ANGEL. Mind you the day she ran across the hills to see her cousin, old Elizabeth?

FOURTH ANGEL. How heaven echoed Elizabeth's greeting and stilled to listen to sweet Mary's song, her glad Magnificat!

FIFTH ANGEL. I often marvel that men did not know. Think that for the Lord of Heaven and Earth, there was no room in Bethlehem's inn.

FIRST ANGEL. Aye, naught but a stable. Mind you the song we sang to shepherds on the hills?

SECOND ANGEL. And how the wise men came, following a star?

THIRD ANGEL. We guarded the sweet Mother and the Holy Child all that long way to Egypt. What wonders then we saw.

FOURTH ANGEL. Afterwards she came here often with Her Son. I can see Him now drawing the water for Her and watching Her with loving eyes.

THIRD ANGEL. Now they walk the way foretold by Simeon and the Prophet seers of old. Within the shadow of Jerusalem, dark Azrael is waiting. The appointed day of sacrifice has come. On Calvary, the darkness falls apace. He is going now and we must watch the spot, made holy by His Boyhood days.

FIRST ANGEL. We guard the children, dearest to His Heart.

FIFTH ANGEL. Hush, dark Azrael is passing. Lo, the work is done and man's redemption is accomplished. At what a cost!

(*They kneel in silent worship.*)

(*Outside "There is a green hill far away" is softly sung.*)

SCENE II: *A week later. The* ANGELS *are in the background unseen by those who come to the well.*

Enter RUTH *and* DAVID.

RUTH. (*Shading her eyes. The* ANGELS *draw nearer.*) All the day the caravans have been passing, David. Yet the folk of Nazareth have not come. I long to talk with Gideon. He promised to come back. I wonder if HE was there.

DAVID. HE? The Prophet? Dost thou think of nothing else?

RUTH. I love Him so, David. The place hath never seemed the same since He left.

DAVID. I just remember Him. But Ruth, folk say that He is mad. He was only the Carpenter and He talks as if He were Messias. If the Rabbi should hear thy words, he would be angered with thee.

RUTH. He is Messias. He ever speaks true. Thou dost only have to look at Him to see it.

DAVID. But Messias cometh out of Bethlehem and He was the Carpenter of Nazareth, Ruth. Thou are just like Gideon. He left everything to follow the Carpenter. He left even you and me.

RUTH. Gideon would have taken me if I had been bigger. But he told me that I must bide to take care of grandmother and thee. The Master knows that I love Him and when He is crowned King in His Kingdom, I shall be there too.

DAVID. What an obstinate little maid thou art.

RUTH. We will not quarrel. Here comes our grandmother. Run and take her pitcher, David, and fill it for her. I will carry it home.

DAVID. Nay, I will do it. The full pitcher is too heavy for a maid.

(*Enter* JUDITH. *She walks feebly but smiles as the children run to her and seat her near the well.* DAVID *fills the pitcher while* RUTH *sits at her feet.*)

RUTH. Rest thee, Grandmother. Thou shouldst have waited for us. We were talking and forgot the time.

JUDITH. About the same thing, I will warrant, little one. Thou dost think and talk of naught but Mary's Son.

RUTH. Aye. I wish that David had not been away the day He came. He talked to us children first, and then in the synagogue, He made it all so plain that God was our Father and that He loves us. I do not see why the villagers got angry and tried to injure Him.

JUDITH. He spoke bold words, my child. Thou didst not understand.

RUTH. He spoke because He knew. I did understand, Grandmother, and so did Gideon. He went with Him that day.

JUDITH. And thou hast never blamed thy brother for leaving thee?

RUTH. No more than thou dost, Grandmother. Thou dost not believe He blasphemed, for thou dost love Him too.

JUDITH. (*Half dreamily.*) Aye, cold argument will never vanquish love. But I am no ruler, Ruth. And a woman's heart doth sometimes play her false. The Rabbi said He spoke of the Lord God presumptuously.

RUTH. I am sure that He spoke true. He was so sure.

JUDITH. Aye, He was sure. But the Lord God hath had His prophets throughout the ages. How could a village carpenter know more than these?

RUTH. He did.

(*Enter the village women*—NAOMI, MIRIAM *and* ESTHER.)

NAOMI. The caravans have come, Judith. See, here come the men and little Jesse. There is strange news they say.

(*Enter* JUDAH, EPHRAIM, NATHAN, ISSACHAR, JESSE *and* BENJAMIN. *There is grave and eager greeting. They group themselves about the well. The men seemed troubled.*)

NAOMI. Were many at the Feast?

JUDAH. Great throngs, good wife. Yet it was a strange Pass-over.

JUDITH. Is aught amiss? Ye all look sad. Where is Gideon?

EPHRAIM. The lad abode behind. Doubtless, he will come later.

MIRIAM. (*Contemptuously.*) Is he still following the Carpenter?

EPHRAIM. Nay, Miriam. That dream is ended. Mary's Son is dead.

(*There is surprise and consternation.* JUDITH *rises with shaking hands.* RUTH *springs to her feet and stands white and frightened.*)

MIRIAM. Mary's Son is dead? How? Where?

JUDAH. In Jerusalem. The rulers seized Him. They delivered Him to the Romans and Pilate crucified Him.

(*The women give cries of horror.* RUTH *clutches at coping of the well for support.* JUDITH *sits down and the girl buries her face in the old woman's lap.*)

NAOMI. Tell us the tale.

ISSACHAR. He came openly to Jerusalem. Jesse and Benjamin know something of it.

JESSE. (*Eagerly.*) He came into the City on the first day of the great week riding on an ass. The folk were strewing garments and palm branches in his path and we, little sons of the Law, ran out to meet Him waving palm branches and shouting Hosannas.

NAOMI. And the rulers did naught?

JUDAH. They bided their time. He came into the Temple daily. He drove the money changers forth and denounced the Pharisees. But He kept the Passover in private with the twelve. One of them was false. Judas the Iscariot. He was a dastard, for whatever we may think of Mary's Son, we of Galilee have little use for traitors. But Judas sold Him to the priests. Thirty pieces of silver was the price, we heard. He led them to His

Master as He prayed in the Garden of Gethsemane and betrayed Him with a kiss lest they should seize on one of the others by mistake.

ESTHER. With a kiss?

EPHRAIM. Aye. I held not with Him but the tale has wrung my heart. They dragged Him to the judgment hall and there condemned Him. Before them all, bound and helpless, He proclaimed Himself the Son of God, Messias. They took Him to Pilate while all the crowd followed.

ESTHER. But surely Pilate cared not for a charge like that?

NATHAN. Nay. They charged Him with sedition. That we know well, was false. And the proof they brought would not stand. But the city was in an uproar and Pilate weakened. He scourged Him and the Roman soldiers mocked Him and put on Him a scarlet robe and crowned Him with thorns. Then Pilate brought Him forth and tried to release Him as the prisoner of the feast but the mob yelled for Barabbas.

ESTHER. If they had lived in Galilee, they would have asked for no Barabbas.

JUDAH. Truly, but who can rule a maddened mob? I saw Him when Pilate brought Him forth. As a Lad I knew Him well. A sad ending.

BENJAMIN. He was a King; He was not afraid.

MIRIAM. Quiet, little son. Such words are dangerous.

JESSE. I would shout Hosanna for Him now. Mother, He was a King. All along the way He went bearing His cross, calm and quiet and unafraid. He never spoke except to bid the women not to weep for Him.

BENJAMIN. He fell thrice. They had to get a countryman to aid Him with His cross.

NATHAN. The boys are right. He was not like the others. Even the soldiers realized it. As they drove the nails home He made no outcry but prayed and kept on saying, "Father forgive them, for they know not what they do."

JUDAH. He was different. To the very last, He called the Lord God Father. It was an awful day. At noontide a strange darkness fell. He was crucified with two thieves and all three crosses were hidden. He had spoken twice before, once to the man on his right—whom He forgave like a King—and once to His Mother.

JUDITH. Aye, what of her? Her heart must be broken now.

NATHAN. He gave her to the care of Zebedee's young son, John. She was there at His cross with Mary of Magdala and John and some other women.

ESTHER. What happened then?

JUDAH. The strangest thing of all. He died just at the evening sacrifice. The priest was approaching the Holy of Holies. But before he could touch the veil, an earthquake shook the Temple. The veil was rent in twain and all could see the altar. God must be wroth with Israel.

RUTH. Perhaps the way to Him is open. Is not the veil to part one day to show it?

NATHAN. Aye, when Messias cometh and sacrifices cease.

RUTH. Perhaps Messias has come. He said—

MIRIAM. Hush, child, if the Rabbi heard thee—

JUDITH. (*Boldly.*) She is right. He called Himself Messias. Mary's Son! I cannot think of Him as dead. I remember when He came here—a child—after Joseph came back from Egypt.

JUDAH. He was born in Egypt. I did not remember that.

JUDITH. Not in Egypt but in Bethlehem at the time of the great taxing. Joseph and His Mother fled with Him, for they were warned in some mysterious way concerning Herod's massacre of the babes in Bethlehem. There was some child of royal birth that he feared or so they say.

DAVID. Perhaps it was He.

NATHAN. How could Herod know aught of a peasant Babe? I went with Him to His First Passover. It was mine too. I mind me well how full of joy He was. Everything spoke to Him of the love of God. God loves us. He taught that even then.

JUDAH. Dost thou remember how He stayed behind, lost for three days? His Mother came seeking Him in our caravan at close of day.

NATHAN. I remember. They found Him at last in the Temple with the doctors. He was listening and actually asking THEM questions. Think of it, a Lad of twelve! They were astonished at His understanding.

JUDITH. I mind me when my Joel died, my youngest born. My arms were empty as I sat here by the well and my heart was sad and bitter as I wept. He came running to me—a mere babe still—and climbed upon my lap. Well—I could not hold my bitterness and look at Mary's Son.

NATHAN. None of us could. I fought with Simeon one day and He came between. It would have gone hard with anyone else who tried to separate us, but somehow in His Presence our anger died. He ever made peace.

ISSACHAR. He did more for me. I was a wild youth enough and that day when Rabbi Obed reproved me, I resented it and started to join the brigands on the hills. Hard and unrepentant was I when I met Him outside the town. Well, it was not what He said but He Himself. To me that day He seemed incarnate purity and truth. He brought me back and I am here today because of Mary's Son.

JUDITH. And He is dead.

THE OTHERS. Aye, dead. The world is poorer; Nazareth is poorest of all, for we rejected Mary's Son.

(*Enter* GIDEON, *running.*)

GIDEON. He is risen, He is risen! He is risen from the dead!

ALL. Who, lad, who?

GIDEON. The Master. Oh blind were we and faithless too. But He is risen. I have seen Him!

JUDITH. Thy grief hath crazed thee, lad. The dead do not come back.

GIDEON. He has come. We laid Him in the garden tomb of Rabbi Joseph. The stone was sealed; a Roman guard was set and we went back to spend a mourning Sabbath. Very early in the morning on the first day of the week, came Mary Magdalene and the other women to see the sepulchre. They found the guard flying from the place with the news of the Resurrection. The tomb was empty and the stone rolled back with all the seals unbroken. There was an angel watcher and he told the women that the Lord had risen. They went to the apostles and they saw Him by the way. But Mary Magdalene was weeping by the sepulchre when He came and spoke to her and turned her sorrow into joy. Later Simon Peter saw Him; and in the evening, He appeared first to Cleopas and another as they walked to Emmaus and last He came to us all.

JUDITH. It was His Spirit, boy.

GIDEON. Nay, it was He Himself. We saw Him and touched Him. It was really He with the wound-marks in His hands and feet. He has come back from death itself, a Conqueror. He turned our sorrow into rapturous joy.

(*The older people shake their heads. They go away puzzled, except* JUDITH *who evidently believes.*)

BENJAMIN. Will He come to us, Gideon?

GIDEON. He ever comes to those who want Him, Benjamin.

RUTH. Thou didst see Him thyself, Gideon? It is really true?

GIDEON. (*Quietly.*) I saw Him. He is risen. He died to conquer death. Did not the Baptist call Him Lamb of God? Was not the Temple Veil rent in twain to show that the way to God was open and the Atonement made? He is Messias. Nay more, He is the Son of the Living God. And yet He is Himself. He loves us and wants us still.

RUTH. *He wants us.* We shall see Him; He will come to those who long for Him.

CURTAIN

SCENE III: *The well by moonlight. The* ANGELS *are grouped there. Very softly one verse of "JESUS CHRIST is risen today" is sung.*

FIRST ANGEL. He is risen, Heaven is glad today.

SECOND ANGEL. And Heaven's songs resound on earth again.

THIRD ANGEL. But some do not believe.

FOURTH ANGEL. Those who do are filled with joy. Some day the whole wide earth will hail Him King.

FIFTH ANGEL. And until then, He comes to simple souls, to those who love and to the children whom He holds so dear.

(*Enter* RUTH, DAVID, BENJAMIN, JESSE *and* GIDEON.)

RUTH. I wonder when He will come to us, Gideon.

GIDEON. We must not be impatient, Ruth. We must hold our faith and wait.

RUTH. I can do that for love of Him. How still the place is, Gideon. Is it because He was so often here that it is full of peace?

JESSE. There are angels here. Dost thou not see them in the gleaming moonlight?

RUTH. I have often felt that they were here. Oh-h—

(*All the children see the* ANGELS *who draw nearer to them.*)

(*Hymn 557 New Hymnal, "God hath sent His angels" is sung. At the end, the children kneel expectantly.*)

(*Outside "The Day of Resurrection."*)

MR. GRASSHOPPER'S EASTER CLOTHES *

By Mirjane Strong

CHARACTERS

Elf
Mr. Butterfly
Mr. Grasshopper
Gypsy Moth Peddler
Mrs. Robin
Sonny Robin
Sister Robin

Elf *is perched on a crimson toadstool, surrounded by buckets of paint of all colors.* Mr. Butterfly *is poised before him having his beautiful swallow-tail wings touched up a bit.* Mr. Butterfly *is a dandy, superbly turned out with a top hat and a large flower in his button-hole.* Elf *is carefully applying paint from a palette.*

Mr. Butterfly. (*Looking elegantly over his shoulder at the work.*) Now, if you'll outline that scarlet with just a suggestion of gold—

Elf. (*Leaning back and squinting critically at his work.*) Don't you think gold will look a little ostentatious, Mr. Butterfly?—Now, *I'd* say a little—ah—*blue,* perhaps—

Mr. Butterfly. (*Raising his eyebrows thoughtfully.*) Blue? —Perhaps. You might try it.

(Elf *strokes the wing daintily with his brush.* Mr. Grasshopper *comes in practicing the latest dance step.*)

Mr. Grasshopper. Oh there you are, Elf— (*Effusively.*)

Good morning, Mr. Butterfly, Sir!

MR. BUTTERFLY. (*Indifferently.*) Good morning. (*Arranging the flower in his button-hole.*) How does the blue look, Elf?

ELF. (*Squinting at the wing.*) It's all right— Yes, it's all right.

(MR. BUTTERFLY *looks over his shoulder.*)

MR. GRASSHOPPER. Simply gorgeous, Mr. Butterfly! Now if you had just a touch of gold—

MR. BUTTERFLY. (*Scornfully.*) Too os—ostentatious, Mr. Grasshopper—much too ostentatious.

MR. GRASSHOPPER. Yes, of course—neat but not gaudy. You have such excellent taste, Mr. Butterfly.

MR. BUTTERFLY. (*Complacently.*) Yes, I suppose I have. It runs in the family. We all dress well.

MR. GRASSHOPPER. Yes, you do—you certainly do. (*He looks enviously at* MR. BUTTERFLY.) Can I offer you some chewing tobacco?

MR. BUTTERFLY. (*Disdainfully.*) No, thank you! (*Aside.*) Filthy habit! Well, am I finished, Elf?

ELF. (*Giving him a last touch.*) Yes, you're done.

MR. BUTTERFLY. (*Flicking an imaginary speck from his coat.*) Just charge it to my account. Good day.

(*With a brief nod at* MR. GRASSHOPPER, MR. BUTTERFLY *goes off.* MR. GRASSHOPPER *chews thoughtfully. He picks a flower and puts it in his button-hole but the effect is not the same. He looks discontentedly at his green suit—everything green.*)

MR. GRASSHOPPER. Elf, I'm tired of green. (ELF *is now retouching the toadstool and does not reply.*) Our whole family has worn green since the beginning of time—no originality at all. (*Still no reply.*) Look here, Elf—how about touching me up a bit—some gold stripes now—though gold might be a little too os—well a little too you know—I want something smart and striking but in good taste, of course. (*Surveying himself.*)

What would you think of putting some crimson spots on my coat and blue stripes on my breeches?

ELF. (*Bluntly.*) I wouldn't think of it.

MR. GRASSHOPPER. Oh come now, Elf, don't be disagreeable. You can see I'm just the color of the grass now and no one even notices me half the time.

ELF. Which is a mercy!

MR. GRASSHOPPER. I shouldn't put up with your insolence, Elf! (ELF *is collecting his paint pots and brushes.*) I'll overlook it if you'll fix me a nice bright suit. (*Taking out his pocket book.*) I'll pay you cash down.

ELF. If your clothes are getting worn or shiny I'll touch 'em up with *green* but that's all I can do for you.

MR. GRASSHOPPER. That's very unreasonable of you, Elf. It's just as easy for you to use red paint as green and I'd be much more attractive!

ELF. You certainly would! Well, I can't do it, that's all.

MR. GRASSHOPPER. Why can't you do it?

ELF. Fairies' orders.

MR. GRASSHOPPER. Do you mean to say—!

ELF. (*Definitely.*) Fairies' orders! And mark me they have a good reason for everything they do.

MR. GRASSHOPPER. Well, I do think I might have been given a more interesting color!

ELF. (*Picking up his buckets.*) Let me know when you want some *green* work done.

MR. GRASSHOPPER. I won't want any! (*He sits down on the toadstool and dejectedly spits tobacco juice.*)

(*The* GYPSY MOTH PEDDLER *comes in carrying a pack. He has a brown insect's face embellished with large round gold ear-rings and a red bandana around the head. His clothes are shabby but gay and dusky brown wings protrude from his back.*)

PEDDLER. Finery and trinkets—a bright scarf or a bangle

for your sweetheart, Sir?

MR. GRASSHOPPER. (*Dejectedly.*) No.

PEDDLER. A fine coat for yourself, then?—or a waistcoat? (*He opens his pack.*)

MR. GRASSHOPPER. (*Impatiently.*) No, no—(*Suddenly.*) What did you say?

PEDDLER. A fine tailed coat for yourself? (*He pulls out a handsome scarlet one with gold buttons.*) Just the thing to set off a figure like yours.

MR. GRASSHOPPER. (*Excitedly.*) What else have you got?

PEDDLER. A very handsome green waistcoat—

MR. GRASSHOPPER. (*Impatiently.*) Nothing *green,* Man. Can't you see I have a green waistcoat!—and green coat and green breeches and green hose and green shoes!

PEDDLER. (*Looking at him for the first time.*) Ah, so you have—hadn't noticed.

MR. GRASSHOPPER. Of course you didn't notice! No one ever does! I'm just the color of everything around here!

PEDDLER. (*Studying him.*) Not much originality. Too bad with your looks. But we'll fix you up— Take the scarlet coat?—and how about some plum colored breeches and yellow hose?

MR. GRASSHOPPER. (*Intoxicated by all the colors.*) I know blue is very good this year.

PEDDLER. Excellent! Here's just the thing! (*He pulls out some blue and yellow striped breeches and holds them up with the coat.*) Lovely with the coat.

MR. GRASSHOPPER. (*A little doubtfully.*) Do you really think so?

PEDDLER. Oh, perfect!—Made to go with it. (*He puts them to one side as if it were all settled—as it is.*) I'll take your old clothes as part payment.

MR. GRASSHOPPER. Good! I'll show Elf and the fairies!

PEDDLER. Here's a pearl gray fedora for you—just the thing.

MR. GRASSHOPPER. (*Hesitating.*) I'd thought of a top hat—

PEDDLER. Too conspicuous—don't want to look dressed fit to kill.

MR. GRASSHOPPER. No, of course not.

PEDDLER. (*Holding up the clothes.*) There now—as neat an outfit as you could have. (MR. GRASSHOPPER, *quite convinced, is eagerly taking off his things, down to his green underwear.*) Here are your yellow hose. (MR. GRASSHOPPER *puts on the new clothes.*)

MR. GRASSHOPPER. What about a new waistcoat for me? Haven't you one that isn't green?

PEDDLER. (*Diving into his pack.*) Waistcoat? Yes, Sir! Purple—just the thing! How about a scarf? Orange? (*He holds one up.*)

MR. GRASSHOPPER. (*Trying the scarf.*) No—no, I think not.

PEDDLER. Right you are—excellent taste. Very!

MR. GRASSHOPPER. (*Flattered.*) Well, one has to know where to stop. As you say, I don't want to look dressed fit to kill.

PEDDLER. No, Sir! (*He has stuffed* MR. GRASSHOPPER's *green clothes in his pack and having fished* MR. GRASSHOPPER's *wallet from the coat pocket, counts the bills and stuffs wallet and all in his own pocket.*) I'll let you have the things for this price— (*He taps the pocket.*) Cheap!

(MR. GRASSHOPPER *starts to protest, but the* PEDDLER *has gone off.* MR. GRASSHOPPER *forgets his money in the pleasure of his new clothes. He smoothes the coat, straightens the waistcoat and puts on the pearl gray fedora at a very jaunty angle. While he is admiring himself, a bustling voice is heard off stage.*)

VOICE. Come children, here's an insect for you—queer looking but edible, no doubt.

(MRS. ROBIN *comes in followed closely by her two children, their big, yellow bills wide open in anticipation.*)

MRS. ROBIN. Why it's a grasshopper—delicious! (*She starts to peck at him.*)

Mr. Grasshopper. (*Terrified.*) Just a minute, Madam! I'm not a grasshopper—can't you see? Grasshoppers are green.

Mrs. Robin. Yes, I know—and extremely hard they are to see as a rule—just the color of the grass. It's very thoughtful of you to wear those funny clothes. I saw you right away. Don't be frightened, Children, it's just a grasshopper— Now which of you had the last bug?—Sonny, I think you did—close your mouth, dear, it's Sister's turn.

Mr. Grasshopper. (*His knees shaking.*) You're not going to feed me to your children!

Mrs. Robin. (*Mildly surprised.*) Does it matter who eats you?

Mr. Grasshopper. I'm sure these bright colors will make them very sick.

Mrs. Robin. (*Calmly.*) Oh, I don't think so. They've eaten worse looking things than you. (*She prepares to grab him.*) All right, Sister, here you are—open wide, it's a big one.

Mr. Grasshopper. (*As* Sister *strains her bill.*) Goodness sakes! That child can't possibly eat me all at once— I'd choke her!

Mrs. Robin. (*Unperturbed.*) Oh, you'd be surprised at the things she swallows. Here you are, dear— (Sister *crowds forward, all bill.*)

Mr. Grasshopper. (*Desperately.*) Mrs. Robin, you wouldn't refuse a last request, would you?

Mrs. Robin. (*Suspiciously.*) What is it?

Mr. Grasshopper. Let me sing a song before I'm eaten— just one little song.

Mrs. Robin. Why?

Mr. Grasshopper. Just to be gay once more before I'm gone.

Mrs. Robin. Well, be quick about it— Sister's hungry— aren't you, dear? (Sister *opens her bill wider than ever if possible.*)

Mr. Grasshopper. This is a very nice song. I hope you'll enjoy it. (*He sings with great feeling, tapping the rhythm out with one foot. He might even have a little fiddle.*)

> "A lit-tle girl once had a cat,
> Sing tra la la la loo—"

Mrs. Robin. (*Interrupting.*) We're not fond of cats. (*She glances uneasily over her shoulder.*)

Mr. Grasshopper.

> "And this little cat grew sleek and fat,
> Sing tra la la la loo.
> His claws were sharp, his eyes were bright,
> And oh, it was a splendid sight
> To see him crouch and spring and bite!
> Tra la la la la loo!

(*The robins are getting more and more uncomfortable.*)

> "The child adored the little cat,
> Sing tra la la la loo.
> Who wouldn't love a cat like that?
> Sing tra la la la loo.
> You'd hear her call him every day,
> She always called the same old way—

(*Raising his voice.*)

> "Come kitty, kitty, kitty, kitty,
> Kitty, kitty, kitty,
> Come kitty!"

Mrs. Robin. (*Screaming.*) Stop it! Stop it, I tell you! (*She looks fearfully over her shoulder, and the children run to her wings for protection.*)

Mr. Grasshopper. (*Innocently.*) But that's the chorus.

Mrs. Robin. Well, leave out the chorus! Don't you know there's a cat in that house up there? You'll have it down here! Come now—you've sung your song—

Mr. Grasshopper. Oh, that's only the first verse! You'll like the rest of it. Something happens to the cat in the end.

MRS. ROBIN. That's good—well hurry up and mind you leave out the chorus!

MR. GRASSHOPPER.

> "The cat grew smarter every day,
> Sing tra la la la loo.
> He frightened all the rats away,
> Sing tra la la la loo.
> They praised him 'cause he was so neat,
> He'd eat a mouse from ears to feet—
> And finish off a bird complete—

(SONNY *and* SISTER *wail.*)

> "Tra la la la la loo!
> The child would call him every day,
> She always called the same old way—

(*Louder than before.*)

> "Come kitty, kitty, kitty, kitty,
> Kitty, kitty, kitty,
> Come—"

MRS. ROBIN. (*Screaming interruption.*) Stop it! I told you not to— Stop it I tell you! Oh, that cat will hear you— Stop it! (MR. GRASSHOPPER *stops.*) I've had enough of your singing. (*She has become very nervous, constantly on the alert for the cat.*)

MR. GRASSHOPPER. Oh, I'm so sorry—you don't like the chorus, do you? I forgot. There's just one more verse and then you can choke "Sister" with me— (MRS. ROBIN *is not going to wait*—MR. GRASSHOPPER *screams.*) If you don't let me finish I'll sing the chorus all the way down! (*He hurries on.*)

> "One day this hungry little cat—"

SISTER. (*Wailing.*) I don't want that horrid bug!

MR. GRASSHOPPER. "Sing tra la la la loo."

MRS. ROBIN. Hush, darling, it'll taste all right.

MR. GRASSHOPPER. "Espied a bird so soft and fat—"

SONNY. (*Howling.*) I want to go home—the cat's coming—

I can hear it! (*He tugs at his mother.*)

MRS. ROBIN. (*Looking quickly over her shoulder.*) Nonsense—

MR. GRASSHOPPER. (*Gaily.*) "Sing tra la la la la loo!"

SISTER. (*Tugging at her mother with a loud wail.*) I want to go home, too! The cat'll eat us all up!

SONNY. Take us home! (*Both children are screaming.*)

MRS. ROBIN. (*Nervously.*) All right, all right! Do keep still, Sister—Sonny. Hush! The cat certainly *will* hear you! (*Tossing her head at* MR. GRASSHOPPER.) There are other bugs in the garden.

MR. GRASSHOPPER. Won't you wait for the end of the song?

MRS. ROBIN. I hope a chicken gets you, you unpleasant creature!

(*She hurries off, hushing the screaming children.* MR. GRASSHOPPER *scarcely waits for a sigh of relief. He looks around desperately for the* PEDDLER.)

MR. GRASSHOPPER. (*Calling.*) Peddler— Oh, peddler!— Oh, where is that peddler!—Some other bird will see me in these clothes. (*Calling.*) Peddler! PEDDLER! (*Desperately.*) What'll I do? (*He takes off the scarlet coat, rolls it up and looks around frantically for some place to hide.*) PEDDLER! Oh, why was I such a fool—!

(ELF *comes in and stops short on seeing* MR. GRASSHOPPER.)

ELF. Well, you *are* a sight! Where did you get those terrible clothes?

MR. GRASSHOPPER. (*With a gasp of relief.*) Oh, Elf! Dear Elf! I traded my beautiful green clothes for these things and now I can't find the peddler to get them back.

ELF. A bird'll eat you while you're standing there talking.

MR. GRASSHOPPER. (*Looking around desperately.*) I know —some robins nearly got me a minute ago.—Oh, Elf—do something!

ELF. I told you the fairies knew what they were about when they made you the color of the grass.

MR. GRASSHOPPER. (*Almost in tears.*) I know— I know— I'm a foolish grasshopper but I'll be an eaten grasshopper in a minute if you don't do something! Paint me green again!

ELF. (*Peering into his paint pots.*) I suppose I'll have to—

MR. GRASSHOPPER. Oh, *dear* Elf!

ELF. (*Taking up his brush.*) I hope you've learned your lesson.

MR. GRASSHOPPER. Oh, yes I have. I certainly have! I'll never be dissatisfied again!—But hurry, Elf—do hurry! (*He struggles into his coat and presents his back to* ELF *as the curtain falls.*)

COSTUMES

The bugs' faces are made by drawing a stocking over the face and sewing it neatly across the top of the head. Large insect eyes are put on the stocking face, high up and far apart, with holes in the center to see through. Antennae can be made of wire bound with cloth or crêpe paper. The insect's "arms" and legs are covered by stockings the color of the face.

ELF: Peaked cap, tight-fitting suit and pointed shoes.

MR. BUTTERFLY: Black stocking face. Black suit with knee breeches (sateen), white vest and gloves. Top hat. White flower in his button-hole. Big wings of crêpe paper wired at the edges and patterned after the swallow-tail—black with a bright border.

MR. GRASSHOPPER: Green stocking face. Green suit with knee breeches.

MOTH PEDDLER: Brown stocking face—gold ear-rings, red bandana. Gay, shabby clothes. Brown wings.

MRS. ROBIN: Gray stocking face with a dark gray cardboard bill sewed securely in place by tabs left on the bill for the purpose. Wings and tail of cardboard, painted dark gray.

MR. GRASSHOPPER'S SONG.

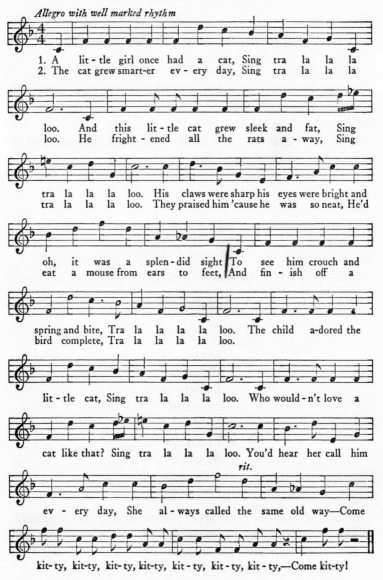

Allegro with well marked rhythm

1. A lit-tle girl once had a cat, Sing tra la la la
2. The cat grew smart-er ev-ery day, Sing tra la la la

loo. And this lit-tle cat grew sleek and fat, Sing
loo. He fright-ened all the rats a-way, Sing

tra la la la loo. His claws were sharp his eyes were bright and
tra la la la loo. They praised him 'cause he was so neat, He'd

oh, it was a splen-did sight To see him crouch and
eat a mouse from ears to feet, And fin-ish off a

spring and bite, Tra la la la la loo. The child a-dored the
bird complete, Tra la la la la loo.

lit-tle cat, Sing tra la la la loo. Who would-n't love a

cat like that? Sing tra la la la loo. You'd hear her call him

rit.

ev-ery day, She al-ways called the same old way—Come

kit-ty, kit-ty, kit-ty, kit-ty, kit-ty, kit-ty, kit-ty,—Come kit-ty!

"Yankee Doodle" will do for a tune if you don't want to go into this.

The wings are fastened to the arms—the tail protrudes from the back of her skirts. She wears a bonnet and, across her red breast, a little white apron.

SONNY ROBIN: Yellow bill, speckled breast, sailor hat.

SISTER ROBIN: Yellow bill, speckled breast, straw hat with streamers down the back. There must be an opening in the stocking faces so the young robins can open their bills. The tabs on these bills must slip inside the stocking opening and be fastened to chin and upper lip.

CARAMINE *

An Easter Pageant

BY ELBRIDGE S. LYON

PERSONS

MATRIA
SARA
CARAMINE
DIAMINUS
ARATHOS
GARIUS
PHEMEON
A VOICE

PART I

SCENE: *A grove of cedar trees with outline of tombs in back. A path and vista leading to right.*

Enter up center aisle two women in Oriental costumes, talking and carrying baskets of flowers and spices.

* For permission to produce, apply to the author, Chatham, N.J.

MATRIA. It is the third day. Let us hasten with our spices before the sun be up.

SARA. Think you He will be risen as some say?

MATRIA. Yes—even so.

SARA. Yet you bring spices as do I.

MATRIA. It is the custom, but I do believe.

(*They step up onto platform.*)

MATRIA. Behold! The stone is rolled away.

SARA. They have removed Him.

MATRIA. He is arisen. Glory to God!

(*Bright beam of light appears from high left across path to right.*)

MATRIA. Look—the Light!

SARA. The Light of the World!

VOICE. (*From above left.*) Whom seek ye?

SARA. 'Tis the voice of an angel.

MATRIA. Our Lord whom they crucified.

VOICE. Had ye so little Faith that ye came here seeking Him?

MATRIA. Tell us where to look that we may find Him.

VOICE. Where your duty is, there is Christ. Wherever your heart leads you in righteous undertaking, there will you find Christ. Go to your homes, follow the Master's teachings, shun all evil and do good wheresoever your hand findeth it to do; and you shall dwell with Christ and He with you.

(*Light goes out. Silently, hand in hand the two women return down center aisle. Enter up center aisle three men hastening; the back one runs to catch up.*)

DIAMINUS. It is the breaking of the third day, let us hasten to the tomb.

ARATHOS. Some say He will be risen.

GARIUS. Nay, say not that again.

ARATHOS. But what if it be so?

GARIUS. Do you consider it possible?

ARATHOS. Yes, I do believe.

GARIUS. Then why this great haste to the grave?

(*They go up on stage.*)

DIAMINUS. LOOK, the stone is rolled away!

GARIUS. (*Peering around behind.*) They have taken Him elsewhere.

(*Bright light shines as before.*)

DIAMINUS. Behold the Light.

ARATHOS. The light of Heaven.

VOICE. Let your light so shine before men that they may see your good works and glorify your Father which is in Heaven.

DIAMINUS. An Angel has spoken.

GARIUS. What light have I that I should let it shine?

ARATHOS. Many there be that are entombed by darkness that with but a word of encouragement would follow the path of righteousness.

DIAMINUS. Let us roll away the stones from their tombs.

GARIUS. You mean the dead?

DIAMINUS. Nay, the dead shall have their judgment, I mean those living dead that dwell in darkness, that know not the light of truth.

GARIUS. There is one I wish were dead, one Phemeon who did me a great wrong.

ARATHOS. Go you first to him, brother, forgive him and ask him also to forgive you that you may be purged before we go on this our great mission.

GARIUS. Nay, I need not purging, indeed! Let him come to me and ask me to forgive him. Him that did me the wrong. Come let us to our homes; why should we go elsewhere?

DIAMINUS. Let us follow this beam of light, mayhap it will guide us.

VOICE. I am the resurrection and the life. They that follow me shall have abundant life. Go ye into all the world and preach the Gospel to every creature.

DIAMINUS. Master, we go. Come.

ARATHOS. Lead on.

GARIUS. We follow.

(*Exeunt, right.*)

CURTAIN

PART II

Flower garden, mostly lilies. Doorway of hut at right. Old lady working around flowers. Enter MATRIA *and* SARA.

MATRIA. Good morning, Caramine, have you heard anything from Garius?

CARAMINE. Well, well, always it is Garius. Look at my lilies, are they not glorious this morning?

SARA. Most beautiful.

MATRIA. We have had no word of him for these many weeks.

CARAMINE. He is doubtless over busy. You will see him as soon as he is sure he can leave the Master's work in satisfactory hands.

SARA. I wish Phemeon would go out and join him. Together they could work wonders.

CARAMINE. Phemeon will do so very shortly.

MATRIA. How do you know that?

CARAMINE. One of my lilies told me.

SARA. I believe you would go yourself if we would let you.

CARAMINE. Weak and old, I can not follow in this glorious crusade. My son is dead, I have no one to send. But for these few plants I raise, I should starve or be an object of charity. I must stay idly here when my heart yearns to be out in the world spreading the Kingdom of God.

MATRIA. YOU? Why you dear old lady, you are doing more than any of us. Everyone comes to you for guidance. You are the inspiration of all our meetings. But for your loving spirit and unselfishness I do not see how we could have kept our band together.

SARA. Think of all the converts you have made right here, even among the soldiers sent to watch us.

CARAMINE. There, there, run along now. You are trying to flatter an old and worthless woman who but does her duty. But you are comforting nevertheless.

MATRIA. Good bye. (*Kisses her.*)

SARA. I will come for you tonight. We meet at my house again. (*Kisses her.*)

CARAMINE. God be with you. Good bye.

(*Exit* MATRIA *and* SARA. *Enter* DIAMINUS. *He kisses her forehead.*)

CARAMINE. Oh, Diaminus. Greetings. You are radiant. How goes the Work?

DIAMINUS. Happily. I know no hardships yet often I travel all night and go without food for days at a time. But how fare you? Cheerful and useful as ever?

CARAMINE. Spreading the Gospel among my lilies which need it not.

DIAMINUS. Every time you raise a lily you resurrect a living Christ. Pure and Holy. Do you see many of the band?

CARAMINE. We Christians meet every night wherever we can for prayer and reading of epistles sent in by the brethren. Great is our encouragement. You must preach for us this night.

DIAMINUS. Would that I could do so; but I am but passing through and must be off at once. I am promised in Christ's name to cure a body in sore pain some few leagues to the North and thence I must to the still further North to see how fares the flock. Good bye, my dear Caramine, some day you will raise a lily that will sing to you for company.

CARAMINE. They sing to me every morning before the sun is up. Good bye, my dear. God be with you and bless you.

DIAMINUS. Good bye, good bye.

(*Exit* DIAMINUS. *Enter* PHEMEON *with packet of parchment.*)

PHEMEON. Here are some letters sent in by Arathos. You are the only one who has learned to read these magic scrolls.

CARAMINE. My son, Phemeon, why have you not joined the glorious force which is out in the world enlightening the heathen? Whole lands there are in need of the Gospel.

PHEMEON. I know it. I want to go but I can not.

CARAMINE. Can not? Why, pray tell? There is no one to hinder.

PHEMEON. One of the missionaries, Garius, did me a great wrong and I can not forgive him. Until I forgive him I am not fit to preach forgiveness.

CARAMINE. Tut—what sort of a Christian are you, after all?

PHEMEON. I know, I do repent but there is Garius preaching repentance, yet he repenteth not.

CARAMINE. Maybe he does not think he wronged you.

PHEMEON. Not, indeed; let me but see him and I will soon remind him.

CARAMINE. You had better pray for your own hard heart. Yet you are a good boy. Please carry this pot into the back shed and refill it with loam for me.

(*Exit* PHEMEON *into hut door.* CARAMINE *continues to work about garden. Enter* GARIUS, *bedraggled and forlorn.*)

CARAMINE. Well, well. Greetings, how goes the work, my dear Garius?

GARIUS. I have failed—utterly. No one believes nor scarcely heeds my preaching. I can cure no sickness not even mine own.

CARAMINE. You have not the faith; the fault is in your own heart. Perhaps you have wronged someone and have repented not.

GARIUS. Nay, not so, but there is one that wrongeth me.

CARAMINE. You must forgive him forthwith.

GARIUS. When he repenteth then will I forgive him gladly.

CARAMINE. There, there, you are tired. I perceive there is plenty of missionary work to be done also at home. Sit on this bench and rest awhile.

GARIUS. Thank you. I am over fagged.

(*Sits in corner of bench and nods.* CARAMINE *works around flowers.*)

CARAMINE. (*Singing.*)

The sun mounts high but soon his tale is told.
Lord, here am I sorrowful, poor and old.
Few are the hours of light, long are the hours of night,
Must I my hope resign? Show me a sign, a sign.

With plants and flowers my busy days are spent,
Through weary hours I learn to be content.
Sweet are the hours of light here with my lilies white.
Lord, take what is thine. Give me a sign, a sign.

(GARIUS *wakes and rises, goes over to* CARAMINE *at right. Large lily in back uncurls petals exposing little child's face. Lily sings. Enter* PHEMEON *hastily; goes to other side of* CARAMINE. *The three are standing with backs to audience watching lily.*)

LILY (*Singing.*)

A lily bud am I,
Opening to the sky
On Easter Day.
From the dark garden bed
I lift my snowy head—
Nature's own sign
Of love divine.

I am a lily pure and white.
I hold a fragrance and a light,
A light—a radiant spirit of the sky
Set free to breathe in immortality.

(GARIUS *and* PHEMEON *slowly clasp hands for a moment behind* CARAMINE'S *back in view of audience.* CARAMINE *turns around and turning* GARIUS *and* PHEMEON *toward each other takes arm of each.*)

CARAMINE. What was this great wrong done you by Garius?

PHEMEON. I know not.

CARAMINE. And what was it Phemeon did to upset your whole life so?

GARIUS. I have forgotten.

CARAMINE. Do you forgive him?

GARIUS. There is some mistake, there is nothing to forgive.

PHEMEON. Forgetting those things which are behind, and reaching forth unto those things which are before, I press toward the mark for the prize of the high calling of God in Christ Jesus.

GARIUS. Come, Phemeon, be my companion. Together we will preach the true gospel of LOVE throughout the uttermost parts of the Earth.

PHEMEON. I am ready. Good bye, Angel Mother.

GARIUS. Good bye, Mother Caramine.

(*Exit* PHEMEON *and* GARIUS *arm in arm.*)

CARAMINE. Good bye, God bless you—my—noble sons.

CURTAIN

PART III (*following immediately.*)

Off stage singing "Christ the Lord is Risen Today" by CARAMINE, MATRIA *and* SARA. *After first verse they walk into auditorium from left, singing, and take seats in front facing audience. Everyone in building joins in the singing. After third verse* CARAMINE *calls on "Brother ————" to offer prayer. (This should be S. S. Superintendent or anyone willing but should not be long.) When he finishes* MATRIA *offers a one sentence prayer followed by several one sentence prayers from any in various parts of room and closed by* CARAMINE.

CARAMINE *then rises and unrolling the scroll which had been handed her in Part II by* PHEMEON *reads the 13th Chapter of 1st Corinthians from scroll.*

Concluding this, CARAMINE *starts singing "Welcome Happy Morning" and is joined by everybody. They sing unaccompanied and without books. After second verse* SARA *and* MATRIA *shake hands and* CARAMINE *shakes hands with both at once, one with each hand and then the three mix with audience and everybody shakes hands with his neighbors.*

THE END

POEMS

RESURREXIT!

By Reginald Wright Kauffman

Lo, He is risen!
In that lowly tomb
That, for a space, had been his noisome prison,
  Buried by night and hidden from the day,
    There was not room
  To hold the immortal, spirit-wedded clay:
  He broke the bars and went upon His way
    Into the Father's glory.—
Thus, since the angel-shape first told the story,
  The type and symbol of our last desire,
    By scourge and fire
  Hath it come down the corridor of years,
    Wafted on dying sighs,
      The vision sought by sad, ascetic eyes,
The vessel freighted with our hopes and fears.

Lo, Earth is risen!
  The enfolding snow
That made her winter sepulchre
  Passes before the Sun-God's eyes;
  The brooks break free, the flowers arise,
    The glad days come, the sad days go,
And bird and beast are glad of her.

Let Man arise!
Whether because that legends dim,
Or Nature's truths, are clear to him,
So to his eyes
There comes the picture of the larger life,
The farther purpose and the broader love,
So in his veins there runs the primal fire,
He shall be armoured for the inspiring strife,
And conquer on the battlefield thereof.—
Because one thing is Duty and Desire,
Because enduring love is but life's breath,
And life and love are one superb surprise,
Trampling beneath his feet the dream of Death,
Man shall arise!

THE MIRACLE AGAIN

BY MAY WILLIAMS WARD

The sky was white with blinding light
When Christ the Lord was born.
Darkness hung from the high arch swung
When He suffered cross and thorn.
When He passed those portals that men pass too,
The gates of death and birth,
The sky flew banners to mark the day.
But Easter comes . . . to earth.

We can recall how He gave all
By our awe when a martyr dies,
And His natal day by the star-bright ray
In a human baby's eyes;
No more need dark skies mark His death
Nor rain of stars His birth,

But what would remind us of Easter time
If Spring did not come to earth?

When leaves come first and tight buds burst
To make the cool air sweet,
Their green and gold pushed through the mold
The miracle repeat.
Oh, God is good, and the whole world should
Be one in praise and mirth,
Remembering resurrection day
As Easter comes . . . to earth.

UPPER ROOM

BY DOROTHY BROWN THOMPSON

They have come back, in the hope they will find what they lack,
They have come back.
Here are others who understand,
Here the press of a hand.

They were so sure—in His power, His Godhead, secure—
They were so sure.
Now all is confusion instead—
Their Master is dead.

The night dulls on (they will visit the tomb at the dawn)
The night dulls on.
And while they grieve darkly, nor heed . . .
He is risen indeed!

EASTER EVE

By Henry Alford

I saw two women weeping by the tomb
  Of one new buried, in a fair green place
  Bowered with shrubs;—the eve retained no trace
Of aught that day performed,—but the faint gloom
Of dying day was spread upon the sky;—
  The moon was broad and bright above the wood;—
  The distance sounded of a multitude,
Music and shout and mingled revelry.
At length came gleaming through the thicket shade
  Helmet and casque—and a steel-armëd band
  Watched round the sepulchre in solemn stand;
The night-word passed, from man to man conveyed;
  And I could see those women rise and go
  Under the dark trees moving sad and slow.

AN ODE AFTER EASTER
From "THE NIGHT OF FOREBEING"

By Francis Thompson

Cast wide the folding doorways of the East,
For now is light increased!
And the wind-besomed chambers of the air,
See they be garnished fair;
And look the ways exhale some precious odours,
And set ye all about wild-breathing spice,
Most fit for Paradise.
Now is no time for sober gravity,
Season enough has Nature to be wise;
But now discinct, with raiment glittering free,

Shake she the ringing rafters of the skies
With festal footing and bold joyance sweet,
And let the earth be drunken and carouse!
For lo, into her house
Spring is come home with her world-wandering feet,
And all things are made young with young desires;
And all for her is light increased
In yellow stars and yellow daffodils,
And East to West, and West to East,
Fling answering welcome-fires,
By dawn and day-fall, on the jocund hills.
And ye, winged minstrels of her fair meinie,
Being newly coated in glad livery,
Upon her steps attend,
And round her treading dance and without end
Reel your shrill lutany.
What popular breath her coming does out-tell
The garrulous leaves among!
What little noises stir and pass
From blade to blade along the voluble grass!
O Nature, never-done
Ungaped-at Pentecostal miracle,
We hear thee, each man in his proper tongue!
Break, elemental children, break ye loose
From the strict frosty rule
Of grey-beard Winter's school.
Vault, O young winds, vault in your tricksome courses
Upon the snowy steeds that reinless use
In cœrule pampas of the heaven to run;
Foaled of the white sea-horses,
Washed in the lambent waters of the sun.
Let even the slug-abed snail upon the thorn
Put forth a conscious horn!
Mine elemental co-mates, joy each one:

And ah, my foster-brethren, seem not sad—
No, seem not sad,
That my strange heart and I should be so little glad.
Suffer me at your leafy feast
To sit apart, a somewhat alien guest,
And watch your mirth,
Unsharing in the liberal laugh of earth;
Yet with a sympathy,
Begot of wholly sad and half-sweet memory—
The little sweetness making grief complete;
Faint wind of wings from hours that distant beat,
When I, I too,
Was once, O wild companions, as are you,
Ran with such wilful feet.

* * *

Hark to the *Jubilate* of the bird
For them that found the dying way to life!
And they have heard,
And quicken to the great precursive word;
Green spray showers lightly down the cascade of the larch;
The graves are riven,
And the Sun comes with power amid the clouds of heaven!
Before his way
Went forth the trumpet of the March;
Before his way, before his way
Dances the pennon of the May!
O earth, unchilded, widowed Earth, so long
Lifting in patient pine and ivy-tree
Mournful belief and steadfast prophecy,
Behold how all things are made true!
Behold your bridegroom cometh in to you,
Exceeding glad and strong.
Raise up your eyes, O raise your eyes abroad.
No more shall you sit sole and vidual,

Searching, in servile pall,
Upon the hieratic night the star-sealed sense of all:
Rejoice, O barren, and look forth abroad!
Your children gathered back to your embrace
See with a mother's face.
Look up, O mortals, and the portent heed;
In every deed,
Washed with new fire to their irradiant birth,
Reintegrated are the heavens and earth!
From sky to sod,
The world's unfolded blossom smells of God.

My little-worlded self! the shadows pass
In this thy sister-world, as in a glass,
Of all processions that revolve in thee:
Not only of cyclic Man
Thou here discern'st the plan,
Not only of cyclic Man, but of the cyclic Me.
Not solely of Mortality's great years
The reflex just appears,
But thine own bosom's year, still circling round
In ample and in ampler gyre
Toward the far completion, wherewith crowned,
Love unconsumed shall chant in his own furnace-fire.
How many trampled and deciduous joys
Enrich thy soul for joys deciduous still,
Before the distance shall fulfil
Cyclic unrest with solemn equipoise!
Happiness is the shadow of things past,
Which fools still take for that which is to be!
And not all foolishly:
For all the past, read true, is prophecy,
And all the firsts are hauntings of some Last,
And all the springs are flash-lights of one Spring.

Then leaf, and flower, and fall-less fruit
Shall hang together on the unyellowing bough;
And silence shall be Music mute
For her surchargèd heart. Hush thou!
These things are far too sure that thou should'st dream
Thereof, lest they appear as things that seem.

Nature, enough! within thy glass
Too many and too stern the shadows pass.
In this delighted season, flaming
For thy resurrection-feast,
Ah, more I think the long ensepulture cold,
Than stony winter rolled
From the unsealed mouth of the holy East;
The snowdrop's saintly stoles less heed
Than the snow-cloistered penance of the seed.
'Tis the weak flesh reclaiming
Against the ordinance
Which yet for just the accepting spirit scans.
Earth waits, and patient heaven,
Self-bonded God doth wait
Thrice-promulgated bans
Of his fair nuptial-date.
And power is man's,
With that great word of "wait,"
To still the sea of tears,
And shake the iron heart of Fate.
In that one word is strong
An else, alas, much-mortal song;
With sight to pass the frontier of all spheres
And voice which does my sight such wrong.

Not without fortitude I wait
The dark majestical ensuit

Of destiny, nor peevish rate
Calm-knowledged Fate.

I do hear
From the revolving year
A voice which cries:
"All dies;
Lo, how all dies! O seer,
And all things too arise:
All dies, and all is born;
But each resurgent morn, behold, more near the Perfect Morn."

Firm is the man, and set beyond the cast
Of Fortune's game, and the iniquitous hour,
Whose falcon soul sits fast,
And not intends her high sagacious tour
Or ere the quarry sighted; who looks past
To slow much sweet from little instant sour,
And in the first does always see the last.

EASTER

By John Richard Moreland

Morning
And a city street
Yellow with laughing sunlight;
A crepe-clad woman
Old and feeble
Tottering beneath the weight
Of dazzling white lilies.
Life and death . . .
Dust and immortality!

THEY SEALED THE STONE, THEY SET THE WATCH

By Nancy Byrd Turner

They sealed the stone, they set the watch.
Day ended, and the dark began.
A stranger night was on the earth
Than ever had befallen man.

No light there was in all the world
Except the cold stars overhead;
No sound except, in measured beat,
The Roman sentry's iron tread.

All night the silence held; all night
The black hill loomed above the town.
The tall Cross stood against the sky.
The stars came up, the stars went down;

They wheeled and set. The watch was changed.
A dreamer stirred but did not wake.
The city slept. And, pure and clear,
The dawn of dawns began to break.

THE LARGER BREATH

By Marion Monks Chase

What fallen column, what ruined shrine is this,
Like some white wreck on an Acropolis?
Before me here, immovable, she lies,
Who once went radiant with life, whose eyes
Shone like two stars reflected in the sea,
The high heart, still, which beat so royally.

How should I not feel anguish for my friend?
Because again is given me to know—
So close and narrow the earth chambers grow—
That in the open there, beyond the ken
Of all save One, the sorest-pressed of men,
Beyond these walls of flesh and pain and death,
The glorious living breathe the larger breath.

"IN NO STRANGE LAND"

BY FRANCIS THOMPSON

O world invisible, we view thee,
O world intangible, we touch thee,
O world unknowable, we know thee,
Inapprehensible, we clutch thee!

Does the fish soar to find the ocean,
The eagle plunge to find the air—
That we ask of the stars in motion
If they have rumour of thee there?

Not where the wheeling systems darken,
And our benumbed conceiving soars!—
The drift of pinions, would we hearken,
Beats at our own clay-shuttered doors.

The angels keep their ancient places;—
Turn but a stone, and start a wing!
'Tis ye, 'tis your estrangèd faces,
That miss the many-splendoured thing.

But (when so sad thou canst not sadder)
Cry;—and upon thy so sore loss

Shall shine the traffic of Jacob's ladder
Pitched betwixt Heaven and Charing Cross.

Yea, in the night, my Soul, my daughter,
Cry,—clinging Heaven by the hems;
And lo, Christ walking on the water
Not of Genesareth, but Thames!

PROSPICE

BY ROBERT BROWNING

Fear death?—to feel the fog in my throat,
    The mist in my face,
When the snows begin, and the blasts denote
    I am nearing the place,
The power of the night, the press of the storm,
    The post of the foe;
Where he stands, the Arch Fear in a visible form,
    Yet the strong man must go:
For the journey is done and the summit attain'd,
    And the barriers fall,
Though a battle's to fight ere the guerdon be gain'd,
    The reward of it all.
I was ever a fighter, so—one fight more,
    The best and the last!
I would hate that death bandaged my eyes, and forbore,
    And bade me creep past.
No! let me taste the whole of it, fare like my peers
    The heroes of old,
Bear the brunt, in a minute pay glad life's arrears
    Of pain, darkness and cold.
For sudden the worst turns the best to the brave,
    The black minute's at end,

And the elements' rage, the fiend-voices that rave,
   Shall dwindle, shall blend,
Shall change, shall become first a peace out of pain.
   Then a light, then thy breast,
O thou soul of my soul! I shall clasp thee again,
   And with God be the rest!

DEATH

By John Donne

Death, be not proud, though some have callèd thee
Mighty and dreadful, for thou art not so:
For those whom thou think'st thou dost overthrow
Die not, poor Death; nor yet canst thou kill me.
From Rest and Sleep, which but thy picture be,
Much pleasure, then from thee much more must flow;
And soonest our best men with thee do go—
Rest of their bones and souls' delivery!
Thou'rt slave to fate, chance, kings, and desperate men,
And dost with poison, war, and sickness dwell;
And poppy or charms can make us sleep as well
And better than thy stroke. Why swell'st thou then?
   One short sleep past, we wake eternally,
   And Death shall be no more: Death, thou shalt die!

TO EXPERIENCE EASTER

By Dorothy Brown Thompson

   The message Easter holds
      Is not revealed,
      But sealed,
   Except as it unfolds

Before him who has known
   The praise of men,
   And then,
Despised, is left alone;

Who, in some upper room,
   His hard fate knows,
   Yet goes
Into the outer gloom;

Who bears, with anguish deep,
   Gethsemane,
   Where he
Finds that his friends can sleep;

Who conquers his own will
   And wins at last
   That vast
Strong faith Death cannot kill . . .

So, having trod the way—
   Then he may kneel
   And feel
The meaning of the day.

MEETING THE EASTER BUNNY

BY ROWENA BASTIN BENNETT

On Easter morn at early dawn
   before the cocks were crowing,
I met a bob-tail bunnykin
   and asked where he was going,
" 'Tis in the house and out the house

a-tipsy, tipsy-toeing,
'Tis round the house and 'bout the house
  a-lightly I am going."
"But what is that of every hue
  you carry in your basket?"
" 'Tis eggs of gold and eggs of blue;
  I wonder that you ask it.
'Tis chocolate eggs and bonbon eggs
  and eggs of red and gray,
For every child in every house
  on bonny Easter Day."
He perked his ears and winked his eye
  and twitched his little nose,
He shook his tail—what tail he had—
  and stood up on his toes.
"I must be gone before the sun;
  the east is growing gray;
'Tis almost time for bells to chime."—
So he hippity-hopped away.

EASTER EGGS

Author Unknown

Humpty Dumpty has country cousins
Who come to the city in Spring by dozens;
They make such a brilliant show in town
You'd think that a rainbow had tumbled down.
Blue and yellow and pink and green,
The gayest gowns that ever were seen.
Purple and gold and oh! such style;
They are all the rage for a little while;
But their visit is short for no one stays
After the Easter holidays.

EASTER

By John Richard Moreland

It happened on an April day,
Bounded by skies so blue and still
And olive trees all hushed and gray,
They led One up a skull-shaped hill,
Followed by a crowd whose piercing cry
Was "Crucify!"

It happened on an April morn,
They nailed a Man upon a tree,
Whose head was circled with sharp thorn,
Lifted Him high that all might see
His agony, His heaving breath,
His awful death.

It happened on an April eve;
The air was cut by one sharp cry
That wine or gall could not relieve:
"Eli . . . lamma . . . sabacthani!"
Then lightning, thunder crack on crack,
The sun was black.

It happened on an April day.
They tombed a Man (the crowd had fled),
Sealed it; and set a watch that way
To flout His words, to prove Him dead;
And show Himself He could not save
From the dark grave.

It happened on an April day,
A tremor shook the paling gloom,

A white flame tore the door away,
Life came a victor from the tomb.
Love cannot die, nor life betray;
Christ rose upon an April day!

SPRING'S IN MY GARDEN!

By NANCY BYRD TURNER

Spring's in my garden!
You'd almost say
A king's in my garden,
It shines so gay.

I can count ten bells
With a band at the rim,
And a silver goblet
With dew on its brim,

And six gold stars
By a flat gray stone,
And a tuft of purple
That stands alone.

My little deep pool
Is bright at the brink
With a flash of crimson,
A flutter of pink.

Green's in my garden—
You might declare
A queen's in my garden,
It shines so fair!

THE GREEN O' THE SPRING

By Denis Aloysius McCarthy

Sure, afther all the winther,
   An' afther all the snow,
'Tis fine to see the sunshine,
   'Tis fine to feel its glow;
'Tis fine to see the buds break
   On boughs that bare have been—
But best of all to Irish eyes
   'Tis grand to see the green!

Sure, afther all the winther,
   An' afther all the snow,
'Tis fine to hear the brooks sing
   As on their way they go;
'Tis fine to hear at mornin'
   The voice of robineen,
But best of all to Irish eyes
   'Tis grand to see the green!

Sure, here in grim New England
   The spring is always slow,
An' every bit o' green grass
   Is kilt wid frost and snow;
An' many a heart is weary
   The winther days, I ween,
But oh, the joy when springtime comes
   An' brings the blessed green!

"IF A MAN DIE SHALL HE LIVE AGAIN?"

By John Richard Moreland

My garden holds a dogwood tree
That winter winds so cruelly knout,
It seems I hear love's voice cry out,
"My God! hast Thou forgotten me?"

And crowned with thorns of frozen rain
It waits through winter's crystal hours,
And then arrayed in starry flowers
Shows forth the risen Christ again!

SPRING IN THE CITY

By Eleanor Graham

Where do they come from? Out of their holes?
Children on roller skates, children on scooters,
Riding on bicycles, sliding down poles,
Angel-faced darlings and little freebooters.

All through the winter this street was so quiet,
Dusk came so early, and nights were so dark;
We had forgotten the boisterous riot
Children can make when they're out for a lark.

Brighter than blossoms and gayer than flowers,
Eager to scatter the laughter they bring!
Cities grow young when the days have more hours—
Spring wakes the children, and children make spring.

APRIL, WHAT WONDER-WORKING

By Lew Sarett

April, what wonder-working beauty in your hand!—
That cups the world this day as craftily
As my five winnowing fingers hold
This lump of drab wet sand
And change it into thin-blown swirling gold
By magic of my breath, the sea
Spangling a foam on it, the sun
Glinting its liquid yellow on the dun.

Your mellow showers that start the cherry's blood
Bounding to every beauty-swollen bud,
Until the petals swarm and swim
Like crimson millers on the cherry limb;
Your breath, so fragrant with wet loam, so cool,
That bends the anemones and billows
The dripping green of ferns and willows
Into each woodland pool;
Your rattling rains that drum
Alert the companies of wild goose-plum—
These quicken the once dead earth,
Call up the miracle of glad new birth,
And conjure the colors of a lovely dream to come.

Hold me, O April, with your cool blue-fingered rain,
And wash me free of winter-bitterness and pain;
Renew me, April, root and stalk and leaf,
As any budding bough or blossoming sheaf.

EASTER

By John Richard Moreland

You who fear death remember April
With her sword of jade
On a thousand hills,
And the warm south wind
That whispers
Of cornel and of purple squills.

You who fear death remember April
With her moon-white trees
And the new-turned sod,—
And the bare, brown branch
That quickens
Like a sudden thought of God!

EASTER EVE

By Bliss Carman

If I should tell you I saw Pan lately down by the shallows of
Silvermine,
Blowing an air on his pipe of willow, just as the moon began to
shine;
Or say that, coming from town on Wednesday, I met Christ
walking in Ponus Street;
You might remark, "Our friend is flighty! Visions, for want of
enough red meat!"

Then let me ask you. Last December, when there was skating
on Wampanaw,
Among the weeds and sticks and grasses under the hard black
ice I saw

An old mud-turtle poking about, as if he were putting his
house to rights,
Stiff with the cold perhaps, yet knowing enough to prepare
for the winter nights.

And here he is on a log this morning, sunning himself as calm
as you please.
But I want to know, when the lock of winter was sprung of a
sudden, who kept the keys?
Who told old nibbler to go to sleep safe and sound with the
lily roots,
And then in the first warm days of April—out to the sun with
the greening shoots?

By night a flock of geese went over, honking north on the
trails of air,
The spring express—but who despatched it, equipped with
speed and cunning care?
Hark to our bluebird down in the orchard trolling his chant of
the happy heart,
As full of light as a theme of Mozart's—but where did he learn
that more than art?

Where the river winds through grassy meadows, as sure as the
south wind brings the rain,
Sounding his reedy note in the alders, the redwing comes back
to his nest again.
Are these not miracles? Prompt you answer: "Merely the prose
of natural fact;
Nothing but instinct plain and patent, born in the creatures,
that bids them act."

Well, I have an instinct as fine and valid, surely, as that of the
beasts and birds,

Concerning death and the life immortal, too deep for logic, too
vague for words.
No trace of beauty can pass nor perish, but other beauty is
somewhere born;
No seed of truth or good be planted, but the yield must grow as
the growing corn.

Therefore this ardent mind and spirit I give to the glowing
days of earth,
To be wrought by the Lord of life to something of lasting im-
port and lovely worth.
If the toil I give be without self-seeking, bestowed to the limit
of will and power,
To fashion after some form ideal the instant task and the
waiting hour,

It matters not though defeat undo me, though faults betray
me and sorrows scar,
Already I share the life eternal with the April buds and the
evening star.
The slim new moon is my sister now; the rain, my brother;
the wind, my friend.
Is it not well with these forever? Can the soul of man fare ill
in the end?

EVOLUTION

By John B. Tabb

Out of the dark a shadow,
    Then, a spark;
Out of the cloud a silence,
    Then, a lark;
Out of the heart a rapture,

Then, a pain;
Out of the dead cold ashes,
Life again.

AN EASTER CANTICLE

By CHARLES HANSON TOWNE

In every trembling bud and bloom
That cleaves the earth, a flowery sword,
I see Thee come from out the tomb,
Thou risen Lord.

In every April wind that sings
Down lanes that make the heart rejoice;
Yea, in the word the wood-thrush brings,
I hear Thy voice.

Lo! every tulip is a cup
To hold Thy morning's brimming wine;
Drink, O my soul, the wonder up—
Is it not thine?

The great Lord God, invisible,
Hath roused to rapture the green grass;
Through sunlit mead and dew-drenched dell,
I see Him pass.

His old immortal glory wakes
The rushing streams and emerald hills;
His ancient trumpet softly shakes
The daffodils.

Thou art not dead! Thou art the whole
Of life that quickens in the sod;

Green April is Thy very soul,
Thou great Lord God!

CHORUS FROM ATALANTA IN CALYDON

BY ALGERNON CHARLES SWINBURNE

When the hounds of spring are on winter's traces,
The mother of months in meadow or plain
Fills the shadows and windy places
With lisp of leaves and ripple of rain;
And the brown bright nightingale amorous
Is half assuaged for Itylus,
For the Thracian ships and the foreign faces,
The tongueless vigil, and all the pain.

Come with bows bent and with emptying of quivers,
Maiden most perfect, lady of light,
With a noise of winds and many rivers,
With a clamor of waters, and with might;
Bind on thy sandals, O thou most fleet,
Over the splendor and speed of thy feet;
For the faint east quickens, the wan west shivers,
Round the feet of the day and the feet of the night.

Where shall we find her, how shall we sing to her,
Fold our hands round her knees, and cling?
O that man's heart were as fire and could spring to her,
Fire, or the strength of the streams that spring!
For the stars and the winds are unto her
As raiment, as songs of the harp-player;
For the risen stars and the fallen cling to her,
And the southwest-wind and the west-wind sing.

For winter's rains and ruins are over,
And all the season of snows and sins;

The days dividing lover and lover,
    The light that loses, the night that wins;
And time remembered is grief forgotten,
And frosts are slain and flowers begotten,
And in green underwood and cover
    Blossom by blossom the spring begins.

MARCH . . . APRIL . . .

By Leonora Speyer

This is a sullen time of year,
The sodden earth is ill at ease
Where lie the roots of trees.

Rigid the hills, the fields austere,
Unwillingly the thought of buds
Occurs along the woods.

A smudge of green is here and here;
A ragged cloud goes limping by
An uneventful sky.

This is a miserly time of year,
Reluctant coming, reluctant going—
And the sap's strength growing, growing!

From SPRING THOUGHTS

By Ernest Crosby

I

The leaves are not out yet upon the mountain, but the red
promise of them begins to tinge its grey flank.

And so my heart flushes with the springtide, and the robins
and blue-birds come back to me also from the South.

For I am part and parcel of it all.

There is no feeling in bird or beast or insect, in bud or tendril,
which has not its counterpart in me.

I am as bold as the bear emerging lean and famished from his
winter dormitory.

I tremble at the sound of the crackling branch with the squirrel
and rabbit, as they prick up their ears and listen with ear
and eye and tail.

The snake and the toad hop and glide within me, though I
would fain deny them.

I am more natural than the nature around me, for the wolf
and the panther have left these woods, but they still have
their lair in my heart, and no advance of civilization will
ever drive them forth from that fastness.

I sleep and dream with the stolid forest trees, lulled by the
south-west wind.

I feel the sap rising in me, and I wake into ardent blossoms.

I struggle for air and sunlight with them all, though we look
so innocent and peaceful.

Every note in the scale of creation from heaven to hell rouses
to vibration some sympathetic chord within me.

I cannot escape a single experience of the universe, if I would.

My cowardice is as futile as all cowardice is futile.

I live with all the life I see.

The spring and summer are mine, and the fall and winter will
just as surely be mine, and after them the following springtime.

I must have all—all.

My lot must be completely bound up with the common lot.

I claim no exclusive privilege.

I will live with them and I will die with them and with them
shall I rise from the dead.

Nature has not slighted me by exempting me from any of her
laws.

II

The willows are signalling with light green streamers the arrival of Spring in the offing.
The soft maples have hoisted the red standard which in their
code has the same meaning.
Sail in with swelling sails, O ship of life, for the ice has long
since ebbed out of the harbour.
Coming and going every year, O ship, bringing the living and
taking away the dead, tell me, where is the other port at
the end of your annual journey?
Do you bring them to life too, and take away their dead?
On the deep, lonely sea is your cargo somehow changed and
transformed?
I half guess the secret of your voyage.
Tell me, is it not true that death is only the seamy side of
birth?

III

The pale-green finger-tips of the sombre firs point in all direc-
tions at the wonders of April.
In the woods the warm days have lured forth the tender leaves
on the young trees, and undergrowth, but the lofty oaks
show hardly a sign of life yet.
A greenish mist of leaves is rising sun-lit from the ground, but
it reaches only half way up their towering trunks.
New yellow sprouts stand upright on the diminutive pines like
candles on a Christmas-tree.
Each sprout, each needle, each leaf, grows forth independently,
obeying only the life within.
O woods,—
Untamed, unheeding woods,—

Ungoverned, unlicensed, unpermitted,—
Asking no one's leave to fulfil your destiny!
In vain I peer and search beneath your branches for a glimpse
    of the State.
Here at least the State is for once well out of sight.
Before your leafy wands the giant Bogey of the ages has van-
    ished with all his spectral train of rights divine.
The only divine rights here are those of beech and chestnut,—
    but that I am here too with the rights divine of Man.
I pledge my allegiance with the forest trees.
Their oath is my oath and their State is my State.
We are the true realists and deal only with facts.
We are not like the sentimentalists in town with their big
    books, pretending that they are practical while they are
    lost in a maze of Laws and Policies and Patriotisms and
    Precedents and countless other shadowy sentiments duly
    capitalized.
We know what they have forgotten, that the one ultimate fact
    is life.
When the leaves of the oak are ruled by a majority rather than
    by the inner life of the tree, then, and not till then, will I
    believe in majorities.

"O WHO WOULD THINK OF SORROW"

By John Richard Moreland

O who would think of sorrow
    When silver rains come down
Like laughter of glad boys and girls
    In some old town?

O who would tell of sorrow
    When warm south winds blow light

And dogwood trees stand like pale saints
In living white?

O who would hold to sorrow
When April sweeps along
In a white dress of wonder,
With lips of song?

APRIL

By Ernest Crosby

See the apple-orchard
Bathing head and shoulders
In the dazzling pea-green
Rising-tide of April;
While an ancient pear tree
In the kitchen garden
Spreads the rugged outline
Of its jet-black branches
Underneath a drifted
Mass of snowy blossoms.
Tinted is the herbage
With unnumbered violets.
Tiny sky-blue butterflies
Like uprooted flowrets
Flirt among the sunbeams.
Hickory-tips are bursting
Into clustering parachutes.
On the white-oak saplings
Pink and folded leaflets
Now uncurl their tendrils
Like the opening fingers
Of soft new-born babies.

Listen, from the marshes
Multitudinous frog notes
Ringing out metallic
Like the ghosts of sleigh-bells;
While a red-winged blackbird,
Eager to be mating,
From a bare twig bugles,
"O-kal-ee,—it's April!"

THE JOY OF THE SPRINGTIME

By Sarojini Naidu

Springtime, O Springtime, what is your essence,
The lilt of a bulbul, the laugh of a rose,
The dance of the dew on the wings of a moonbeam,
The voice of the zephyr that sings as he goes,
The hope of a bride or the dream of a maiden
Watching the petals of gladness unclose?

Springtime, O Springtime, what is your secret,
The bliss at the core of your magical mirth,
That quickens the pulse of the morning to wonder
And hastens the seeds of all beauty to birth,
That captures the heavens and conquers to blossom
The roots of delight in the heart of the earth?

SPRING SONG

By Bliss Carman

Make me over, mother April,
When the sap begins to stir!
When thy flowery hand delivers

All the mountain-prisoned rivers,
And thy great heart beats and quivers
To revive the days that were,
Make me over, mother April,
When the sap begins to stir!

Take my dust and all my dreaming,
Count my heart-beats one by one,
Send them where the winters perish;
Then some golden noon recherish
And restore them in the sun,
Flower and scent and dust and dreaming,
With their heart-beats every one!

Set me in the urge and tide-drift
Of the streaming hosts a-wing!
Breast of scarlet, throat of yellow,
Raucous challenge, wooings mellow—
Every migrant is my fellow,
Making northward with the spring.
Loose me in the urge and tide-drift
Of the streaming hosts a-wing!

Shrilling pipe or fluting whistle,
In the valleys come again
Fife of frog and call of tree-toad,
All my brothers, five or three-toed,
With their revel no more vetoed,
Making music in the rain;
Shrilling pipe or fluting whistle,
In the valleys come again.

Make me of thy seed tomorrow,
When the sap begins to stir!

Tawny light-foot, sleepy bruin,
Bright-eyes in the orchard ruin,
Gnarl the good life goes askew in,
Whiskey-jack, or tanager,—
Make me anything tomorrow,
When the sap begins to stir!

Make me even (How do I know?)
Like my friend the gargoyle there;
It may be the heart within him
Swells that doltish hands should pin him
Fixed forever in mid-air.
Make me even sport for swallows,
Like the soaring gargoyle there!

Give me the old clue to follow,
Through the labyrinth of night!
Clod of clay with heart of fire,
Things that burrow and aspire,
With the vanishing desire,
For the perishing delight,—
Only the old clue to follow,
Through the labyrinth of night.

Make me over, mother April,
When the sap begins to stir!
Fashion me from swamp or meadow,
Garden plot or ferny shadow,
Hyacinth or humble burr!
Make me over, mother April,
When the sap begins to stir!

Let me hear the far, low summons,
When the silver winds return;

Rills that run and streams that stammer,
Goldenwing with his loud hammer,
Icy brooks that brawl and clamor,
Where the Indian willows burn;
Let me hearken to the calling,
When the silver winds return,

Till recurring and recurring,
Long since wandered and come back,
Like a whim of Grieg's or Gounod's,
This same self, bird, bud, or Bluenose,
Some day I may capture (Who knows?)
Just the one last joy I lack,
Waking to the far new summons,
When the old spring winds come back.

For I have no choice of being,
When the sap begins to climb,—
Strong insistence, sweet intrusion,
Vasts and verges of illusion,—
So I win, to time's confusion,
The one perfect pearl of time,
Joy and joy and joy forever,
Till the sap forgets to climb!

Make me over in the morning
From the rag-bag of the world!
Scraps of dream and duds of daring,
Home-brought stuff from far sea-faring,
Faded colors once so flaring,
Shreds of banners long since furled!
Hues of ash and glints of glory,
In the rag-bag of the world!

Let me taste the old immortal
Indolence of life once more;
Not recalling nor foreseeing,
Let the great slow joys of being
Well my heart through as of yore!
Let me taste the old immortal
Indolence of life once more!

Give me the old drink for rapture,
The delirium to drain,
All my fellows drank in plenty
At the Three Score Inns and Twenty
From the mountains to the main!
Give me the old drink for rapture,
The delirium to drain!

Only make me over, April,
When the sap begins to stir!
Make me man or make me woman,
Make me oaf or ape or human,
Cup of flower or cone of fir;
Make me anything but neuter
When the sap begins to stir!

EASTER JOY

By Nancy Byrd Turner

Look, everyone, look!
Leaves are lovely on bush and bough,
Robins build in the treetops now,
    A song sounds in the brook!

Run, every child, run!
Flowers are shining by hollow and hill,
Buttercup, violet, daffodil,
   All bright in the sun!

Bells silverly ring!
With grass and flowers and buds uncurled,
Easter is back in the beautiful world—
   Sing, everyone, sing!

ESSAYS

THE TRIUMPH OF LIFE

(EDITORIAL IN NEW YORK TIMES, APRIL 9, 1939.)

Easter is the supreme religious festival of the year for all adherents of the Christian faith. At the same time it is intimately connected, in origin and place in the calendar, with the long non-Christian history of the Mediterranean and North European races. The Crucifixion took place, as the biblical narratives tell us, on the day of the Jewish Passover. The name under which Easter is known in the Romanic languages is derived, through the Greek, from the Hebrew word for Passover. Behind this link are many traditions and observances which show that men's imaginations were caught, centuries before the Christian era, by the mood expressed in Solomon's words:

For, lo, the Winter is past,
The rain is over and gone;
The flowers appear on the earth;
The time of the singing of birds is come.

Men of all faiths and all philosophies can read in the rhapsodies of Hebrew shepherds and prophets, tending their sheep or making their journeys over the hills of Palestine under million-starred night skies, in the teachings and sufferings of the great Prophet of Christianity and the lesser saints and prophets, the origin of that spiritual quality which, with the Greek intellect, was to create the modern world. When that spirituality—ripening through the ages into freedom for the human mind and soul—is threatened, the Christian churches will find allies in many a diverse creed and many an individual who has lapsed from formal religion.

This Easter we know that the hand of death is on civilization in many parts of the world. An unseasonable kind of Winter hangs over them, even though seeds are germinating in the ground, grass growing green, fruit trees putting out blossoms. But it is not easy, nor fitting, to be hopeless in springtime, nor, above all, on Easter Sunday. Death in times past has been called by many names, for which its new ones, doctrinal and political, are only synonyms. The secular as well as the religious lesson of Easter is that death has never won a lasting victory.

SPRING

From Kavanaugh

By Henry Wadsworth Longfellow

Ah, how wonderful is the advent of the Spring!—the great annual miracle of the blossoming of Aaron's rod, repeated on myriads and myriads of branches!—the gentle progression and growth of herbs, flowers, trees,—gentle, and yet irrepressible, —which no force can stay, no violence restrain, like love, that wins its way and cannot be withstood by any human power. If Spring came but once a century, instead of once a year, or burst forth with the sound of an earthquake, and not in silence, what wonder and expectation would there be in all hearts to behold the miraculous change!

But now the silent succession suggests nothing but necessity. To most men, only the cessation of the miracle would be miraculous, and the perpetual exercise of God's power seems less wonderful than its withdrawal would be. We are like children who are astonished and delighted only by the second-hand of the clock, not by the hour-hand.

ACTIVITIES

GETTING READY FOR EASTER

A Unit for Primary Grades

By GARDIE KIRKMAN

I. Teacher's aims.
  A. To increase the children's vocabulary.
  B. To increase their interest in reading for specific purposes.
  C. To develop independent thinking.
  D. To create an interest in planning activities.
  E. To increase their ability to express themselves in complete sentences.
II. How the unit developed.
On Thursday, two weeks before Easter, the following note was posted on the bulletin board. A picture of a rabbit with an Easter egg on its back was above the note.

> The Easter Rabbit is coming soon.
> What would you like to do for Easter?
> We could do something nice.
> Let me know what you want to do.
> Miss Kirkman

As the children came into the room, several stopped and read the note. The sentence, "Come and read," was printed with a small printing set and tacked above the note and the rabbit.

In one corner of the room there was another bulletin board on which hung a large printed calendar. The children marked the date every morning, and had been counting the number of days until Easter.

After the calendar was marked, one child said that she could read what was on the other bulletin board. She was allowed to do so. No one made any suggestion as to what he would like to do for Easter.

On Friday morning, the children found this note added to the first one on the bulletin board.

This is Friday, and you have not told me what you would like to do.

The Easter Rabbit will run away if you do not hurry.

Miss Kirkman

As the children came into the room, several read the note but made no comment. Later in the day, a child said that she could read what was written. She did so, and then I asked what we should do. As the children gave their suggestions, they were written on the blackboard.

What We Can Do for Easter

1. Make Easter rabbits.
2. Make Easter baskets.
3. Dye some eggs.
4. Make Easter nests and eggs.
5. Write an Easter poem.
6. Make a rabbit pulling a wagon.
7. Have an Easter hunt.
8. Make an Easter calendar.
9. Read an Easter story.

The last thought came after the reading lesson. There is an Easter story in our reader. Although we had read only about halfway through the book, the vocabulary did not prove too difficult. After the story was read and discussed, a child suggested that we dramatize it. Another child directed the dramatization.

Since there were nine things to do, and nine days until Easter, we decided to write the names of the days on the blackboard and put a number by each day, so that we would know what we were to do each day.

Every morning a note was put on the bulletin board, telling the day of the week and what was to be done that day. As the children came into the room, they read the note. Later a child was asked to read it aloud and also to find the day of the week written on the blackboard. The sentence in the original list which corresponded to the number was located, and it was read to the class.

One day an Easter picture to be colored was on the bulletin board, with the statement that a certain girl should color it. She failed to find the request, and a boy found it. I had him tell her what she had missed, and he was allowed to color it. She remarked that she would always look to see what was on the bulletin board.

Two days before we were to dye our eggs, I requested the class to select some children to ask permission to use the kitchen for dyeing the eggs. A girl and a boy were selected. They went to the office, and the principal came back with them and gave the class his permission. The children thanked him.

The next day the following note was on the bulletin board.

This is Tuesday.
We must make our rules of how to behave when we dye our eggs.

The following rules were made, and the title was suggested by the class.

How to Act

1. Talk quietly.
2. Walk softly.

3. All can't stand around the stove.
4. Wait for our turn, and color with crayons while waiting.
5. We must not push.

One child told how to dye eggs, and expressed himself in well-chosen sentences.

The next day the note read as follows.

This is Wednesday.
Look on the blackboard and find the rules which tell us how to act when we dye our eggs.

The rules were read in the morning, and again for the principal, and again before going to the kitchen.

While some of the children were dyeing eggs, others were in another room with crayons and paper. Some forgot the rules of conduct, but the majority behaved very nicely in the new experience.

The next day this note was found.

This is Thursday.
Have you had a good time getting ready for Easter?
I hope that the bunny brings you many eggs.
A Happy, Happy Easter.

Miss Kirkman

This note was written on the blackboard.

Don't you think that we should thank the principal for letting us use the kitchen?

Miss Kirkman

The following note was dictated by the class and all of the children copied it for the writing lesson. The three best were taken by the children and put on the principal's desk.

Dear Mr. Nash:
We thank you for letting us use the kitchen to dye our eggs.
1A Grade
(Child's name)

The following poem was dictated by the class. It was copied and illustrated by each child.

> Easter Bunny, Easter Bunny,
> Bring me some eggs,
> Come to my house,
> Come, hop, hop on your little legs.

The activity had a happy ending with an egg hunt and an ice-cream party in the park. The party was a surprise from one of the mothers.

III. Outcomes.

A. Forty words were added to the children's reading vocabulary.

B. A greater interest was created in reading from the bulletin board.

C. A greater interest was created in planning activities.

D. A new number experience developed in finding out how many dozen eggs were needed for the group.

E. Courtesy was expressed by thanking the principal for the use of the kitchen and the mother for the nice surprise.

F. Consideration for one another was shown by agreeing to divide the eggs after the hunt.

G. An interest in writing for specific purposes developed.

EASTER FAVORS

By S. E. Evalyn Hammond

Miniature hat standards with Easter bonnets placed on them make interesting Easter favors or place cards.

Each standard is made of a $2\frac{1}{2}$-inch button mold, or any wooden circle, and a $\frac{1}{4}$-inch dowel 6 inches long. Nail the circle to one end of the dowel. Sandpaper the top of the dowel, making it slightly rounded. Paint the standard in pastel colors with oil paints.

The bonnets are made of paper envelope linings, tissue, crêpe, or any other soft, fancy paper. Manila drawing paper, or paper of about the same weight, is used for the foundation.

For the hat shown at the right in the illustration, cut two circles of heavy paper 4¼ inches in diameter. Cut a hole 2¼ inches in diameter from the center of each. The resulting pieces are for the brim of the hat. Cut them so they can be lapped, to make the brim droop slightly. Paste. Cut a circle 3¾ inches in diameter from colored paper, and gather it around the edge. Draw up the gathering string until the paper fits the inside edge of the brim, thus forming the crown. Paste the edge of the crown to the underside of one of the pieces for the brim. Line the brim with the other piece. Add trimmings as desired.

For the bonnet in the center, cut a circle and a semicircle, 3⅝ inches in diameter, from colored paper of contrasting colors. Cut a heavy-paper semicircle 3⅛ inches in diameter. On one side of the heavy-paper semicircle paste the colored circle so that it extends ¼ inch; on the other side, for a lining, paste the colored semicircle, keeping the outside edge even with the outside edge of the colored circle. Gather the edge that is not re-enforced, to form the back of the hat. Roll back the front edge to show the lining. Trim as desired.

For the hat at the left, cut two strips of heavy paper, ¼ inch by 2½ inches. Cross them at the center and paste together. This forms a foundation for the crown. For the band, cut a strip of heavy paper ½ inch by 5 inches. Lap the band, and paste the ends together. Paste the four ends of the frame to the band, spacing evenly. Cover the band with colored crêpe paper. Cut three 3¾-inch circles of crêpe paper the same color as the band. Slash the edges toward the center ½ or ¾ inch. Cut a 2½-inch circle of contrasting color. Slash the edges about 1 inch. Sew the three larger circles to the top of the frame. Paste the circle of contrasting color on the large circles.

THE EASTER PARADE

By Alma May Rodgers

The art work in our school for the week preceding Easter is always devoted to the making of egg dolls and toys. I bring two or three of my own designs to school, as suggestions only.

One little girl made an excellent likeness of "Felix the Cat." She drew the features on a hard-boiled egg, pasted on black ears, a black paper collar and tie, and colored the entire egg black. Another girl braided black darning thread, wound part of it and pasted it firmly on the top of a brown-shell egg, leaving the unwound braid free for a queue. With crayons she drew a Chinaman's face on the egg. Other dolls made were a schoolmaster with his tiny paper spectacles and collar, and the "Skipper" with his beard and little cap.

AN EASTER BOOKLET

By Inez C. Sundberg

The children of my second grade made a "Signs of Spring" booklet. They discussed in detail the various signs of spring, and then illustrated the things discussed. Each child drew a fence and pasted pussy willows on it, making them look like cats sitting on a fence. Each child made a picture of a broken egg and a baby chick, a picture of a cocoon and a beautiful butterfly, a picture of a nest filled with baby birds and a mother bird hovering near, a picture of a rainy day, and one of a sunny day. Another picture showed flowers blooming. In language class several short poems were studied, such as "In the Heart of a Seed," and "The Little Brown Bulbs." In penmanship class the children copied these poems on paper the same size as that on which the pictures were drawn. Then each child bound all his pictures and poems into a booklet, and made a cover, decorated with bright yellow daffodils.

On the last page of each booklet there was a picture of an Easter lily. On the first page was written an Easter greeting to the child's mother and father. On the Friday before Easter each child took his booklet home to his parents.

EASTER GREETINGS

By Marie Marsh

Children of all grades will enjoy making spatter-work Easter cards. Sketch a simple pattern on paper which is heavy enough to stand the wear and tear of use. Leave enough space about the various parts of the design to prevent the paper from tearing, and ruining the pattern. The stencil is then made by cutting out the sketch with either scissors or a razor blade.

Place the stencil on a card and pin all points down securely. If a border of spatter work is desired, make the pattern a fraction of an inch smaller than the card on which the spatter is being placed. If there is to be no border, see that the stencil is larger than the card to be decorated.

Spread out several newspapers before beginning the spatter work. An old toothbrush with not too stiff bristles and a nail file or dull knife are needed. The paint should be quite thick. Opaque water colors are excellent to use. Dip the brush into the paint; then quickly and gently scrape the brush with the knife.

Leave the stencil on until the paint is dry. Use as many stencils as colors, for only one color may be applied at a time. After the spatter work is completed, the greetings on the cards may be either written or printed.